I0754728

THE

BLACK MAN;

OR,

HAYTIAN INDEPENDENCE.

DEDUCED FROM

HISTORICAL NOTES,

AND

Dedicated to the Government and People of Hayti.

By M. B. BIRD,
Nearly Thirty Years a Resident Missionary in the Haytian Republic.

NEW YORK:
PUBLISHED BY THE AUTHOR.
TRADE SUPPLIED BY
THE AMERICAN NEWS COMPANY,
117, 119, *and* 121 *Nassau Street.*
1869.

John J. Reed, Printer, 43 Centre St., N. Y.

Official Report of the Commission,

FORMED BY THE HAYTIAN SECRETARY OF STATE, FOR THE EXAMINATION OF THE GENERAL MERITS AND BEARING OF THE PRESENT VOLUME.

PORT AU PRINCE, HAYTI,
November 14*th*, 1867.

SIR,—The Commission having gone through the examination of the work on Hayti, by the Rev. M. B. BIRD, now forward you their report on that Manuscript.

1st. Although it does not profess to be a full and entire history of Hayti, it begins with the discovery of the Island; gives a sketch of the French Colonial system, shows the difficulties and struggles connected with the establishment of the Independence of our Republic, and continues a line of Haytian history down to the fall of General Geffrard.

2nd. The entire history, as it is given, is in the spirit of a friend, and at the same time, with perfect frankness: the details of domestic manners are evidently given in the sense of one greatly attached to our country.

3rd. The Republican institutions of Hayti, and their political influence upon the masses, are given as facts, without entering into the supposed motives by which they may have been dictated.

4th. The Commission recommends and encourages the publication of this work, as useful to Hayti itself, as well as to its foreign friends. We wish its author to receive every support, and we do not hesitate to say that its publication would be to the interest of our branch of the human family, first in the English language, which is so widely spoken both in the West Indies and on the American continent.

5th. Hayti has great need of Immigration, hence it is desirable that the seven or eight millions of African descendants in the new world, which speak the English language, should understand the merits and resources of Hayti.

6th. The Commission, under the influence of these views and convictions, sincerely desire the publication of this work, and they earnestly hope that Mr. BIRD may be assisted in every way in his good intentions.

The Commission, Mr. Secretary of State, beg to assure you of their highest consideration.

(Signed)

W. G. SMITH, M. D., Chairman of Commission;
GENERAL ST. LUCIEN;
GENERAL J. LAMOTHE;
JUDGE BOCO;
J. B. DEHOUX, M. D.;
A. AUDAIN, M. D.;
S. PRESTON, ESQ.;
J. J. RIVIERE, Ex-Mayor of Port au Prince,
GENERAL A. TATE, Secretary of State;
P. ETHEART, Under Secretary of State;
J. B. HEPBURN, Esq.;
D. BOWLER, ESQ.;
C. PRESSOIR, Esq.;
O. RIVIERE, Esq.;
JUDGE LACRUZ, absent by sickness;
G. LOPEZ, Editor, etc.;
G. LAFONTANT, Esq., called away.

PREFACE.

VARIOUS views having been entertained, even by the friends of Hayti, as to the real merits of its Independence, it is only due to the Haytian Republic, that a fair statement should appear before the world on this subject ; hence, one of the leading purposes of the present work is, to show what that Independence has been ; nor has it been thought that this could be fairly done, without bringing out both the merits and demerits of this interesting question ; the national faults, therefore, are brought out in the sense of true and sincere friendship, and pointed to as rocks to be shunned in the nation's future course.

Hayti herself makes no pretensions to superiority ; her enlightened sons are conscious of national defects ; it must, however, be acknowledged that injustice has been done her, especially when the great and extraordinary difficulties of her career are fairly considered from the beginning ; difficulties which must have rendered Independence, in her case, impossible, had there not been real stamina somewhere.

From the title-page of this work it will be seen that it designs to show what Haytian Independence has been, rather than what it might or ought to have been ; its real merits, after a candid examination of what is here advanced, must be left to the fair and honest judgment of mankind.

It is of the highest importance to remember in Haytian history, that although the Haytians fought for the maintenance of their freedom, they did not themselves choose or seek Independence ; this was rather forced upon them by circumstances which they never sought, and which were utterly beyond their control. The wish of Hayti, evidently was, to remain faithful to France, but the history of the case will show that this ultimately became impossible ; in fact, the case is clear, that Toussaint L'Ouverture would have remained faithful to France, but he was convinced at last that her purpose was to re-enslave his people.

The purpose of the present production is neither eulogism nor censure, but rather to make a fair statement of facts and circumstances as they have occurred, and thus to bring out a picture which has been the production of extraordinary Providences, ruling in the storms of human passions ; a picture made striking by the great Master of events ; in fact, the whole case of Hayti seems to indicate something altogether unusual, a special purpose on the part of Providence in rendering her independence inevitable, seems to be singularly manifest ; it will, therefore, be easily understood that the hope of rendering service to Hayti herself, constitutes one of the leading motives of the work now before us, and may ultimately lead to its translation into the French language. But the fact of seven or eight millions of the descendants of Africa in the new world, speaking the English language, seems to render it desirable that it should first appear as an English work, the more so, as one of the leading objects is, the general interests of the " Black Man."

Reasonings and opinions of different shades and bearings have indeed been expressed and pursued in the course of this work, as the result of long experience and continuous observation, and with an earnest desire for the welfare of the descendants of Africa in the new world ; but they must, together with the general subject in which they have all originated, be left before the tribunal of a Christian public.

The present volume might be considered as a plea for independence, whenever the indications of Providence seem plainly to point to it, for whatever reasons, hence the present work is preceded by an introduction, having for its object the general development of this important question, and especially as it is here meant.

It will, therefore, be seen that independence, as it regards both Hayti and Liberia, is here considered as a vital point, not indeed in any exclusive or isolated sense, yet still, in the strictest sense of national identity, which might, and should be, compatible with the same liberality towards foreigners, as is practiced by France, America, and England, and as unquestionably will ultimately be imposed, by the power of universal light and interest, upon the human race at large, as the natural and inevitable result of that close contact, into which all the nations of the earth must ultimately be brought, by means of electricity and steam.

It has been thought that the present moment is peculiarly adapted to the appearance of these "Historical Notes," etc., for it is undeniable, that the course of events with regard to the descendants of Africa, has brought out, by extraordinary means and circumstances, the clearest and strongest proofs of a Divine rule in human affairs, that were ever made visible to mortals ; hence we have recently seen, both in America and Europe, some of the greatest struggles which have ever been known among men, followed by such an extraordinary remodeling of nations, as was never before recorded on the page of human history, the well pronounced supreme will having been, that some should entirely disappear, while others should stand fast, with even great acquisitions ! Many are the indications which might be regarded as expressions of the Divine will, that Hayti should remain an Independent Nation ; this, however, will not hinder the coming on of a power of circumstances, which will compel her to develop and practice those true principles of Liberty, which alone can secure her destiny, independence and permanent prosperity.

It will be seen, both in the introduction and also in the body of this work, that the formation of national independencies, by the Black and Colored people of the American continent, is freely entered into, as a question which can now involve no injury to any interest or community. Political Justice having finally placed all shades of complexion on the same level, this question is made both an open and a fair one, and like every other, is to be either received or rejected, as opinions may prevail.

The subject of Independence, in the sense here advocated, is not of recent adoption by the author, as may be seen by the "Liberia Herald," under the title of "A Voice to Liberia," for 1858 ; nor are the convictions which constitute the subject of that piece, in the slightest degree lessened by passing events.

It will, however, be seen that isolated independence is not here advocated, but simply that which constitutes the glory of France, England, and America, compatible with the strictest identity, and at the same time with the most unbounded intercourse with the whole human family, without which, these last named nations never would have been what they now are.

The discovery of Hayti and its aboriginal inhabitants are but glanced at in this work ; nor has it been possible to enter very extensively into the Colonial system under the French, although it should not be forgotten that the leading minds in the Haytian Revolution had been fostered under Colonial rule ; and it is due to Hayti to state here, that one of her ablest and most worthy citizens,* has done justice to his Colonial Black and Colored predecessors, in the great work of Haytian Independence, by transmitting to posterity both their names and deeds.

The following extract, from the author just referred to, will become this preface :

"Before the proclamation of Independence, or the final organization of the Country, there were men among us who did not

* Beauvais Lespinasse.

hesitate to sacrifice themselves for the future happiness of the African race, and it would be impossible not to admire the courage shown, by some of them, in the midst of slavery and prejudice, while the volunteered, and self-inflicted hardships and privations of others who sheltered themselves from despotism, in inaccessible mountains, is worthy of note.

"What anguish, what tribulation prepared men for the hour of bloodshed in the cause of liberty and independence !

"Would Julien Raymond, Ferrand de Baudieres, Ogé, Chauvannes, Boury, Pinchinat, Bauvais, Lambert, Rigaud, Villate, Boukman, Jean Francois Biassous, Polverel Santhonasse, Toussaint L'ouverture, Moise, Charles Belar, Sylla, Sans Souci, Lamour Derance, leave us at rest in our work of 1804 if we did not acknowledge the services they rendered us ?"

The author himself admits their excesses ; it must, however, be confessed that but few of the noted leaders of mankind have come out of the great battle for human liberties unstained.

It will doubtless be evident that it has been the design of this work to bring out the religious and general moral bearing of Hayti. This, to the sincere Christian, will be deeply painful and distressing ; it is, however, hoped that this question is made sufficiently clear, not only to show the national character in this sense, but also to convince the Evangelical Churches of America and Europe, that if Hayti had had the attentions which were unquestionably due, not only to her peculiar and extraordinary circumstances, but to the spirit of religious liberty which she has so long manifested, her position, in a moral point of view, might at this moment have been wholly different to what it is, as may be easily and justly inferred from the statistics of Protestantism, here given, showing an extent of success which, in so Roman Catholic a country, is certainly worthy of special notice ; the more so, when the very limited means by which it has all been accomplished, are fairly considered.

But we now leave this production, with all its defects, before the world, as having originated in a desire to maintain right principle, and render it triumphant, by doing justice to Hayti ; for, whatever may have been or still are its defects, they have resulted from that depravity of fallen man, which is so fully recognized by the Christian Church, and which she binds herself to correct, by her declarations to the world that she possesses all that is necessary for the healing of the nations !

A residence of nearly thirty years, among a newly formed nation such as Hayti, as in some sense a Teacher, will perhaps be a sufficient apology for a didactic tone, now and then seemingly assumed, sincerely meant as a friendly warning of those rocks ahead, on which so many nations have already wrecked.

INTRODUCTORY REMARKS

ON THE ADVANTAGES OF

NATIONAL INDEPENDENCE,

AS A GENERAL QUESTION.

The realm of liberty alone, I call
My home!

THE present production on Hayti is by no means intended as a full history of that country, although the events recorded are generally placed in chronological order, and it is presumed that the main out-lines of its history may be found embodied in the work.

The main design of the present effort is to bring out one great and important fact, which the great Ruler of all things has so manifestly established, by those various divisions of the human race, which at present make up the great family of man.

The fact in question is, simply, that the spirit of emulation, which doubtless has designedly resulted from the divisions and independencies which at present exist among mankind, is most salutary and powerful, bringing out as it does and must, not only the capacities of our being, but also the vast resources of nature in general ; this same principle is also actively and perseveringly developed between families and communities, and is evidently intended to keep the entire human family in the most productive activity; hence history has made it manifest that this great moving principle has ever been the most active and powerful among the most advanced nations in all ages of the world; nor is it less powerful at present than it has ever been in any former age of human history; in fact, never did this principle work with such driving power as in the present advanced state of everything.

We find yet that the most distinctive peculiarities attach to all the great divisions of mankind. The Anglo-Saxon, Celtic, and Teutonic branches, as well as others, have their various and distinctive peculiarities, while at the same time this is to be understood, simply in the sense of fact, not at all in the sense of excluding barriers, or in the slightest degree interfering with mutual and cordial intercourse.

That Africa, therefore, and its descendants should form a distinct branch of mankind, would seem to be only in the natural order of things; nor does it follow that this should be understood in any exclusive sense, but simply in the sense explained by God himself, in what is so plainly to be seen in the various ranks and orders of human beings, scattered over the face of the earth, in the forms of families, tribes, and nations, all of which have ever instinctively recognized a universal brotherhood!

Hence Independence, as it is distributed by Divine Providence over the world, shows a just and salutary principle; there is nothing in it exclusive, and its useful working among the nations is evident, yea, the hope we derive from it is great and good, serving as it does as one of the mainsprings in the general welfare of the world.

We may, therefore, take it up as a great fact, that the civilized divisions of man never would, or could, have been what they are but for their independence, and that as a whole, the grand spectacle of human activity and development, commercially, scientifically, and even religously, would never otherwise have been what they now are. The emulating power which has ever existed among them all, has produced that admirable and ever working whole, which now offers to the general gaze of universal intelligence.

With these views before us, it will be seen that the work in question, bearing the title of the "Black Man," etc., has for one of its objects, to show, that the divisions of the human race are only a part of the order of things, and that, therefore, Africa, and her widely spread children, constitute one main division in this great whole.

That Hayti should be at the head of an African subdivision cannot be any matter of surprise, nor can the design of her independence fail of being recognized.

Hence our present direct purpose is to bring out the fact, that the Haytian Republic possesses in itself every material, and resource of every kind, to place it on a level with any other nation as to general merit, and at the same time to show what the Haytian people are, mentally, morally, or otherwise.

It will also be the aim of the following pages, to demonstrate from the history of Hayti itself, that she never could have been what she now is, but for her independence, whatever may have been, or still are, the defects of her Government, or the management of any of the departments of the national interests, which it need not be concealed are many.

The great imperfections of Hayti stand out before the world, and although the intelligent Haytians themselves are ever ready to recognize them, yet they justly demand that the exceptional circumstances of their origin as a nation, over which they had no control, should be fairly considered, not indeed in the sense of justifying error of any kind, but rather as explanatory, especially as the Haytians, as a people, can only be considered as simply on their way to understand the true principles of free Government, they never having been transmitted to them by their wiser French predecessors.

The present volume is also intended to remind all who are disposed to think fairly and dispassionately on the national character of Hayti, that nations, as well as individuals, invariably receive the stamp of the circumstances which gave them birth, and which, should they have been unhappy, cannot be effaced but by long years of every kind of improvement.

With this fact in view, it will not be difficult to understand the peculiarities and characteristics of the people in question, for Hayti must, after all, be judged by the depths of error and injustice from which she, as a nation, has risen into existence ; she did not, like some, spring from free institutions, notwithstanding they were her aim—she indeed rushed toward them, but to arrive at the accomplishment of her wishes, she had to make her way through fiercely conflicting elements of every kind ; the instinctive longings for liberty were there, but how to use it, when once seized, was yet to be learnt.

It is not, however, intended by anything here advanced that nations, as well as individuals, never create their circumstances, or that they are not responsible for their need of reformation, whenever progress and amelioration may have been at their command, nor is it pretended here, for a moment, to justify the present condition of the masses of the Republic of Hayti ; guilt is unquestionably at her door in this matter.

The history of this Republic has yet to be written, and whenever it is fairly brought out it will show that the intensest fervor in the cause of Liberty—without that wholesome moral power—which is to be found in Christianity only, places a nation on a dangerous track.

The bare events, making up this general history, are already well recorded and detailed by several Haytian authors of deserved celebrity, particularly by T. Madiou (Fils), and B. Ardouin ; but to bring out all the lights and shades of that phase of humanity, which a full and entire history of Hayti in all its bearings must present, remains yet to be done, and doubtless will be accomplished by some able Haytian pen at a future day, to the advantage not only of the great African family, but to man at large—a work the more to be desired from the fact, that the enemies of the African race are not yet entirely silenced.

The dark shades of Slavery, which for many years have hung over mankind, withering and concealing so much of real worth in man, and especially as to the true character of the African, are now rapidly dispersing, and the clear light of simple truth is breaking forth, which shall ultimately expose all false reasoning and demonstrate that man is man, of every hue. Clouds, indeed, still roll over us, and long will, but the glorious sun of truth is, nevertheless, rising to its zenith !

The forming power of Independence upon nations and individuals, is too evident to need any reasoning ; those who have well noted the influence and power of national institutions upon collective masses, as well as upon individual character, will be prepared to understand the difference, between the Black Man independent, and, in a national sense, in his own house, under a Government of his own formation, and the one under the influence of a foreign element, although probably with vast advantages.

It is not intended that there are no advantages to be derived from contact with a superior element, but it is maintained that there is an ennobling power in true and well-managed Independence ; and that general contact, in this sense only, has its full effect, when the soul of Independence is present ; hence the manly bearing of the Haytian, which is unquestionably the result of his own national institutions, independence, and education.

It will, of course, be understood that we are not here speaking of the ignorant masses of the people, although even with them an air of conscious independence is manifest. The

Haytians, however, have more than ever to learn, that their independence must fail in true dignity, without sound moral principle universally diffused.

We have, indeed, pointed out the Black Man as especially benefiting by independence ; this has been done in the sense of a general principle, and is, therefore, as applicable to him as to the rest of the human family ; perhaps, indeed, there are peculiarities in his case, as relating to the present age, which might make this great principle specially applicable to him, and render the designs of Providence, as to his independence, yet more clear and striking.

Already the Haytian commerce, as resulting from independence, is comparatively great ; nor should it be lost sight of, that the public revenues are created by the same organized and legalized system of Patents, Customs, Licenses, etc., as in all other civilized countries.

It is an interesting and important fact, that Hayti is at this moment, and for a long time past, has been carrying on an extensive and increasing commerce with the United States of America, which, for some time past, has been said to be worth three millions of dollars per annum ; this is to be understood as relating to the French part of the Island only. Also, with England, France, and Germany much is doing commercially ; and it is not to be supposed that the extensive correspondence, and constantly calculating intercourse with foreign nations, can be without its general and powerful results upon the interests and civilization of this nation, especially when it is remembered that Scriptural education has, during the last quarter of a century, widely sown the seeds of truth, while at the same time thousands of Haytians, although not converted to God by a new birth unto righteousness, have nevertheless opened their eyes to see that true religion is, God in man, and that alone ; and as far as convictions are concerned, have shaken off the iron yoke of error in many things, as incompatible with real moral progress,—

that all these powerful elements should have been so long at work without effect, is not to be supposed.

Let the thinking part of mankind open the details of these facts, and it will most certainly be seen that national Independence is the road to dignity ; this, it is true, has never been doubted of the White Man, nor has there ever been any real reason to doubt it in the case of the Black Republic of Hayti, notwithstanding much error, and the fact that she has yet much to learn.

Time was, when the idea of the formation of an African Independency, in any sense, from the vast Black population of the United States, was looked upon with suspicion and a frown ; fear was felt that the great cause of Justice before the law would suffer, by weakening the ranks of those who would thus be left to struggles for rights supremely dear, but the arm of the Almighty has now been revealed, right has triumphed over wrong, and an Independency under present circumstances would, therefore, be simply another competitive power in the earth, bringing out and completing the boundless resources of human beings ; showing also, that the sons of Africa are not sent back to savage life by Independence, as both Hayti and Liberia attest, where wealth and learning have at least commenced their elevating power, and will, doubtless, by the aid of general knowledge, true religion, and commercial intercourse, raise them ultimately to rank with the most civilized and prosperous nations of the age.

Truly, the great principles of Liberty and Independence, rightly understood, are the glory of our times ; so much so, that, Liberty a failure ! has now become too absurd, both as an expression, and even as a thought, for use ; rather it is Despotism and Slavery that have proved to be utter, and, let us hope, eternal failures ! Men are now beginning to see what they long refused to see, or understand, viz., that universal freedom is universal wealth !

But the burden of our song is Independence ! Nor does

the admitted fact that Hayti ought to, and might have done better, in any way diminish either its glory or its dignity. If Hayti has at all risen from her starting point, as she unquestionably has, then has she demonstrated to the world, that she possesses both the elements and capacity for Progress.

The fact of Law, Mathematics, Literature, Commerce, etc., forming fields, where intelligence has unquestionably shown powers which do honor to this branch of the human family, demand just notice ; while at the same time, Independence in this case, having placed the nation in official intercourse with the leading Governments of the day, has brought out state-documents not inferior to those of other nations, as will appear from the following "Historical Notes," while the Haytian Bar, with the Medical Faculty, show men of all shades worthy of their professions.

In fact, the wealth already accumulated, both in intelligence and gold, afford ample proof that Independence in Hayti is not, and cannot be a failure ; swarming evils, indeed, abound, which even seem to threaten every good ; the fact of the utter corruption of human nature is as evident with Independence as it is under the greatest despotism, hence the great stress laid on the necessity of moral culture, as applying to every individual in a nation, rich and poor, high and low.

Let it not, however, be supposed that the Independence advocated in these pages, in reference to the "Black Man," is in any sense exclusive ; it is rather that which belongs to man as a social being, and which forms the glory of England, France, and America ; an Independence which, while it extends shelter to all, retains at the same time a perfect national identity, while it tells upon every child in the nation, stamps its character upon each family, is seen in the peasant's gait as he strides his mountain tops, and in the more developed townsman is visible as he paces his own streets.

Unconscious, bold, instinctive are the airs,
Of those who feel as if the earth were theirs !

Hayti and Liberia have, indeed, been exclusive in their Independence ; but this, it must be admitted, has been rather from necessity than choice, as the history of each country will show ; this necessity, however, no longer exists in either case, and it is for them to judge whether they will not, by perpetuating such defiant attitudes, in excluding those who now freely open their doors to them, expose themselves to the sarcasm of the age ;—*exclusiveism* cannot belong to man as a family ; hence all walls of separation between mankind must everywhere speedily fall ; the utmost intercourse, or legitimate amalgamation, being in no way incompatible with the most complete national Independence and identity.

It may be thought by some, both Black and White, that the tendency of the present work, in favoring a separation between two of the main branches of the human race, is more lowering than otherwise to the dignity of the " Black Man," the contrary, however, is most unquestionably the aim of the author of these pages ; in fact, it would be difficult to show that Independence is, or can in any way be, degrading, nor could any one sincerely entertain such a thought ; most certainly, Haytian Independence does not mean, or even suppose, separation, in any isolating sense ; hence her capitalists are mainly foreigners, who may be viewed as among even the greatest supporters of the national Independence.

If we enquire into the origin and cause of the various divisions which have taken place among men in former ages, we shall find that in most cases they have been nearly the same ; hence, the case of Lot and Abram's herdmen is highly illustrative of the question before us ;—circumstances which men call accidental, have doubtless mostly originated their needed and salutary divisions throughout the earth, and we are probably right in concluding that one great law of Providence is, that the interests of the earth should be developed and worked out, upon the principle of national Independence ; nor have the divisions among men, in this sense, ever involved the idea of degradation ; they have rather been upon the instinctive supposition, of each and all acting independently for themselves, each thus exploring for himself, and bringing out the general resources and wealth of nature.

Still the question might fairly be urged, has not a man a right to remain in the land of his birth ? To which question the only possible reply is or can be, that he has ! But if there did not, with this great truth, exist the right in every individual of the human family to change their place of residence, or their circumstances, and, if possible, better them, either by emigration or any other fair means, it would be most unhappy for the world.

On this principle, the island of Great Britain, had long since been too small for its ever increasing population ; and, in fact, many other places in the world would, long ago, have become intolerable from density of population, had there existed no right to change.

The undisputed right, therefore, to remain in one's native land, is indeed poor, compared with the right to be unrestrictedly at large—at full liberty, to make the best of the world, and, so to speak, lay it out to the best advantage !

Hence the question of right, even to abandon one's birth-place, needs no further consideration. This not even forming any part, properly speaking, of the subject now before us, the right of all men and all communities to do and act for the best for themselves and their children, in the course of public events, is universally recognized ; and they are wise and happy who know how thus to appreciate true freedom for themselves and posterity. This is that true Independence which becomes every man upon earth.

It was upon this sound principle of independence that the immortal founders of those Colonies which ultimately terminated in the formation of the present great North American Republic, wrenched themselves and their families from their native shores. Notwithstanding their entire rights in the beloved land of their birth, they simply, from motives which appeared to them sufficient, preferred the bleak and cheerless wilds of the New World, to what they conceived to be the despotism of their native land, which they felt destroyed the happiness of their homes and ancient fire-sides ; hence they literally flung themselves upon the world, and even wandered about in the dens and caves of their new-found land, to save themselves from the fury of untutored man ; and yet this painful exchange was even sweet to them—of oppression for liberty ! as the free and spontaneous praises of Jehovah, which rose from their noble hearts, breaking the long silence of the primeval forests now before them, attested—although they were not insensible to the endearing sweets of their ancient homes which they had left behind. Nor is it to be wondered at, that the grandeur of such a genuine spirit of independence should have impressed itself upon a nation, which may now be said to be one of the glories of the age.

The principle, therefore, here advocated, is one which must and does command the attention of mankind. There may, and indeed will be, various views as to its present application to the "black man" of the United States ; but the fact that national independence is the highest dignity to which either he or any other branch of the human family can attain, is not to be controverted.

Nor ever did it occur to any of the descendants of the Pilgrim Fathers, that their great progenitors in any sense ignored either the cause of freedom or their friends, by thus departing from their country, and leaving behind them the great struggle for liberty in which they had so long been engaged ; or that they in any sense descended from their dignity, in leaving the land of their birth, for the carrying out of the great purposes which they had in view. Rather their own fathers applauded them, as they wafted from their ancestral shores, and voluntarily gave up all right to their own birth-place ; while they themselves were cheered with the hope of establishing their own just principles of religious liberty on those far-off shores, towards which they had now set their faces. And great have been the results of their bold and daring energy—results which have amply demonstrated the soundness of their principles, thus annihilating all doubt as to the carrying them out in modern days, by the simple force of preference and principle, for whatever reason might be deemed sufficient.

It is not meant here to insinuate in the remotest manner, that either the ruling power or people of the United States intend in any sense the oppression of the "black man." Nothing can be more evident, than that at the present moment honesty and justice are in the ascendency in the great American Republic, on the African question ; nor is it to be supposed that the rivers of blood which have been poured out as the purchase-price of justice, laid down before God and man, in awful conflict, will be in vain. But the fact is before the world, that the slavery and degrading bondage of past ages, so fertile in every conceivable evil, and so ruinous to all ranks and conditions of men, giving even to liberty itself a sickly hue, and perverting noblest minds, have left behind them false views and unhappy effects, from which independence would prove a shelter. Such were the noble Lincoln's views. Such, too, were those of Toussaint L'Ouverture ; and if all Africa could speak on such a subject, it would be with no uncertain words. Nor will it be surprising that the thought of a black independence, rising out of the great numbers of the sons of Africa in the United States, should have found birth in a Haytian element, or that it should appear here, although only in the form of a question.

Astonishing as it may seem, it is a fact that political strife in Hayti has sometimes laid hold of the question of color, between the blacks and those of mixed blood, for the accomplishment of base purposes ; nevertheless, the man who would presume to think more of his lighter hue, and in any sense act upon it, would, in the land of Toussaint, find himself greatly mistaken, and would soon feel himself under the necessity of concealing his empty vanity, in the presence probably of his darker superior, whose education might possibly have left him in the shade. In fact, it is seen in Hayti that a complete education is a withering power to the vague hate of color.

But men in all ages have been guilty of absurdities; hence the justly celebrated Macaulay informs us, that in an age not very remote from our own, the Irishman was looked down upon with absolute contempt, by his lordly and conceited English brother; nor does the great historian fail to make this singularly plain. And such, too, has been the course pursued in all ages; shades and straws have been the causes of rivers of blood, and peace has often come about only from sheer exhaustion.

Nor would it be difficult to understand that thousands of recently freed men, from similar circumstances, might gladly avail themselves of an open door of deliverance from elements which are in contact with God himself, and cannot but be productive of anguish. It might, indeed, be said, Live them down! But there are various ways of doing this; nor can there be any doubt of the effectual power of a Christian and well-ordered independence in such a case. We, however, are here reminded that the social question is not settled as a mere matter of right. The "black man" must command, intellectually and morally. His well-formed soul must be the power. This must be his demonstration that "all men are equal!" This, too, is the great truth which would justify a constantly open door to a well understood independence, for all who might wish, from any consideration, to change either their place of residence or national style of life, where the "black man" might rise in independent freedom.

Hayti and Liberia—whatever their past history may have been—are now free and independent nations, and are both advancing in all the interests and prosperity of the age. They are giving proof of the soundness of the great principle which it is the aim of this volume to illustrate, and which constitutes the glory of their national existence.

An exodus in any sense is not here meant. All that is thought of in the present reasonings, should be the result of unconstrained choice, whether for or against. "Let each one be fully persuaded in his own mind." All motives being entirely Christian, all will be safe.

The black man, or any other, who might wish an element of yet greater freedom in any respect than that which he now realizes, is only the renewed case of thousands of every past age. Like his predecessors of all the past, he withdraws to wherever he pleases, and from whatever motive he pleases. He does not ask about his right to remain here or to go there. He, as a Christian, follows his moral instincts, and what may seem to him the leadings of Providence.

Let even millions move. Nothing need be feared from the utmost liberty of action, while the honor of man of every shade is the sole motive and aim.

It will be easily understood that the ground-work and elevation from whence all these views are taken, is Hayti; nor can anything be more certain than that the reasonings here adopted, as well as the feelings here expressed, are very decidedly those of the enlightened and educated portion of the Haytian people; while it cannot be denied, whatever be the national defects of Hayti, that the present educated classes of this country are sufficiently numerous and powerful, fully to establish and demonstrate the great question before us, that independence is its true dignity.

That there ever should have been an entirely uneducated class in Hayti, is to be deplored; but this evil is now recognized, and its sole cure is now well understood. The Christian Churches, therefore, that have ears to hear, "let them hear!"

With regard to the great mission of Hayti, as given it by

God, in a Christian, national sense, and in the order of Providence, which we may presume was to prove that man of every hue is man, many Christian men, to whom great deference is in every respect due, have seemed to hesitate as to the success realized in this respect. Whether this hesitation has been well founded, or whether there has been in all such cases a sufficient knowledge of Hayti, to warrant the conclusions arrived at, remains to be considered. Much, in such cases, would depend upon the amount of expectation which may have been entertained. If the class of persons referred to have expected of Hayti a model Republic, in which all the details of free institutions and free government should be entirely developed, then there might well be hesitation. The question, however, is, whether such an expectation was fair and reasonable. Can we fairly overlook the inevitable distance which there must, in the nature of things, be between national infancy and national maturity? This overlooked, disappointment would become certain.

Let, then, the law of nature and plain truth be here carried out, and all difficulty in the case will cease; by this law it will be at once evident that we only reap that which we sow; and without any reasoning, we understand that that which was never sown at all, can never appear.

The question, therefore, which naturally arises in this case, is—What has been sown in Hayti, morally, politically, or otherwise? This question demands fair and serious attention; for if the evil seeds of false and pernicious principles, religiously, intellectually, and politically, have been sown broadcast, all further hesitation must evidently cease.

Nevertheless, the mission of the Haytian nation was, it may be presumed, to develop and establish the character of the black man. This may not have been done as probably many expected it to be; but it is certain that the great law of God and nature, as we have just referred to it, has been carried out and fulfilled.

An Anglo-Saxon ancestry might have placed everything on a different track in Hayti ; yet it would not be difficult to show that the land of Toussaint has not been the least amongst its sister Republics in the new world, whose origin has been more or less similar.

Hayti has already demonstrated the fallacy of much that was once said of the African, and to our great astonishment, is still persisted in by a deservedly distinguished traveler of our own day, who has perhaps immortalized his name by his African discoveries ; but whose views as to the African as a man, do not appear to harmonize with those of the great Livingstone.

To one who has resided long in Hayti, it is somewhat amusing to hear that the Negro, after a certain age, is worth little in literature or mental power. It would be a curious enquiry to examine on what ground this is said—how and why is this vitality lost ? and is it in harmony with the experience of five and twenty years educational labor in Hayti ? Men that have had romance enough in them to face black savages, and sometimes tremble for their lives among them, are not always the best judges of the mental powers of such branches of the human race.

The blacks of Hayti, who have received a good education either in France or in their own country, know how to prize it. Those who think differently might make many a test in that country, where some well educated blacks might be found who, mentally, are yet youthful at sixty !

In fact, such reasoning is simply the abandonment of truth ; and in the case of the great traveler just referred to, goes to show that it is possible for even great men, of a certain mental style, to travel amongst the savages of Africa until they arrived at the conclusion that they were, in their origin, "pre-Adamic !" or as impious mortals might suppose, a preliminary essay of creative power, intended to produce a man of inferior order. Can this be seriously meant ? Rather is it not an empty freak of an irreverent imagination? It is not, however, uncommon for the reasonings of able men to lead to erroneous conclusions.

The conclusions of the traveler in question, as to African incapacity, were doubtless those also of Julius Cæsar and his attendants, as to the ancient Britons, when they first landed on their shores. Whether, therefore, the final decision of the class of men now referred to, that all attempts to raise such branches of the human race is useless, either by Christian missions or otherwise, is well founded, may be very safely left to the results of experience. The facts on this subject, both in Hayti and elsewhere, are indeed stubborn, nor do they leave any doubt on which side the real visionary is found on this question.

Most unhappy would it be for uncivilized humanity to be left to the tender mercies of those who are quite undecided as to whether human beings, under certain circumstances, are men at all.

Hayti has at least demonstrated the existence of sound mental material in the African; and although this is a great and triumphant step, it must nevertheless be admitted that she might and ought to have done better still.

CONTENTS.

CHAPTER IX.

CHAPTER X.

CHAPTER XI.

CHAPTER XII.

HAYTIAN INDEPENDENCE.

CHAPTER I.

Discovery of Hayti.—Native Indians.—First rupture with the Spaniards.—Gold discovered.—Indian and Negro Slavery.—Arrival of the French.—The American Colonies rise.—Case of Ogè.—First French Expedition.—"La Crête à Pierrot."—Exports.—Religion in the Colony.—Vandouism.—French Revolution, Spirit of, in Hayti.—Liberty proclaimed in France.—Toussaint faithful to the French.—Toussaint declines being King.—He Rules the whole Island.—His rule severe.—He is captured by the French.

The great Columbus, star of modern days,
Went westerly, and glowing, stood, over
A new found world!

HAYTI was discovered by Christopher Columbus, on the 6th of December, 1492.

The name of the island is said to have meant, in the native Indian language—among many other things—" High, Mountainous Land," but Columbus, on discovering it, thought it greatly resembled Spain, and therefore gave it the name of " Hispaniola," or little Spain: subsequently, St. Domingo, or St. Domingue, was for many years the name by which it was generally known in Europe; since, however, the Declaration of Independence by the Haytians in 1804, the ancient aboriginal name has been revived and adopted. This large and important island is now, therefore, generally known by the name of Hayti.

The entire island is upwards of four hundred miles in length, from east to west, and about one hundred and eighty miles in breadth. It is situated between 17 and 18 degrees north latitude, and between 71 and 79 west longitude from Paris. Its situation with regard to the adjacent Antilles, is peculiarly central, having Cuba twenty-two leagues to the northwest, Jamaica forty-five leagues to the southwest, and Puerto Rico about twenty leagues to the east-southeast.

The native Indian population, at the time of the discovery of the island, has been variously estimated at from one to three millions. The aboriginal tribes have generally been represented as a mild and hospitable race, and were governed by chiefs, bearing the title of Caciques.

The whole island appears to have been divided into five different States, each one being ruled by a Cacique.

With regard to the primary origin of these ancient races, but little or nothing can be said with certainty. It is, however, evident, that on their discovery by Columbus, they were not what might be termed savages, but were rather a mild and interesting people, possessing a certain type of civilization ; and although greatly astonished at the sight of their new visitors, they were quite disposed to receive them well. We can, however, here only refer to history for the full details of all the facts and circumstances connected with the discovery of this island.

It would appear that the first rupture between the

Indians and the Spaniards took place in 1493, at the garrison left by Columbus some few leagues from Cape Haytien, on his first departure for Spain.

History informs us that the Spaniards, having ill-treated the Indians, were fallen upon by them, and utterly exterminated. This unhappy event led to all the rest of bloodshed and murder which afterwards took place between the Spaniards and aboriginal habitants of Hayti,* thus showing how utterly vague is all merely nominal Christianity, either in the form of national creeds or otherwise.

Various indications of gold having presented themselves, the love of that idol was soon vehemently developed, and the unhappy Indians were ere long dragged forth from the quiet of ages past, and as slaves, to which state they were soon reduced, were compelled to hunt the worshiped metal, either in the streams or mines. But the Indians of the tropics soon sunk beneath this weight of woe, and even speedily disappeared, to the perpetual dishonor of their rapacious, although nominally Christian masters.

The use of the blood-hound, it would seem, contributed much towards the bringing about of this fearful result; hence we are informed, that even Columbus, on the 5th of April, 1494, when the natives of Jamaica opposed his landing there, let loose a blood-hound upon them. Justin Martyr, also, a well known name of those days, observes: "Our people availed themselves of the blood-hound, in their struggles with natives." †

Such were the perverted views of Christianity in

* T. Madiou. † Schelcher on Hayti.

that age; and yet it must be admitted, that there were good Christian men among the Spanish clergy of that time, who had found their way to the new world, and who also were faithful in their remonstrances against the wanton cruelties then practiced.

The great scarcity of hands for the working of the gold mines which had been discovered, and other exhausting toils, which were quickly imposed upon the Indians, soon originated the idea of seeking help elsewhere; hence, Africa was thought of, from whence the white man delayed not to drag by thousands the unhappy Africans from their ancient shores; and having shackled both soul and body, promptly set his more hardy limbs to work, thus soon lashing from him unbounded wealth. But the horrors of both Indian and Negro slavery have now long been before the world, and it will not be necessary to recapitulate them here, except as incidental circumstances, in the course of narration, may render necessary; suffice it to say, for the present, that the wealth and splendor of St. Domingo, as the result of French slavery in after days, were beyond compare, as to anything the West Indies had ever previously known; but injustice of every kind ever carries with it the elements of self-destruction.

The arrival of the French in Hayti was gradual, and according to the united testimony of history, commenced with a few adventurers, who settled themselves on a small island,* about opposite the town, now called Port de Paix. They were a class of men called fillibusters, or buccaneers. Their numbers gradually increasing, they soon came into con-

* Latortue.

tact with the Spaniards, who now had long been masters of the whole island. Conflicts, fearful and destructive, were the result. There is, however, reason to believe, that the French government sent out in the end men capable of protecting their subjects; hence contests for territory soon came on, which at last ended in taking possession of a portion of the main land, and the ultimate establishment of the little town of Port de Paix, already alluded to. This point once gained, it will be easily understood that encroachments went on, until in the end, limits were formally agreed upon between the Spanish and the French governments, and the island thus became divided into two colonies, the French part bearing the name of St. Domingue, understood in English as St. Domingo, which at that time was less than a third of the whole island.

The elements and resources of every kind of wealth being found on these fertile shores, the active spirit of the French soon turned all to good account, and the result of their industrial powers became a subject of both wonder and admiration, although to the philanthropist, the whole of the West Indies and all the nations interested in them, had tarnished their honor by the use of slavery.

Horned cattle had now long been introduced into Hayti by the Spaniards, and were, when the French commenced their career in the island, quite abundant.

The Spaniards had already commenced the importation of Africans. Slavery had begun its horrid course, and the French, like their predecessors in this foul scheme, from equal thirst of wealth, drove on the fearful system with dreadful energy, so that from about 1650, which was soon after the commencement of African slavery in Hayti, till about 1737, the entire population of the French part of the island, including all classes and colors, amounted to 600,000; and this, too, in an age when the means of traveling and general transport were very far from the facilities of the present day. Such, too, had been already the development of the unbounded resources of this fertile land, that it soon acquired the distinguished title of "Le Paradis des Français!"—so great was the wealth that had been wrenched from the now annihilated Indian, and from the still lashed and groaning African.

But slavery had by this time become a thoroughly consolidated system. The Spanish, English, French, and other nations, had forced its galling yoke upon the whole of the West India islands.

In the French part of the island, the increased activity arising from an intense eagerness for wealth, brought on all the cruelties peculiar to slavery, and this passion became more and more intense: the exhaustless resources of the country were brought out, until in the end, riches and luxury assumed a scale of even grandeur, as may be seen at the present day in the northern part of the present Haytian Republic, by such remains of ancient seats as plainly indicate the style of former days, when the positions of both high and low were almost fabulous in their extremes of misery and ease.

It is true that the French colonists frequently resided on their foreign properties, and their homes and general establishments, therefore, corresponded with their wealth and rank—a habit exceedingly advantageous to the colony, making it as it did superior in production to the British colonies, where absenteeism, as to land-holders, was the general rule.

French and other writers unite to give a glowing picture of St. Domingo, of which the details would doubtless be interesting here; it will, however, for the present, be impossible for us to enter into any of the particulars of the internal management of this splendid colony, under the French; suffice it to say, that as to slavery, it was carried out in all its fearful and revolting details, while at the same time, the most rigid order was maintained throughout the entire system of things, civil, military, and religious, as it then existed. But amidst all this luxurious ease, so much sought and adored in the relaxing heat of the tropics, the instinctive throes of oppressed humanity would sometimes shake the foundations of society, a fact which ought to remind all posterity that truth and justice alone can render our homes safe, or make the future bright.

During the eighteenth century, the seeds of fearful principles had not only taken root, but had risen up and borne their awful fruit. France broke her ancient chains, but in her fury, she confounded all order, and for a moment let loose upon herself overwhelming ruin.

The North American Colonies, under British rule, also rose, and asserted their solemn resolution to be free, and constitute themselves an independent people. The convulsions necessarily associated with these gigantic efforts amongst mankind, are always great; nor was it possible that such bold and mighty struggles for liberty, of every kind, should have been without effect, on such a population as that which was now found in St. Domingue, especially when it is remembered that the materials which made up the general state of society at that time, were peculiarly liable to ignite and explode, as will be easily understood when it is remembered, that in so many cases, the sons of the white colonists had been sent to France by their fathers, for their education, where they had acquired not only the general elements of literature, but where they had imbibed the political life and spirit of the times, from which such fearful and overwhelming storms broke forth.

The simple but important fact of an European education having been given to many of the sons of the French colonists, should by no means be lost sight of in the history of this country, for it may be truly regarded as a hinge, on which so much that is interesting and important turned, in the general course of events which followed; it was, in fact, the root and spring of Haytian manhood as a nation.

It was in France itself, therefore, let it be remembered, that the colored sons of Hayti learnt to know what they were; there it was that they were taught, at the expense of their own white fathers, residing in their native land, that they were men, and that righteous heaven had made them heirs of liberty, without reference to color or any other condition; and yet, on the return of these well-prepared sons for liberty, their own fathers refused them those common rights of men, for which they themselves had fitted them, and even despised their darker hue.

That flames of discord should burst forth from such

conflicting elements, cannot be at all surprising to any who have read human history, or studied human nature.

The case of Ogé will throw a melancholy light on this deeply interesting part of French colonial history in St. Domingue.

This individual, the colored son of a white colonist, had, by his education in France, acquired a full sense and consciousness of his dignity as a man, and on his return to his home, boldly demanded of the colonial government his rights as such. It should be understood that this demand was not simply for himself, it was in the name of his fellows; but it was received by those on whom it was made, both with contempt and indignation. A mock trial was the result of this demand, and the end of this iniquitous proceeding, in the name of law, was, that this unhappy, although noble minded man, was, with another, led out to execution, and in open day, before the great church of this noted city, was publicly, and with the most humiliating ceremonies, broken on the wheel, his thighs, legs, arms, and loins, being broken by blows, inflicted with heavy bars of iron. This disgraceful scene took place in the city of Cape Haytien, on the 25th of February, 1791.*

It is not surprising that the general course of oppression, which led to the barbarous execution of Ogé and others, should at last have roused and set fire to the fiercest passions of our nature. This was, indeed, the case. Struggles and contests came on, and the passions rose to fury, until opposing armies of mutual hate were formed. Nor was it to be sup-

* T. Madiou's History of Hayti.

posed that France would lose so splendid a colony, without making the utmost effort to keep it. We therefore here give a statistic sketch of the great armaments, and immense expense, so promptly and unsparingly put forth by the home government, as the beginning of this dreadful struggle, which has taken its place upon the page of history.

The following statement will enable us to form some idea of the forces sent from France to St. Domingo during the years 1802 and 1803:

FIRST EXPEDITION.

Troops of all sorts, sent from Brest, under command of

Vilaret Joyeuse, on board eighteen-men-of-war	6,600
On the Lorient, and two others	900
A squadron, by Admiral Gauthcaume	4,000
A squadron, by Admiral Latouche	4,000
A squadron, by Admiral Linois	2,000
A squadron from Havre	1,000
A Dutch squadron, Admiral Hurtzwitch	1,500

SECOND EXPEDITION.

In June, "Expeditionnaire"	1,600
On board the Formidable and Annibal	1,600
On board three men-of-war, in August	4,000
On board the Vautour	700
On board the Lodi	2,000
On board the Egyptian	2,570
On board the Prudent	512
On board the Jeanne Edouard	227

THIRD EXPEDITION.

A division under Rochambeau	6,000
A division under Admiral Bedout	6,000
On board several men-of-war	4,000
On board several vessels	1,500
On board the frigate Infatigable	1,000

LOSSES UNDER GENERAL LECLERC,

During nine months, according to statistics given by the French General, Pamphile Lacroix.

Whites of both sexes, murdered in various ways	3,000
General officers of all sorts, by sickness or war	2,000
Soldiers slain in battle	5,000
Soldiers lost by sickness	20,000
Sailors by war and sickness	8,000
Sailors of merchantmen, by war and sickness	3,000
Men in Government employ, civil and military	
Lost by war and disease	2,000
Men engaged in commerce	3,000
Natives killed in war	0,800
Natives lost by disease in Government service	1,800
Blacks and colored by war	7,000
Blacks and colored, drowned and murdered, judicially	4,000

In these harrowing details, we see the price which it cost, not to retain, but to lose this splendid colony The elements themselves fought against the Europeans; in fact, that which sheds so deep a gloom on this already dark and melancholy picture, is the unhappy fact, that the leading purpose of this mighty armament, involving such an immense expenditure of gold, life, and suffering, was, not to liberate mankind, and thus carry out the great principles of liberty, for which France had convulsed all Europe, but it was a gigantic effort to re-enslave those who, having already drank the gall and bitterness of bondage, were now beginning to taste the sweets of liberty—France herself having declared all men free and equal! So uncertain are even the greatest gusts of political winds, which are raised by hollow and exaggerated principles.

Doubtless, the climate, which was so unfriendly to

European constitutions, became a powerful weapon in the hands of the Haytians against their enemies; and, like men of war, they knew how to turn every means to their own advantage, which they most certainly did in every conceivable manner. Yet it cannot be denied, that they fought bravely, whenever necessity placed them in the front of their enemies, notwithstanding their army was composed of men who had but just come forth from the withering darkness of slavery. In fact, that an army composed of almost chaos itself, should have shown phalanxes of good order and rigid discipline, was not to be expected; still it is not to be denied that the Haytian arms, in connection with the fiery elements of the tropics, etc., did confound and triumph over some of the best troops that ever left the shores of France. But the fact is, that neither intelligence, discipline, or bravery, can successfully maintain war against such deadly powers, especially when they are at the command of those who are at home in them, who know well how to use them, and above all, who have right on their side.

Although it is not the design of this volume to enter fully into the details of those sanguinary wars, by which the Haytians won their liberty, it is but just to the memory of the brave that fell in this great struggle, and also to those who nobly stood by them when they fell, to record those deeds of valor, which in all ages have ever been appreciated and applauded. One narration of this nature may be due to Hayti. This was the attack of the French army in the affair of what is called "La crête à Pierrot."

The place thus named, was a fortification in the

northern part of the island, which in itself was said to have been comparatively insignificant, and was originally built, it would appear, by the English, being situated about a mile from the village, in the plain of the Artibomte, called "La Petite Riviere." One side of this fortress is nearly perpendicular, while from the north and south the approaches are difficult, and are covered with a considerable quantity of underwood, and some large trees, under cover of which, the French made their attacks. Three unsuccessful assaults were made by the French, in their attempts to take this memorable fort. According to General Pamphile La Croix, who commanded one of the divisions of the French army on that occasion, the attacking force amounted fully to twelve thousand men, while the native garrison could not have been more than twelve hundred, under the command of Le Chef de Brigade Lamartinière.

The amount of the attacking forces in this affair would scarcely have been credible, had not the account been transmitted to us by an evidently generous enemy in the French army.

The little army holding the fort against such fearful odds, being sorely pressed, and very naturally despairing, resolved at last to sell their lives as dear as possible, and therefore came to the final resolution of cutting their way through the superior forces of the French; hence they rushed forth—their dash was furious; nearly one-half of them fell as they drove through the ranks of their enemies, the remaining half victoriously joining the main Black Army beyond.

This feat is justly celebrated as a great and deadly

one in Haytian history, and is admitted to be such by the candid French military historian, already named, who was present at the time, and who relates this extraordinary case, with a frankness which commands admiration. This event took place in March, 1802.*

Men of renown in arms, although many of them without any other education than that which was imprinted on their souls by the existing circumstances which surrounded them, had now risen up in Hayti. Toussaint, Dessalines, Christophe, Petion, Rigaud, with many others, were already high in military fame, and in that cause of independence which long has been the glory of Hayti. They had all shown themselves to be no ordinary men, having secured the liberties of an oppressed people by feats of valor and renown. It may indeed be said, that they were men of fury and of blood, nor is it to be denied that such was the case, although certainly not more so than their opponents, whose arms, in this case, were tarnished by the defence of an unrighteous cause, as well as much needless cruelty.

Nevertheless, such were the leading Haytian spirits of this remarkable epoch—men who had been raised to their elevation in the affairs of their own people, by circumstances over which they had had no control. Nor is it to be denied that they were singularly fitted for their times and circumstances. They were indeed men of war, and therefore they used the sword unsparingly, and without hesitation, whenever it was needed. Nor let it be forgotten, that whatever barbarities were practiced, when the passions rose, they

* Mackenzie's Notes on Hayti.

were only the imitations of an enemy with which they had to contend, whose pretentions to superiority in all respects were sufficiently great. It were, indeed, an easy task to show that the provocations of the Europeans of those times, in too many instances, consisted of the most barbarous atrocities that ever tortured human nature. But the white man's provocations doubtless commenced in the theft of human beings on the coasts of Africa, and were continued through generations of such slavery as was never surpassed in cruelty and oppression by either Egyptians, Greeks, or Romans.

Here doubtless will be found the root and origin of all Dessaline's fury and cruelty. Here, too, was the false starting-point of those who brought superior minds and arms to this great contest; and if the dignity of independence is to be judged by the extent of life, blood, and treasure, laid down for it, then indeed will the merits of Haytian independence appear to be great. But injustice and oppression have never, in the whole history of mankind, failed ultimately to work out their own destruction.

The Haytians, therefore, in their wars, have simply shown themselves to be as other men, nor will history fail to do them justice, for the leading minds among them at their national birth, were evidently, in many respects, equal to some of the most advanced spirits of that age, on the great questions of human rights and general liberty.

But war has not always been the only phase of Haytian existence; although, like many other nations, this was the fiery element through which it rose into form and power.

For a moment, therefore, let us turn our thoughts back to the commercial, educational, and religious interests of this remarkable community, during its colonial existence, especially as many of the elements of the present national peculiarities of Hayti are derived from the colonial regime, which was certainly not without some few good and interesting features.

With regard to commerce, it can easily be understood that the great and exhaustless resources of an incomparably fertile soil, together with an insatiable desire for wealth, would certainly, with the power of life and death in hand, drive on industry at a rapid, yea, fearful rate. In fact, the sum total of the produce of St. Domingue became the wonder and admiration of Europe, although the thought but rarely occurred in those days, that this was all iniquitously drawn from Africa. But with this power in hand over a population of about 700,000, the result of industry would be immense. It will not be astonishing, therefore, that in 1801, the produce was—

Sugar of all sorts	18,535,112 lbs.
Coffee	43,220,270 "
Cotton	2,480,340 "
Logwood	6,768,634 "
Cocoa—Chocolate	648,518 "
Sirup	99,419 "
Gum	75,519 "
Indigo	804 "
Mahogany	5,217 ft.

Besides which, an immense traffic was carried on in skins and a variety of woods.

In this year were found in the French part of the island—

Horses	37,782
Mules	48,852
Horned cattle	247,612 *

* Madiou's History.

Such, in fact, was the amount of wealth, resulting from the tremendous pressure of oppression, which the system of slavery brought to bear upon the great mass of the slaves, that the aristocracy of the colony lived in splendor seldom equaled, as may be seen by some of the French historians of that day, as well as by the mansion-like remains, which are still standing in the northern part of the present republic.

But a system which outraged every feeling of human nature, could not, in the nature of things, consolidate; sooner or later, in such a case, all must change, either by reasonable or violent means.

On the subject of education, under the colonial dispensation, it will be easy to conceive that anything like a really developed, or widely extended system of tuition, would not even be thought of, simply because it was not compatible, or even possible, with the existence of slavery. In fact, with any kind of despotism, the one thing needful is ignorance. The elevation and instruction of every and each individual in a community belongs rather to our own day.

At the same time, the various historians that have written on St. Domingue, inform us that education was not altogether neglected in the colony, and that here and there were individuals of both the clergy and others, who manifested more or less interest on this subject. But in all such matters, we have simply to bear in mind the tendency and spirit of the age. Still, there were even in those days, some few establishments founded, for both monks and nuns, with doubtless good intentions; but the centres of real good were indeed few, and their aims were limited. This indeed, at this time, was the case throughout Europe; in fact, up to the end of the eighteenth century, even in the most advanced portions of the civilized world, the education of the masses was rather dreaded than sought.

The great movement in Hayti did not, therefore, begin in a thirst for knowledge, nor was it the offspring of a widely diffused or national education; it was rather the effect of the French revolution, which was the great event of that day, and which, notwithstanding all its horrors, nobly declared all men to be free!

Whether the fierce leaders of that astonishing convulsion of humanity remembered that the descendants of Africa in St. Domingue had ears to hear, and hearts to feel, on this great question, need not now be discussed; although it must be admitted, that the colored people of the French colonies were honorably treated, and well received in France, as the representatives of their people.

On the subject of religion, although it was much more widely diffused than education, yet that it was such as really regenerates the heart, may be fairly questioned. On this subject, two things are to be noted:

First, that the ceremonies and general ritual of the church of Rome prevailed, as far as Christianity was concerned.

Secondly, that African superstitions were believed and practiced to an awful extent. In fact, to enter fully into detail on this question, would require a volume of no ordinary size, and would most certainly bring out some awful developments. Certain it is, that the presence and pernicious influence of African superstitions was the constant complaint of the colonial writers. Doubtless there were in this colonial community many well intentioned people. But the foundations of society here were wrong, and the very structure of things was incompatible with true Christian principle.

One of the leading superstitions introduced from Africa was Vandouism, of which the presiding god is called Vandoux. The disciples of this creed are generally formed into organized and united societies, which are bound by solemn oath to secrecy.

We are informed by a French writer* that the word Vandoux is said to mean, in the African sense, an almighty, omnipresent, and omniscient being. We are also informed that this being is represented by a snake or serpent, not venomous. But whatever may have been the original meaning of the word in question, it is impossible to suppose it to have been so understood by the Africans themselves, unless we are to understand it as a proof, that an advanced state of civilization at one time existed in Africa—an idea in perfect harmony with much that has been said of the main divisions of the human family.

But the ceremonies and rites connected with the Vandoux worship, are minutely detailed by the author last referred to. They are painfully interesting, and lead to the inevitable conclusion, that the climax of the system is immorality and perdition.†

* Morau St. Méry.

† The Vandoux dance, in which both sexes engaged—frequently under the influence of intoxicating drinks—would lead on to a sort of religious phrenzy, which terminated in the greatest obscenities.

Such was the general state of things under the colonial system in St. Domingue. Commerce and wealth were abundant, but all was the effect of brutal force, and not the happy fruit of spontaneous industry;—literature and education, with very little exception, being excluded.

The details of this unhapy state of things, as here given, are not indeed minute. But perhaps enough has been said, for our general guidance, in forming our ideas on the question in hand, and to enable us to see that the forming materials for this nation consisted principally of masses of human beings, which had been brought over by ship loads from Africa, each mind being steeped in foul and gloomy superstitions, which had been handed down from generation to generation, for many ages past, unaccompanied by any ray of light, on any really good and useful subject.

True, the imported Africans now found themselves in contact with light and intelligence, which they had never known before. But in the case of their now white masters, the melancholy fact stands clearly out, that religion and knowledge were wielded as mighty powers, to awe the enslaved masses into the degrading belief, that they were really inferior beings. Nor is it to be questioned, that this ruling idea, so essential to the security of an unrighteous power, was worked out and acted upon, until all sense of manhood was at last annihilated, together with every noble feeling, even of their former savage state; all was degradation, both to the high and to the low. Hence the whole course of things was ruinous to all parties; the master dared from fear, and the bondman submitted from the same base motive, until all was error, tyranny, and corruption.

Such a people seizing their liberty, and wresting it by force of arms, from an enemy vastly superior to themselves, would inevitably involve the necessity of a military system, as the only means under such circumstances of protecting their liberty. They had indeed beaten off their enemy, but there was reason to believe that his purpose was to re-enslave, as was evident in the case of some of the other French colonies, where slavery had been recommenced.

Hence the sword, which had become the deliverer, became the protector, and ultimately, the ruler of the nation. Justice, therefore, compels us to admit, that the character and style of the Haytian Republic, as to public institutions, were formed under the most unhappy circumstances; and it might perhaps safely be said, that this nation stands alone as to the circumstances of its origin and formation. Nevertheless, there were among the originators of Haytian independence, minds well formed, and of enlarged views, as to what a free people ought to be, as may be understood from the fact already mentioned, that many of the sons of the colonists had received their education in France. Yet it will be easily understood, that these men, with their educational advantages, were greatly embarrassed by a mass of ignorance, of which they were greatly in advance, and yet without which they could not act, although they could not in all cases control them.

It is, however, an extraordinary fact, that even from the uneducated masses of those days, men would almost suddenly appear, who often seemed to be singularly fitted for the work, which divine Providence evidently meant them to accomplish in behalf of their people.

The spirit of the French revolution, with its general bearing, became well known to and understood by the Haytians; but the details of its influence and general working upon this infant people, must be left to the future historians of events relating to Hayti. We, however, must not lose sight of the revolutionary spirit, which thus innoculated this nation from its very birth, and which, from want of the habit of free and open discussion, political or otherwise, have been, in a certain sense, the only safety-valves of the nation.

From the general working of circumstances and events, rose that remarkable man, Toussaint L'Ouverture, who as a slave, faithfully served his kind master, Mons. Bayou, as coachman. Toussaint, in gratitude to his benefactor, who had given him more or less education, not only aided him in his flight to the United States, but also in supporting him in his exile there; and being then at liberty, joined the insurgents under Jean François, by whom he was rapidly promoted.

Toussaint, in this case it would seem, simply fought for royalty, under the impression that it was the form of government best suited to his people. This royalist party was then in connection with Spain. But Toussaint L'Ouverture soon left the Spanish service, and was accepted by the French General Laveaux, by whom he was made a general. Toussaint was soon recognized as a man of great ability, and as such, his influence over the blacks would naturally be very great. He now promoted the French interests, and soon drove the Spaniards in all quarters.

Ultimately Toussaint L'Ouverture was invested, by the French Commissioners, with the office and dignity of General-in-Chief of St. Domingue.

The conviction that the French were sincere in their declarations as to Liberty, doubtless won Toussaint back to them:

On the 14th of February, 1794, entire liberty to all men was proclaimed by the French Republic, intentionally involving the abolition of slavery, and this was ratified by the reception of Black and Colored Deputies, which were sent from St. Domingue to represent that branch of the French Empire; nor should this remarkable circumstance, connected with the great Freneh Revolution, be lost sight of, or slightly passed over; for it ought to be remembered that nations, which in those days made far greater pretentions to Christianity than Revolutionary France, then, and even long after, held men in chains.

The declaration in France of universal liberty was, in this case, practically carried out; and the proof of sincerity, at least in the dominant party of the day, with regard to the entire equality of mankind, was seen in the great fact that all shades of color, as Representatives from St. Domingue, took their seats with their White Brethren, now their recognized and acknowledged equals, as in fact they were in intelligence, civilization, and education.

Whatever horrors, therefore, distinguished the unparalleled convulsion produced by the French Revolution of the latter part of the last century, the recognized equality of mankind, on the subject of color, was an honor which no other nation, however Christian, had at that time acquired, and which, even at this day, we are compelled to applaud, at least as to all who were really sincere in this matter; for, it must be admitted that subsequent events proved but too clearly that they were only a portion, however powerful, of the French nation whose views were thus liberal.

The French Commissioners in the Colony of St. Domingue, it should be stated, had, in an hour of alarm, proclaimed the Emancipation of the Slaves, who were now in great excitement from fear of being again re-enslaved; but, under the power and influence of Toussaint, as General-in-Chief, they were soon marshalled into a body of industrious free laborers.

Up to a late period of his life, Toussaint remained faithful to the French, who long were indebted to his unlimited influence over the masses; but he was also inflexibly true to the great cause of Liberty; yet his fidelity to France is seen in the fact, that while he served the French, he maintained and kept up the produce, prosperity, and general industry of the country; a fact which, in connection with the undeniable injustice and oppression of the White Colonists, throws the guilt of all the blood which was shed in the Revolutionary struggles of St. Domingue upon the Whites; who, by plain honesty and impartial justice, might have saved their lives, their country, and their fame.

During the time of Toussaint L'Ouverture, the English had been called in from Jamaica by the

French White Planters, and they soon began to display their power, ultimately establishing themselves at Port-au-Prince and other places; but their military force was always comparatively small, and they at last evacuated; to this day, however, several forts, in various parts of the country, are pointed out as having been built by the English.

It is said by a French author* that the British, during their stay in the country, offered Toussaint to create him King, and to sustain his Independence; this, however, he is said to have declined, notwithstanding he was, like most men, ambitious of power; while at the same time the sending of his two sons to France for their education, strongly indicated his entire fidelity to that country, and that he did not aspire to anything beyond the honors which he then enjoyed, and of which he had shown himself worthy.

In 1805, Toussaint decided on extending his rule through the Southern part of St. Domingue, where General Rigaud had long presided as Military Chief. Toussaint having the masses with him, and being himself popular, it was, perhaps, to be expected that Rigaud's party should disappear, although headed by a man of no ordinary character.

Toussaint prevailed, and having thus made himself master of the whole of the French part of the Island, he now marched upon the city of Santo Domingo, the ancient city of the Spanish part of Hayti; here also his arms were victorious, so that the extent of his Empire was the entire length and breadth of the Island; his rule was severe and rigid; indeed, one Haytian historian speaks of him as having been exceedingly cruel. †

* Pamphile la Croix. † St. Reny de Cayes.

There is, indeed, something significant in the two last named campaigns; a full narration of them would, doubtless, be exceedingly interesting; that they had a definite object in view is not to be doubted, but notwithstanding the well demonstrated honor of Toussaint, the suspicions of Napoleon were probably roused by his great successes and power, as in fact became quite apparent in the end.

After the conquest of the city of Santo Domingo, Toussaint convoked an "Assemblée Constituante," composed of the leading Generals of his army; from this body emanated a document in the form of a Constitution, the proclamation of which was offensive to Napoleon I., who, on hearing of it, declared that Toussaint, by this act, had thrown off the mask and drawn the sword from the scabbard for ever. How he could have arrived at such a conclusion, is difficult to understand; Toussaint having, in all good faith, sent him a copy of all the proceedings for his examination and approval; the French, however, from this time ceased to consider Toussaint true to them.

That the rule of Toussaint L'Ouverture should have been harsh and severe, is not astonishing, for he had resolved to keep up the produce of the Island, and having himself been trained to do this by brutal force, he probably deemed it the only means of accomplishing his purpose; nor are we to lose sight of the fact, that he could not be expected to have had any really correct idea of free Institutions or free Government.

Toussaint, however, remained true to the French as long as they themselves remained faithful to the leading principles of their own great Revolution, in relation to universal Liberty; nor is it to be supposed that his own nature could go beyond this; but on the arrival of the last army sent by Napoleon I., under General Leclerc, the suspicions and fears of the Haytians were greatly excited by the fact, that while the highest pretensions and the strongest assurances were made as to sustaining the liberties of the Haytians, the other French West India Colonies had been again reduced to slavery. Here, then, was fearful reason for any change which might show itself in Toussaint. He was faithful to the liberty which the French Revolution had proclaimed, and he was resolved to maintain it; but the French Islands of Guadaloupe and Martinique having been again compelled to bow to the iron yoke of slavery, he concluded that it was impossible that the richer colony of St. Domingue should remain free.

There was great dignity in the stand of the noble hearted Toussaint L'Ouverture for Liberty; nor will the true historian of Hayti fail to give him all due honor; while posterity will never cease to deplore that he was seized by order of General Brunet, put on board a French man-of-war, and carried off to France, where he was thrown into the Fortress of Joux, in the Department of Jura. Toussaint L'Ouverture was taken on the 11th of February, 1802 and died, it is said, of starvation in the month of April the following year, within the walls of the above-named fortress.

CHAPTER II.

French cruelty to Haytians.—Dessalines proclaims Independence.—800 Whites fall at St. Marks.—Ferrand's Proclamation.—Dessalines marches on Santo Domingo.—Viet flogged to death. Dessalines retreats.—Christophe carries off hundreds.—Dessalines shot.—"L'Assemblée Constituante"—Report to Christophe on Petion's Constitution.—Christophe marches on Port au Prince.—The Republican's routed.—Christophe retreats.—The Senate provides for Northern exiles.—Laws of Christophe on Marriage, etc.—"Ou'peut on este mieux," etc.—The two States compared.—Rebecca Port de Paix.—Lamarre Gardel, etc.—Gen. Borgella joins the Republic.—Christophe proclaimed King.—Christophe's Cruelty to his Servant.—The Constitution read by every Haytian.

The great primeval chaos of the earth
Compared with that which from foul passions bursts,
Was order!

The French now having the strongest assurance that the blacks of St. Domingo were fully bent on maintaining their freedom, gave way to every evil passion, perpetrating the greatest atrocities, and the foulest barbarities; hence the pangs through which this infant people rose to independence were indeed great. They, however, helped to form the nation, and compelled its independence.

The unhappy Haytians were seized, and drowned by hundreds in the harbors; others were shot, bayoneted, or gibbeted, until hate, anger, and revenge had reached their horrid climax.

In 1802, Petion and Clairveaux revolt from the French, and are soon joined by Dessalines, whose superior authority was recognized by Petion, and he soon became General.

The black and colored people were now finally resolved on liberty, but the horrors of their struggle were great. All parties became furious. The French had now yielded to the despair of their threatened and exciting position, their mortified passions rosé high, and this soon brought on the pitiless and retaliating massacre of the whites by Dessalines, whom the fearful circumstances of the times had turned into a fury.

The details of the mutual cruelties of all parties are fully entered into by the Haytian historian already referred to, whose work has been officially acknowledged by the Haytian Government as authentic.*

Nothing could be more deplorable than the state of things at this time, as described by the historian just referred to; indeed it is impossible not to read in it the simple truth that right, whether civil, political, or religious, cannot be trampled upon with impunity; sooner or later, if not in one generation, in another, a fearful reckoning comes on, for man is destined to rise to the dignity of right, nor can mere shades of color hinder it.

The year 1803 was rendered remarkable by the entire breaking up of the French power in Hayti; the now roused indignation of an incensed people, led on by able and daring men, who had justice on their side, and were true to the great and righteous cause

* Madiou (Fils.)

of liberty, proved to be too much for the abettors of slavery, although backed by all that France could do; nor is it for a moment to be doubted that the utmost efforts of a great people were here brought out, for St. Domingue had now long been the "Paradis des Francais," and it was not to be supposed that it would be given up without a struggle.

The bravery and energy of Dessalines were great, and he was very naturally considered by the Haytians to be the great hero of the day; but he had been inured to slavery, tyranny, and blood, nor had his mind been softened by education; yet he was the man for the moment, and he had risen to eminence amongst his fellows by military feats which had swept away the enemies of liberty.

This man, fearing neither France nor all the legions she had sent forth, or the yet greater she might still send, on the 1st of January, 1804, in the city of Ganaives, solemnly and fearlessly proclaimed the independence and sovereignty of the Haytian people, and at the same time abolished for ever the name of St. Domingue, as a name which would only bring to remembrance the deepest horrors, and re-established the aboriginal name of Hayti.

Thus singularly did a comparatively weak people triumph by the mere justice of their cause—a people which probably it would have been easier for France to have annihilated than to have subdued.

Thus too may it be said that slavery received its first great blow in modern days; and as far as Hayti is concerned, 1804 may be considered as an epoch of no ordinary note. The fact is, that the honor of the first great shock to this gigantic evil of modern times, is due to Hayti.

> Hayti thus dared the fiends of all the earth ;
> They fled before the glory of her birth.

Dessalines, in the giddy whirl of victory, declared himself an emperor. It is, however, worthy of note, that he created neither nobility nor privileged class of any kind. True, indeed, the vanity of this extraordinary step was quite enough without it. His rule was marked by the fierceness of his nature ; nor can it be for a moment surprising that such a man should have been in an exclusive sense fitted for this one great object, viz., that of defying France, by sweeping slavery for ever from the shorés of Hayti, and proclaiming the sovereignty and independence of his country ; thus boldly starting the great principle that independence is the dignity of any people, to which God has given in any sense or manner a special destiny.

The barbarous drowning and gibbeting of the Haytians by the whites, doubtless provoked their wholesale murder by the infuriated Dessalines, under whose relentless sword men, women, and children, in the town and neighborhood of St. Mark's, fell—both the provocation and revenge remaining as foul blots upon the page of history ; so true it is that in all senses we reap that which we sow.

Eight hundred of all ages, and of both sexes, are said to have been swept off, at one fell swoop, by the ever-memorable Dessalines, at the last-named place.

These dreadful events are minutely brought out

by the faithful historian; nor will truth and justice spare the guilty, of whatever color or people.

In 1805, the French General Ferrand, then commanding the city of Santo Domingo, the capital of the Spanish part of the island, issued a proclamation, by which all Spaniards living on the frontier were empowered to reduce to slavery any of the Haytians which they might be able to capture. The natural effect of this iniquitous measure was the wrath and indignation of Dessalines, who immediately decided on marching against the ancient Spanish capital, and without provisioning his army, he arranges everything for departure; pillage, therefore, would become the only means of subsistence for this army of 30,000 men. This too was intended by Dessalines as in some sense punitive, although it unquestionably suited the poverty of his resources.

The country through which this mass of men had to march, was in many places mountainous and rugged, and frequently without anything worth calling a road. The troops from the extreme west end of the island had not less than 193 leagues to march, before reaching Santo Domingo.

In addition to other difficulties, it must be remembered that, in the Spanish part of the island, several formidable rivers would have to be forded, or crossed in large ferries, bridges being out of the question; but this numerous army was driven through every difficulty and privation by the brutal proclamation of Ferrand, which, as might be supposed, had produced a fearful effect.

In due time they arrived at the well-known pass between two mountains, in the neighborhood of

Azua, where a few well-directed cannons might defy even a powerful army. Here Ferrand considered that the Haytians would certainly be entombed. Instead of this, however, to the great astonishment of the French and Spaniards, they took the Fort, which it was thought would have commanded everything, in such a position.

Many prisoners were taken by the Haytians on this occasion, and among them the commandant of the Fort which commanded this pass, named Viet, who was brought before Dessalines, and was recognized as an old colonist, who had been exceedingly cruel on his plantation.

This unfortunate man was ordered by the Emperor to be flogged to death, which was no sooner done, than a Haytian soldier opened his breast with one stroke of the axe, and taking out his heart, devoured it before the army. The man that did this abominable deed, was from a cannibal tribe in Africa. Such an act was indeed horrible to think of; and yet it is a humiliating fact that during the French Revolution of 1792, cases of furiously devouring human blood are recorded.

Dessalines entered Azua on the 1st of March, and on the following 4th of the same month, he challenged Ferrand under the walls of Santo Domingo.

Christophe's division had had to contend with the French and Spanish forces, before reaching the main body of the army.

The force of all arms in the city could not have been more—if even so many—than 5,000; but the Haytians had no artillery, and could not therefore contend with the heavy pieces of this ancient Spanish fortification, which the besieged did not fail to use furiously against the besiegers.

Soon, however, great murmuring commenced against the French General in Santo Domingo, in consequence of a great want of provisions in the city. But help soon arrived, and Dessalines hearing that Ferrand still expected more, called a council of war, in which it was decided that the assault on the city should be commenced on the 26th of March, which indeed took place; but Dessalines, fearing that French forces were landing on other parts of the island, and despairing of success against an artillery to which he had none to oppose, raised the siege and withdrew, laying everything in his retreat under fire and sword.

Christophe, as he advanced with his retreating columns to the north, set fire to St. Jago, it is said with his own hands, and ordered the butchery of twenty priests, who were found in the burying-ground of the place.

The Haytian historian* also informs us that this General, during his retreat, took with him 349 men, 430 male children, and 318 girls, who had been doubtless captured wherever they could be found.

The siege had continued some twenty days.

But the empire of Dessalines—which had begun on the 8th of October, 1805—was destined to be of short duration. Although he had been the most daring friend of his country against its enemies, disgust and impatience at his tyranny soon ripened into revolution, respecting which Dessalines is said to have declared that the entire south—where in all

* T. Madiou (Fils.)

probability this revolt against him originated—should be drenched in blood, and left a desert, where not even a cock should be heard to crow!

On the 17th of October, 1806, Dessalines left Arcahaie, where he had arrived from Marchand, his favorite retreat, in the neighborhood of the town of St. Mark's, on his way to Port au Prince, his object being to put down the rebellion against his government which had just commenced, not doubting for a moment of success.

Arriving at "Pont Rouge," a bridge within half a mile of Port au Prince, and which he reached about 9 A. M., on the last mentioned date, he found himself surrounded by a revolutionary army, which had decided on his destruction. When the two parties met, a confused conflict took place, in which he was picked out by one in the opposing ranks, and shot.

Thus fell the founder of Haytian independence, and it will be for posterity to judge the case of this first revolution recorded in Haytian history.

The death of Dessalines, just or unjust, was doubtless brought on by the despotic course which he had pursued with his own people, who, had he only been just, would have made him their idol. His very looks are said to have inspired terror. Daring to the utmost, he doubtless was the right man to defy France, and break its iron yoke.

After his death, some cut off his fingers; others took the ornaments from his person; such was the eagerness to have some relic of this extraordinary man.

A Constitution had been drawn up under Dessalines, which was considered to be suited to the times and circumstances of Hayti. The main thing, or rather the most prominent feature, in the National charter thus drawn up, was the article which was then justly deemed indispensable to the national identity and independence of Hayti, viz., that the whites should be excluded, as land proprietors, from the territory of Hayti—a measure only in harmony with that day, and can now be viewed only as a necessary evil.

Exclusiveism can never, indeed, be considered as the order of God, and hence can never be perpetuated, without ultimately bringing on the ruinous effects of stagnation; free moral currents must sweep through all the earth, nor can it be doubted that this grand day of safe, healthy, and universal freedom is coming on.

It is indeed to be deplored that the internal storms and conflicts of this small, but now independent nation, did not terminate with the political exectuion of Dessalines. This, however, was not the case. Yet far greater difficulties were in the future. The epoch now before us seems to have been a hinge upon which the hopes of the nation turned. It was indeed a critical moment. Nothing, however, is more deceptive than human nature. Peace might have been looked for even at this critical juncture of affairs; but so long as it is not a principle in the human heart to covet the lowest place, rather than the highest, the assurance of peace must remain shaken. The highest place in this young nation, which was but just starting into life, was even already too much adored, and there were many who thought themselves equally entitled to and capable of all the power, dignity, and honor which this country could offer.

General Christophe was now a prominent character on the stage of Haytian affairs—he also having been renowned for his daring against the French. Hence, after the death of Dessalines, he was named by a military council, not only as commander of all the forces, but as the provisional chief of the nation. This honor was conferred upon him provisionally, until the National Assembly should be called. This great meeting was to be called "L'Assemblée Constituante," and was invested with authority by the same originating source as clothed Christophe himself with the power and dignity which he had received—which was doubtless the first Senatorial body.

This great "Assemblée Constuante," which must be considered, historically, as one of the starting points of free and constitutional government in Hayti, took place on the 18th of December, 1806, in the cathedral church of the capital, which at that time was Port au Prince.

Christophe's residence was in the northern part of the island, at Cape Haytien. His ideas of government were well known to be in favor of great powers and prerogatives confided to the Executive. In fact, it is probable that he had inherited from Toussaint L'Ouverture the idea of a monarchical form of government; for although the latter is said to have declined a crown of British offer, and under British protection, yet it is probable that if he had remained in Hayti, he might ultimately have become an independent monarch—there having been great reason to believe that his ideas ran much in this channel. On this subject, Christophe's views had been gathered from his general conversations. But in the West, where General Petion resided, all was enthusiastically in favor of Republicanism. In these two great facts—the difference of political views and principles between Petion and Christophe—doubtless commenced the unhappy division between the northern and the western portions of the French part of Hayti.

Republican views and feelings, it would appear, prevailed in the National Assembly, notwithstanding the agents of Christophe were many, and his power and influence very great.

After much warm and even violent discussion, a constitution was finally drawn up, on the most liberal principles, and Christophe was chosen President of the Republic of Hayti, for four years.

In this constitution, the articles excluding the whites as land owners, was continued, and the Roman Catholic religion was recognized as being that of the Haytian nation, without any reference to other creeds, in the way of toleration.

During the framing of this constitution, one named Juste Ugonin is said to have written to Christophe, and to have observed to him that if he accepted it, he would have no more power than a corporal!

On the 27th of December, 1806, the final meeting of " L'Assemblée Constituante" took place. All was anxiety; and an ably drawn up Introduction to it was read by General Bonnet, who was a man of known ability; and this highly important national document, which had absorbed the attention of its framers until after sunset, was by them, amidst high hopes and expectations, signed by candle-light.

It is a remarkable fact that it had been proposed to hold this important National Assembly at Cape

Haytien; but Christophe, having all confidence in his own power and influence, opposed the proposition, lest it should afterwards be said that he had in any way influenced their decision; yet he never scrupled to make it known that if the new Constitution should not suit him, he would reject it. In fact, his love of rigid and oppressive rule was already known, and even felt, as will appear from the fact that desertions from the northern army to the western had already commenced, and were not even uncommon, which Christophe hearing of, would, as commander-in-chief of the forces, send to Petion, at Port au Prince, requesting that such men should be sent back to join their regiments; but his messages were generally coolly received, and severe letters passed between these distinguished Generals on the subject.

Christophe was kept well informed of all that was passing at the capital; and on hearing the general character and bearing of the Constitution just drawn up, he unwisely concluded, that being the responsible President of a Republic, he might at last, like Dessalines, fall under the power of the people. His rash and final conclusion, therefore, was to march at once upon Port au Prince. This decision formed, he issued a proclamation, in which he accused Petion and the Generals of the western part, of having so arranged matters with regard to the framing of the Constitution, and organization of the Republic, as to have all power in their hands, with a view, ultimately, to reduce the whole nation under the yoke of their own power, hence he calls upon the people to take up arms in defence of their liberties, and at the same time promises full and free plunder to the army.

We therefore find ourselves here at the starting point of innumerable evils for Hayti. Christophe was legitimately at the head of the nation; this was fully and fairly recognized by all; there was no disposition anywhere to deprive him of any honor that was due to him. But the plain fact seems to be that he had resolved to hold all power, and to be without control, notwithstanding there were many at tnat time who were his superiors as to mind and education. Posterity, therefore, must and will blame this man as a despot, both in his principles and passions. Hayti as a nation cannot here be blamed. All had been well arranged; in fact the nation had in the most open and legitimate manner chosen a Republican form of government, and they had accorded to the right man its highest honor; but he chose to be a despot, and rose in arms against his own people; nor is there anything here but what was in harmony with the general history of mankind, however much to be deplored.

On the 26th of December, 1806, Christophe was at St. Mark's, about half way to Port au Prince from the Cape, with an army of 18,000 men.

Petion left Port au Prince on the 1st of January, 1807, with some 3,000 men. He probably reckoned on increasing his army as he proceeded through the country; but arriving at a place called Sibert, which was a plantation, these opposing armies met, and a contest fierce and terrible commenced, between men and brothers, who not long since had been firmly united against their common foe.

Petion was entirely routed, his General's hat rendering him a mark at which the enemy had already eagerly aimed. A young officer named Jerome Coutilien Coutard, snatched it from Petion's head, and putting it on himself, saved his General, who had seriously began to think of committing suicide, under the impression that he was about to be taken prisoner. The young officer, however, fell a victim to his noble feelings of devotion, while Petion, with one or two more, escaped, and reaching the sea shore, a canoe which was standing off came at his call, and took him from the Arcahaic side of the great bay of Port au Prince, to the opposite side, within a few miles of the capital, where his fate was not yet known. Some feared he had been killed, while others feared he had been taken prisoner.

In the mean time, Petion's army had collected at Port au Prince, having been hotly pursued by Christophe, so that the battle now raged outside of Port au Prince. General Yayou had taken (provisionally) Petion's place, and maintaining his ground, had kept off the enemy during the whole of that day; but the next day Petion himself appeared, and was received with great joy and enthusiasm as their beloved head.

The struggle between Christophe and the Republicans was great, but all turned and was decided in favor of the latter. Even women and children are said to have helped, from sheer dread of the name of Christophe, so entirely was this man's name associated with the idea of horror.

This great contest commenced at 3 A. M., on the 6th of January, 1807; and on the 8th, the arms of Christophe having totally failed, were on their way back to the north, leaving the Republicans in possession of their capital, their constitution, and their liberty.

At an early period in Haytian history, a military chief named Goman, in the South, occupied an important position, and occasioned much anxiety and trouble to the legitimate rulers of this Republic. But the details of this matter would be impossible; for the present it must suffice simply to mention the fact of such a case, and refer for the details to the larger histories of Hayti.

Here, then, we come to the complete, and for the present final division of this small, and but lately self-liberated nation—a separation which was evidently occasioned by the determination of one man to subdue a nation to his own views of government. No unknown rock, this, of pride and vanity, but one on which many of the mightiest of the earth have dashed themselves to pieces.

Christophe not unnaturally thought that his adversary, Petion, would have pursued him. This, however, was not the case; and for this the conquering General was severely reproved by General Gerin, who declared that had Petion appeared in the North at that moment, the people would certainly have joined the arms of the Republic. But Petion's opinion was, that Christophe's ferocity would soon ruin him, and that any further effusion of blood was needless. Christophe, left thus to himself, re-took Arcahaic, by a division under General Larose. The people of this place were well known to be altogether Republican in their preferences, and therefore by this monarchical General they were given up to be pillaged, and several among the most prominent of this village were sent on to Marchand, where Christophe had halted with his troops, and were there executed by his orders.

Christophe, intending to make his seat of Government at Cape Haytien, transported all the wealth which Dessalines had amassed to his intended capital, from whence he issued an address to the inhabitants of the North, in which he promises liberty, warns the enemies of his cause, and urges the people to give themselves fully to industry of every kind.

At Port au Prince, the Senate had assembled, and appointed General Petion to the maintenance of order in the Western Departments; General Gerin being at the same time, and by the same authority, charged with the command of the South.

Several of the representatives from the North, having voted in "L'Assemblée Constituante" for the Republic, could not consequently return to their homes; and being therefore involved in loss and difficulty, their cases were taken into consideration by the Senate, and suitable provision was made for them, while at the same time Christophe was declared to be entirely outlawed, and the Constitution which he had rejected was adopted, and proclaimed with all due solemnity. This important and memorable event took place on the 27th of Dec., 1806.

The power of the Senate thus established, they at once sent a military force, under command of Petion, to re-take Arcahaie for the Republic, for which it was well known that place was inclined. This undertaking was successful; and many of the Northern troops, who had been taken prisoners on this occasion, became citizens of the Republic. But Petion hearing of a revolt in the Southern part of the Island, deemed it prudent to return promptly to Port au Prince; notwithstanding the army demanded to be led on from Ascahaie to St. Mark's, which he considered would simply involve the shedding of blood uselessly, and therefore persisted in his purpose to return to the capital. Petion, however, did attempt to win over Christophe's principal General, Larose, by addressing him a letter, but the Northern General tore it up without even reading it.

Petion being now returned to Port au Prince, the Senate sent a strong force to subdue the revolt in the South, and to re-establish order there; after which this legislative body proceeded to the regulation of the general finances of the State, on which subject General Bonnet read to the Senate a long and able address.

During this time, Christophe sent back a military force to Arcahaie, the only object of which was to entirely destroy that place. The inhabitants fled to the woods, but were pursued by a furious soldiery, whose orders were nothing less than extermination.*

These unhappy people had fallen victims to the fury of Christophe, simply because they were well known to be sincerely attached to the Republic. General Gerin and his party, in this case also, reproached Petion for having suffered this massacre to take place, while he had 10,000 men at his disposal; nor indeed is it easy to understand such a seeming neglect.

Christophe now began to organize his affairs, and a Constitution promptly appeared, in which Havti is

* Madiou.

declared to be a State, with a President at the head. This Constitution was inaugurated with great pomp and ceremony; and General Christophe, who was now Chief Magistrate of the new State, attended the "Te Deum" which was sung in the Church at Cape Haytien, at the close of which the new functionary received the most flattering felicitations of the people at large, and especially of his Generals.

It is indeed remarkable that a man whose fierce and unfeeling character had already manifested itself, should have become so popular; but he was known to have enlarged views of things, hence, with all his defects, he was at that time considered an extraordinary man; and what ultimately in him degenerated into ferocity, was in the commencement of his career great and unusual energy.

On the 25th of February, 1807, Christophe's Council declared its power and authority over the entire Island, not only in opposition to the West, but in defiance of Spain and France. The same was done by Petion and his Republic, in the West; while General Ferrand, in the name of France, at Santo Domingo, in the East, declared his power over all Hayti. Here, then, were three claimants for this Island, and each one pretending to unlimited power. These, however, were mere declarations; for although they each led to their separate consequences ultimately, yet for a moment all were anxious for a pause. Breathing time from past exhaustion was now needed by all parties; and by the time the needed pause had ceased, views, feelings, and circumstances underwent important changes.

Christophe, during 1807, established regulations,

the object of which was the promotion of morality in the State. One was, that public functionaries, military and civil, including public schools, should be expected to attend public worship. Another was, such laws on inheritance by legitimate children only, as should cover the issues of concubinage, adultery, and incest, with shame and disgrace. Such regulations must indeed have been keenly felt by a population, the vast majority of which must have been at that time out of the pale of honorable marriage, and tends to show the fearful evils which must have been entailed upon that generation by slavery.

In the meantime, the Republicans in the West proceeded to organize their now fairly started Republic. A more definite Executive was necessary, and the two principal candidates, it would appear, were Generals Gerin and Petion. The former, it would seem, was so certain of his election, as history informs us,* that he actually ordered and directed the making of his official coat! It turned out, however, that the votes were very decidedly in favor of Alexander Petion, who, on the 9th of March, 1807, became the first President of the newly-formed Republic of Hayti, then confined to the Western part of the Island.

On the 10th—the following day—General Petion appeared before the Senate ; the Senators receiving him sitting, with their hats on. The General at that time was suffering from rheumatism, and was therefore leaning on crutches. Receiving the newly-elected President thus covered, was indeed significant, and seemed strongly to indicate that they considered the Executive to be the servant, not the master, of the people.

* T. Madiou (Fils.)

Uncovered before the Senate, President Petion took the following oath of fidelity to the Constitution, which had been accepted by the people, who were understood to be represented by the Senatorial body :—

"I swear faithfully to fulfil the office of President of Hayti, and to maintain, to the utmost of my power, the Constitution.

"May those arms confided to the people for the defence of liberty, be pointed to my breast, if ever I conceive the audacious and infamous project of violating their rights; or if ever I forget that it is after having punished with death a tyrant, whose existence was an insult to the nation, and after having aided to proscribe another, whose ambition has lighted up civil war among us, that I now find myself President of Hayti."

Certainly it must be admitted that, on all sides, true republicanism is here fully recognized, and is yet more completely sustained by the following statement, that, at the invitation of the presiding Senator, the now accepted President took his seat on his right hand, while the band immediately struck up—

"Ou peut on etre mieux,
Q'au sein de sa famille?" *

Joy beamed in every countenance, both among foreigners and natives, and the speeches of the Chairman, the Senate, and also of the President of Hayti, were ordered to be printed.

With the great majority of the Republicans, the choice of Petion was decidedly popular. There was, however, one whose influence was considerable, and whose mortification at the loss of the great honor of presiding over the Republic, was the more deeply

* Where can one happier be,
Than in one's family?

felt, because of his entire confidence that he would have obtained it himself.

Few, perhaps, had ever felt greater assurance in their expectation of such an honor, than had General Gerin and his party ; nor could anything be more deplorable than the fact that jealousy, with its many evils, should have been the result with the losing side in this affair, which ultimately developed itself in the form of a conspiracy. All, however, was useless. Petion was the man of the people, and it was want of dignity of spirit in this case to oppose him.

The following is a comparison made by a Haytian historian, between the Constitution of the Republic in the west, and that of the "State" in the North :*

In that of the "State," the Chief Magistrate commands all the forces, naval and military, and also could name a successor, but only among the generals of the army.

In the Repubiic, of that day, the President at the head was under the control of the Senate.

The President of the "State" was for life.

The President of the Republic was for four years.

In the "State," the Legislative Council was confided to a Council of State.

In the Republic, this was confided to a Senate chosen by the people.

In the "State," the President nominated to all offices and honors.

In the Republic, this was done by the people, through the Senate.

A wide field of discussion as to the merits of the two Constitutions, is indeed open. It is, however, worthy of note, that the handling of such subjects, in such a manner, is strongly indicative of an ad-

* T. Madiou.

vanced intelligence, at least on the part of those concerned.

That the masses of Hayti were at this time really prepared for the unbounded freedom of a genuine Republic, cannot for a moment be supposed. The reins of power held by one leading mind, of good faith, and of thoroughly patriotic feelings, might probably, have been better. If, however, the necessity of good faith is to be admitted in one case, it must be in the other; and hence we are driven to the conclusion that where righteous principle and feeling reign, the form of government is but of secondary importance. Justice and good faith in any administration, will secure the public weal. Time and experience, however, have shown in Hayti itself that the abuse of any form of government, although good in itself as to theory, must and does lead to confusion and unhappiness.

On the 12th of March, President Petion was allowed by the Senate to nominate all his civil and military officers—reserving to itself the power of refusal or change.

On the same day was proposed the law relating to the administration. The document drawing up this great measure was an able production, by the justly celebrated General Bonnet, who evidently was a man of very comprehensive mind and views, as may appear from the fact that, with but few modifications, the same general law has been in force ever since, notwithstanding all the revolutions and changes which have subsequently taken place.

The first and vital point relating to the tenure of landed property, which, at such a time, and under such peculiar and trying circumstances, must have been singularly intricate and difficult, appears to have been ably settled, as may be seen fully detailed in the pages of the historian already so often named;* and affords another amongst many other proofs in the history of this country, that European education has furnished leading and able minds for the management and direction of national interests and circumstances, which even in general history will appear as of no ordinary character.

About this time it was decreed by the Senate that, in case of a siege, the Senators should appear on the ramparts of the city in full costume,† to encourage the energies and activity of the people. At the same time, all who had submitted to the authority of Christophe, were declared to be rebels against the Republic. The case, however, of those who were living on the frontiers, and who by fidelity to the Republic had lost all their property, was considered; such in many cases having been driven from their homes, it was decided that gifts of land should be made to them, in compensation for their losses.

About this time also, Boyer was promoted to the rank of colonel, and attached to the staff of the President.

In the meantime, Christophe was not inactive. It is, however, to be deplored that even at this early period of his power, notwithstanding many wise and good measures, symptoms of severity, and even

* T. Madiou.

† To this day the Senators, and also the Representatives of the people, wear a uniform, consisting of a blue coat, with yellow buttons, a cocked hat, and sword. The Judges wear cocked hats, black coats, and swords. The real simplicity of Republicanism has yet to be learned in Hayti.

tyranny, began to appear in his general proceedings. His institutions were in may respects good, and upon the whole adapted to the charactor and circumstances of the people; but he did not conform to them himself; and it is complained of him that the laboring classes, under his power, were more in the position of serfs than otherwise. It is not, therefore, surprising to learn that a rising against Christophe took place at Port de Paix, where the Republic under Petion was decidedly preferred.

An officer in Christophe's army, named Rebecca,* having been reduced to the ranks, under the influence of revengeful feelings, availed himself of what he knew to be the dominant preference of the people of Port de Paix and its neighborhood for republicanism, and raised the standard of revolt; but notwithstanding all his reasonings on the tyranny of their Chief, he failed to win over to his own side Christophe's officers.

One very singular and even extraordinary feature in this rising was, that none sought posts of honor or emolument. Rebecca, it is said, commanded in this affair simply as a grenadier private; and the same simplicity appears to have been manifested by all who had attached themselves to him: a rare but interesting exception to the general rule in such cases, both in Hayti and elsewhere. This man, however, persisted, and succeeded in raising the whole population of that neighborhood against Christophe.

After taking Port de Paix, Rebecca learned that Christophe was near at hand on one side with his

*It is singular that the name of a woman should be borne by a man; this, however, is still to be found in the Haytian army.

troops, while one of his generals, named Romain, was approaching with his forces on the other side; but strange to say, Rebecca's men had so abandoned themselves to pillaging the town, that as the only means of gathering them, he set fire to the place, and even then he could only muster some forty of them. Instead of flying, however, notwithstanding great odds, he attempted battle with Christophe's superior forces; and, falling wounded, was taken alive and brought before General Romain, who inquired of him why he had taken up arms against Christophe. "Because," said he, "I consider him to be a tyrant, who, in the name of liberty, is re-establishing slavery; and I consider you, General Romain, as the vile instrument of a monster!" At this the General became furious, and asked him what he meant, and what he wanted. Rebecca's reply was, "Death!" upon which his head was immediately severed from his body, and carried to Christophe, who ordered that it should be put upon a pole, and placed before his army.

The Senate at Port au Prince had raised Rebecca to the rank of Colonel, but his death occurred before the brevet reached him. The Senate, however, on hearing that he had fallen a victim to his love of liberty, voted a pension to his widow, and one also to his bereaved mother.

President Petion, without loss of time, issued a proclamation, calling upon the people for military aid, and at the same time commenced collecting a land and naval force, with the design of attacking Christophe at various points; but the base and unhappy thirst for plunder on the part of Rebecca's men, had already ruined their cause. Had they remained honest and united, they would doubtless have been able to present a bold front; at least they might have held out until the republican forces from Port au Prince had arrived, when in all probability the power of Christophe might have received a severe blow, and possibly might have been entirely broken up. This, however, was not the case, and the unhappy people who had revolted were compelled to fly to the woods and mountains; but Christophe, acting both humanely and with good policy in this case, sent some of his men into the woods, to endeavor to win over the insurgents. In this, however, he failed; for the very name of Christophe, and the bare sight of his men, filled them with terror, and the wretched people therefore persisted in their flight.

Christophe's troops continued their course until they reached the Mole, which is the western extremity of the Island on the north side, where it would appear that many women and children had taken refuge; but the historian of Hayti informs us that on the approach of Christophe's army, many of the unhappy mothers who had fled here for safety, preferred throwing themselves into the sea, to falling into the hands of the northern despot.*

The forces of the Republic being now organized, General Bazelais was sent, with a naval armament under his command, and with orders to take St. Mark's; or, if that was impossible, to proceed to Port de Paix. Bazelais, on reaching St. Mark's,

* The details of the whole of this affair were related to the historian Madiou by General Alaire, who commanded Port de Paix at the time of Rebecca's revolt.

found it so prepared for an attack, that he decided to continue on to Port de Paix. Here he entirely succeeded; and soon also took Gonaives.

During the interval of preparation at Port au Prince for the defence of Port de Paix, Colonel Nicolas Louis, of the latter place, who was an ardent friend of the Republic, hearing of the decision of the Senate with regard to the rising at Port de Paix, and being thus encouraged with the expectation of the speedy arrival of Petion's forces, entered the Fort of that place with a few men during the night, Christophe's party having neglected to place a garrison there; the surprise, therefore, of the northern soldiers was great, on hearing the 4 o'clock drum the next morning from the Fort.

At daylight, Colonel N. Louis mounted the wall of the Fort himself, and calling to General Romain, told him that he begged to hand him a proclamation from President Petion, at Port au Prince; to which Romain very significantly replied, "I am just getting ready to come and take it!" and immediately moved forward with a couple of columns, to take both the Fort and the proclamation. In this, however, he failed. Three violent and fierce attacks were made, and even a fourth, in which he not only failed, but was wounded, and returned to the Cape, pursued by Nicolas and his few men for a considerable distance.

By this time, great manifestations of feeling appeared against Christophe, in the plains of the Artibonite.*

* A beautiful and extensive level country, through which a river of that name meanders, in what is called the northern part of the Island.

In fact it is easy to understand that the contrast between the two States must have been great; and in the nature of things, the working of a free system by the side of real despotism must have told powerfully upon the latter. In the one reigned a freedom which could not string up the energies of an uneducated people to a sufficiently high tone of industry; and in the other, a discipline which amounted to oppression, was becoming gradually insupportable to an untrained, uncultivated, and but recently liberated mass. Christophe's system, therefore, rapidly ripened, rotted, and fell.

On the 26th of May, Petion left the capital for the North, and on the 28th and 29th was himself engaged in bloody conflict with Christophe's troops; nor had he much repose until the 10th of June following, when the Republican Generals Bazelais, Lamarre, and Lanoix, were driven from Gonaives by the northern forces, and even narrowly escaped with their lives.

Petion, who about this time was in the neighborhood of St. Mark's, recognized his own fleet off that port by which he knew that the Republican army had been compelled to retreat; and inferring from what he knew must have happened, that Christophe's whole force would therefore soon be upon him, with his comparatively weak numbers, he immediately decided on returning to Port au Prince. On his arrival however at the capital, he found that intrigues had been carried on in his absence against General Yayou, who had been left in command; but the presence of the President soon made all right.

But the inhabitants of Port de Paix, who had

shown such attachment to the Republic, could not be abandoned, Petion, therefore, promptly organized another expedition for the north, and confided the command to General Lamarre, who was instructed to hasten to the succour of Port de Paix.

Lamarre set sail with 800 men; and the Senate having addressed the people on the necessity of flying to the help of their brother Republicans in the North, their number was soon augmented.

In the meantime, Christophe himself reached Gonaives, and from thence, on the 20th of June, arrived at Cape Haytien, where he was received by the most enthusiastic welcome of the people.

Having now a few days rest, the Chief of the Northern State set to work about commercial arrangements, and the formation of other laws which were needed for the general welfare and prosperity of the nation.

Meantime, Colonel N. Louis was still contending with Christophe's army, when on the 2d of July, General Lamarre announced to him his own arrival, with Colonels Gardel, Weillard, and Adjutant General Delva; on the same evening of their arrival, they commenced their march to join Nicolas Louis, and came up with him at a place called Moustiques.

The united forces of the Republicans amounted to about 2,000 men. This, however, was a long and tedious struggle, and lasted from 1807 until 1810, when Lamarre died, and Christophe became master of the Mole.

History informs us that on one occasion of great peril, Soulouque* stood faithfully by the side of Lamarre.

* Who subsequently became Emperor of Hayti.

During all this struggle, Goman, in the South, disturbed the public peace, and both himself and party declared themselves in favor of Christophe.

In 1810, Rigaud arrived in Hayti, and finding a party, under Gerin, ready for revolt against Petion, he placed himself at the head of it; the following year, however, he died, and the Republic gradually gained strength.

General Borgella, whose name is celebrated in Haytian history, as a brave and honest man, was elected as Rigaud's successor in the Government of the South. He, however, ultimately sent in his adhesion to the Western Republic.

During this year, Petion was re-elected for four years as President of Hayti; nor can there be any doubt that this distinguished individual, notwithstanding a seeming want of energy, which was felt throughout his administration, was worthy of the high esteem in which he was held by his countrymen; for whatever may have been his errors, he was honest and brave, having enlarged and liberal views of government.

On the 2d of June, 1811, Chistophe became king, under the title of Henry I., and surrounded himself by a privileged nobility of princes, dukes, barons, etc., who assisted him in carrying out his own harsh views of government, and compelling activity and industry by an insupportable oppression, which ultimately lost everything they aimed at; it must, however, be admitted that an amazing amount of industry was thus wrenched from the people, by mere terror of their Chief.

It is indeed to be lamented that less than half the

Island should have been thus divided into two small nations, and especially that they should so repeatedly have been brought into fierce and deadly conflict with each other, whatever may have been the motive of either party. Such, however, is human nature, for our business here is not so much to judge of motives, as of facts and principles, with their tendencies, as shown by the light of history.

Independence, which is the element and dignity of any distinct branch of the human race, is frequently only gained at an awful cost; yet it is this cost, in the form of daring feats of valor, and triumphant struggles with mightier foes, which constitute the glory so boldly sought, " even at the cannon's mouth." Nor can we refuse to any nation which has victoriously passed through the dreadful ordeal of arms and blood, a fair amount of dignity—whatever may be the opinion as to military systems, or even as to the use of arms at all.

In 1810, this comparatively small territory, of less than 500 miles in length, and of less than 200 miles in breadth, was divided into not less than four different governments. The Spaniards in the east, Christophe in the north, Rigaud in the south, and Petion in the west. Christophe's regal sceptre, to all human appearance, at one time seemed to be held by a firm hand. His capital was Cape Haytien, which at that time was, notwithstanding many ruins from fire and war, rather a handsome little city; but the favorite retreat of the newly-made king, in the north of Hayti, was his palace at " Sans Louci,"* a few miles only from the city of the Cape.

* "Free from care !" A name certainly very far from true in this case.

Cape Haytien is described by an English traveler, who visited it in 1809, as a beautiful city, and as being a most agreeable residence as to climate, etc.†

With regard to the government of Christophe, it must be admitted that there was much that was good in it, and that he really did raise his kingdom to a high degree of industry and wealth; it must, however, be remembered that the system in operation for the accomplishment of this, was such as to render its overthrow inevitable. The white colonists before him, whom he had so powerfully aided to drive out, had also succeeded in winding up the Colony to a high pitch of energy and wealth, by sheer brutality.

Some have indeed said that Christophe erred on the right side; but how can that course be in any sense right, which at last plunges the man who pursues it, with all who are dependent upon him, into utter wretchedness and ruin? All, therefore, that was good in the system of Christophe, was neutralized by overwhelming evils, which will send down his name to posterity as a sanguinary tyrant; so much so, that to enter into a full detail of his cruelties, in floggings, executions, imprisonments, etc., would be far too sickening and disgusting. One case only we will state here, which will suffice to show the man; and this is stated by the traveler last named, who was informed of the abominable transaction by one who was an eye witness of the whole affair.

One of the king's servants, it would appear, had stolen a quantity of salt fish. The case having come to the knowledge of Christophe, the man was ordered

† Mackenzie.

to be laid down in the kitchen, and in the presence of the monarch, was literally scourged to death, notwithstanding earnest entreaties in behalf of the culprit.*

That a government impregnated by the spirit of such a man should perish, is only natural; nor, in fact, can it be any matter of regret that slavery, whether crowned or in the name of liberty, should be abolished.

It is true, we are not to forget that this king had become what he was, not only from his own natural ferocity, but from a system under which he had been born and trained, and under which he had seen men, far superior to himself in education, etc., practice the most horrid and barbarous deeds.

In fact, Christophe's whole system degenerated into low oppression; its ruling power became absolute, and the liberty of both pen and tongue was annihilated; while the general bearing of the western Republic, and the presiding spirit of Petion, may be seen in one of his splendid mottos:—

"Let every Haytian, with the Constitution in his hand, know what he can do, and what he ought to do."

Here it is fully seen that the leading aim of this ruling and noble mind, was to raise the people to the level aud dignity of an unsophisticated liberty. Had this great and good intention only been carried out, and accompanied by well-timed, well-placed and persevering energy on the part of Petion himself, there can be no doubt but that the Haytian Republic would have risen rapidly in civilization of every

* Mackenzie.

kind, and prospered to the entire satisfaction of its best friends; while at the same time it would long ago have confounded much empty reasoning on the African character in general, which to develop and demonstrate doubtless constitutes the great mission of the Haytian people, in their existence as a nation.

Every Haytian, with the Constitution in his hand, and the ability to read it and make it his national guide, necessarily involved that every Haytian should have sufficient education at least to be able to read; from this, therefore, would result the primary instruction of every man, woman and child in Hayti! so that the entire nation would have been placed on the high road to that dignity which it must be confessed it has never yet reached, and which it never can, but by the elevation of the entire mass of the people.

Such a measure, carried into effect in the spirit of true republicanism, would have superseded the necessity of degrading rural codes, which inevitably suppose a degraded and sunken people. In fact, the education of the masses, as here supposed by Petion, is the only true law by which real wants, and therefore real industry, can be created, and at the same time the dignity of a nation secured and promoted.

It must, however, be both admitted and deplored, that the grand defect of Petion's government was want of energy; hence the best plans and soundest principles were frequently paralyzed in their execution. Could the energy of Christophe, the humanity of Petion, and the daring of Rigaud, have been brought into united action, under one government Hayti might have won the admiration of the world.

But the demon of discord broke loose in this land of freedom; and notwithstanding every means and element existed in Hayti to sustain the dignity of an an elevated, wealthy and praiseworthy Independence, disappointment has afflicted both Hayti and its friends; but these same elements still exist, nor is it by any means too late to bring them out into full and successful development.

CHAPTER III.

Distribution of Lands.—Senatorial Plan.—Petion a Dictator.—Republicanism the choice of the Educated.—Five Carreaux of Land given.—Ardouin on the Distribution of Lands.—Petion Re-elected.—He is envied.—Christophe attacks the Republic.—Desertion to the Republic.—Christophe fears.—He kills the Colored People at St. Mark's.—He builds Laferriere.—His Palace.—Candler's Description of it.—$30,000,000 lodged at Laferriere.—Idea of Purchasing the Spanish part.—Case of Medina. Chistophe's Schools.—Falls out with his Bishop.—Is smitten with Apoplexy.—Fails in mounting his horse.—Commits Suicide.—His Biography.—Indemnity to France.—Commissioners from Louis XVIII.—Presidency for Life.—House of Representatives.—Esmongart to Christophe.—Petion offers Indemnity.—Bolivar in Hayti.

The nation rises, power and form assumes,
When plains, hills, mountains, with their boundless wealth,
To her brave sons are fairly meted out.

The distribution of lands by Petion was doubtless one of his master-strokes of policy, as to its general effects upon the Republic over which he presided, particularly at a time when the nation needed some such popular measure for its final organization and consolidation. In fact, it is almost difficult to conceive how this small nation, which had just broken loose from law and order, had existed up to the present moment. By this means, however, it soon began to assume a definite form; and the contrast which the free and simple western Republic formed with Christophe's more pompous and almost feudal system in the north, was great; nor were the northern people blind to this.

The measure in question, relating to the distribution of lands, doubtless told well in its influence and power on the nation: in fact, it created a consciousness of national existence; and yet it is a singular fact that this great measure did not pass through the Senate without great difficulty. Why this should have been the case, we will not now enquire, especially as the measure itself was a great, good, and vital one.

Petion's proposal was, that lots of land, of from thirty to sixty or more acres, should be distributed to such individuals in the army as had in any way distinguished themselves in the service of their country. This, doubtless, would have reached a great number of deserving persons in the nation, and would have had a powerful effect in diffusing strength throughout the entire Republic; but the Senate, from some mysterious cause, either did not or would not see this, and the consequence was painful and unhappy throughout the nation—dissensions and conspiracies being the result.

Such is human nature, that to avoid differences of opinion appears to be neither desirable nor possible, either in politics or religion, and yet common sense ought to preserve peace. The measure in question was undoubtedly one of paramount importance, and if carried with unanimity, would have raised the nation, both in strength and dignity. Whether selfish and ulterior aims really operated in this case, we will not say; but certain it is that the question itself, important as it was, offered nothing intricate: it was plain, straightforward, and simple.

The Senate, however, drew up a plan of their own.

Why they should not have adhered to that of their President, or why the President himself should not have sought some understanding with them, rather than disperse them, whether by military power or otherwise,* will be for posterity to consider. The Executive, ruled by the majority, has yet to be understood in Hayti.

The leading idea of the Senatorial plan was thus expressed :—

> "That those fathers and mothers who should have the greatest number of legitimate children, resulting from honorable marriage, should be favored with concessions of land."

The measure of the Senate was unquestionably good; yet when we place before it the fact that the entire population which had fought for the liberties of the country, had been taught by men of superior acquirements vastly different things, and that there had not been time or opportunity yet for the formation of domestic order, or the establishment of morality, in a national sense, we are compelled to pause before this measure, although in itself good.

Concubinage and libertinage had been taught the blacks by the whites, and it would be useless to shun a truth which reveals the fact of the almost total absence of honorable marriage at that time in the country; hence, notwithstanding the measure was

* S. Larnour, still living, who was attached to the Senate at that time, denies that military power was in any sense resorted to by Petion in this case.

L. Ardouin, in his Essay on Haytian History, declares that the Senate dissolved itself involuntarily.

M. B. Ardouin, in his Studes sur l'histoire d'Hayti, declares that Petion threatened military force, and that the Senate then dissolved.

good and laudable in itself, yet neither the practice or neglect of marriage could lessen the desserts of those who had fought and bled in their country's cause; while the execution of the Senatorial measure must have produced great embarrassment, by circumstances which had resulted from causes over which no one had had any control, and for which no one was or could be responsible; but the main object of Petion was, a prompt and immediate effect upon his own people, and also upon those who were under the spell and power of Christophe. It is not, therefore, surprising that the measure of the Senate should have become unpopular with the people, or that it should have been decidedly opposed by Petion.

The whole measure, consequently, was postponed; and in the meantime the Senate demanded of the President, their Executive, a general account of his administration. The President, in reply, takes up the position that he was not responsible to them for his proceedings; we have, however, seen that it was this Senatorial body, as the representative of the people, which had created both himself and his power, as President of the Republic, and that it was to them, as such, that he had sworn fidelity to the people.

But things now rose to so high a pitch between the parties, that Petion dismissed the Senate abruptly. The consequence of this measure was, that Petion rose immediately to the power of a Dictator, which for a short period he certainly exercised, until it was feared that General Rigaud, who was now in the Southern part of the Island, might sympathize with the violently-dissolved Senate, and by this means sap the foundations of Petion's Republic.

The President, therefore, created another Senate; but it will be easy to understand the position, character and freedom of a Senate so formed.

President Petion was at this time surrounded by many difficulties; nor was it to be expected that they would be lessened by interference with the civil power just referred to—a case in which we see a well-intentioned man was compelled to act contrary to his wishes.*

Christophe was indeed Petion's chief opponent; but he had now become, so to speak, an external enemy. Party feeling within ran high, and it would appear that Petion and his friends were not heartily in favor of a periodical Presidency. This, doubtless, must have been more or less known to their opponents, and is the more to be regretted from the fact that General Gerin had from the beginning been the avowed and well-known rival of Petion.

This may doubtless be considered as an important epoch in Haytian history, and posterity can now judge of the propriety of the contemplated change in the Constitution.

Whether the continuation of a periodical Presidency would have been less productive of revolutions than has been a life Presidency, is now a fair and open question. It is not, indeed, here intended to decide this matter; but whatever may be the probabilities of either side, the fundamental principle of Republicanism is that the people should govern, and

* It would be unjust to the memory of Petion, to infer from this trying case that he was ever in any sense despotic. This was far from being his character. It must be admitted that the course pursued by the Senators in this instance is quite inexplicable.

not an individual—the Executive being their servant, not their master.

The British view of such a case would be, that if the Executive is perfectly controlled, and made responsible to the people, change would be needless.

The American view would be, that change in the Executive would be as necessary as elsewhere.

A free, sound, and responsible Government is the great thing needful for either Hayti or any other country; and with this boon, all else is of minor consideration.

It might, indeed, be said that the masses in Hayti at this time were utterly unable to govern themselves; than which, perhaps, nothing could be more true; but on this subject we have only to remember that it was the intelligent portion, and not the ignorant masses of the nation, which originally chose the Republican form of Government; and that the same amount of intelligence which was capable of choosing its form of government, was capable of working it.

But a nation with its masses in deep ignorance, is exposed to the greatest danger that can well be conceived. Let the intelligent classes of such a nation differ among themselves, and the ignorant masses—especially in a free Republic—will become the mere tools and dupes of both parties, while the general result will be the wreck of the nation. Nor can it be denied that such has been the lot of Hayti, to a fearful extent; so much so, that its only hope and resource at the present day, is in the primary Christian education of every individual throughout the entire Republic. This may, indeed, seem to be an impossibility; but however great and insurmountable this might appear to be, from the beginning it should have been the conscientious and persevering aim of every government; nor will there ever be any other means for this nation to reach that degree of population, dignity, and wealth which the Christian world has a right to expect in it.

No mere system of policy, however good, can do this. Every man, woman, and child in the nation must be something. There must not be thousands upon thousands of nonentities, from sheer ignorance and vice, who as to intelligence and industry, are utterly unproductive from inanity. Systems of politics will then find their right shape, and the springs of the nation being well tempered, will be prepared to work; while arms and reason will also both find their right places. But Petion persevered in his great plan for the distribution of lands. The opposition on the part of the Senate is indeed to be deplored. The President, however, was bent on his purpose, and his measure was popular.

During the short Dictatorship which, as we have seen, took place, Petion called a council of the leading officers of the State, both civil and military; and the measure which he had so much at heart, and which it must be confessed was so adapted to the then peculiar circumstances of the Republic, was carried into execution, with this difference, however, that five Carreaux (or some twelve acres) of land should be given as the smallest donation, instead of ten, as had been proposed to the Senate—hence title deeds are said to be still in existence, having the signature of Petion during 1809.

It must certainly be admitted that this was one of the greatest measures ever carried out in Hayti. By this means the former slave was made to feel himself a man; and even the uneducated and free citizen became doubly interested in his own country, while he also became attached to the soil, in a manner which induced him to try its virtue by cultivation. Great will be the regret of all posterity that knowledge was not deemed as essential as land for the people.

The following are the remarks of an able and well known Haytian writer on this important and interesting subject:—

> "From this time, a new era for the country commenced; property thus distributed without distinction or respect of persons, but awarded, it might almost be said, to the masses, has done more to consolidate our institutions, and for the maintenance of public peace, than all the other measures of the Legislature put together."*

And yet, great as this measure really was, time has shown us that in a national sense, one thing was wanting with this, viz., sound primary knowledge.

Great wealth distributed to a people not possessed of the light and judgment needful for its just and proper use, would simply be in danger, first, of not being increased by judicious industry; secondly, of being thrown away altogether, in the name of sale or otherwise, from inability to appreciate it.

This great national boon to the masses, the accompanying one of national education being absent, lost more than half its value and power. Education even on a limited scale, had it been possible at this early

* M. B. Ardouin, editor of "Le Temps."

stage of the national existence, would have taught them that their lands were worth more to them than gold.

The difficulties of a popular education were unquestionably great under the circumstances of those times; but the question is, whether anything of the sort was any where really at heart. Nothing but an intense Christianity filling a ruler's heart, could have led to this; certainly a mere national creed would not. At the same time, it may safely be said, that until this becomes a question of heart and conscience, on the part of the reigning power, the difficulties of such a work will ever be deemed insurmountable. It is therefore much to be regretted, that the sound policy which dictated the enriching of the people, did not also strike out some bold plan of universal education. Had this been done, the crime of Jacob, who sold his birth-right for a trifle, might perhaps never have been heard of among the new possessors of land in Hayti; for it is well known that in some cases they were shamefully sold. It is, however, gratifying to be able to say that these instances were not common.

It will not be astonishing that many of the larger lots of land should have remained uncultivated, even to the present day, while the smaller portions have been better attended to. This is explained by the fact that the small lots generally fell into the possession of such men as would not hesitate to cultivate their little properties with their own hands; while the larger lots became the properties of such whose rank in life was not, in their own estimation, compatible with manual labor. Such has been the curse of slavery wherever it has existed, that labor has ever been considered as degrading; want of capital, therefore, with these individuals, would render them helpless with their lands.

On the 9th of March, 1811, Petion was re-elected President of Hayti; but the involuntary dissolution of the Senate, which first created his power and gave him his elevation, induces the fear that the Senate which now re-elected him was not so perfectly and absolutely free as the former one; and although there can be no doubt but that Petion stood high in general estimation, yet it would have been still more satisfactory had his re-election been accompanied with, and resulted from, the straightforward and honest working of the Constitution, and of those institutions to which he had in so manly and frank a manner, sworn fidelity. It would, however, be unjust to the memory of Petion, to overlook the strange conduct of the Senate which he was obliged to dissolve, and the difficulties which resulted therefrom to him; nor will any error of judgment in this case shake the confidence of posterity in this noble-minded man, who, it must be confessed, was far in advance of his people generally.

Yet that there were men in the nation at that time, who were perfectly competent to hold and guide the helm of public affairs, history abundantly testifies; and if these men did aspire, legitimately, to share in the Presidential honors, it must simply be remembered, that this was honorable to them. It must, however, be borne in mind, that no man had taken a more active part in the general organization of the institutions of the country, than had Petion himself; nor can there be any doubt that his original idea in consenting to a periodical Presidency, was, that such a measure would afford the means of saving the nation from anarchy and confusion, by fairly opening the means of gratification to honest, although ambitious men, who also had rendered the greatest services to their country, while at the same time it placed in the hands of the nation the means of ultimate relief from either an overbearing or indolent ruler.*

Petion was re-elected; but it soon became evident that the means by which this re-election had been brought about, so surrounded him by secret and open enemies, that his life became unhappy. Nor can there be any doubt, that he would have saved himself many a pang, and have prolonged his useful and valuable life in the service of his country, had he more rigidly adhered to his own first principles of popular government. Had he set the example, which would have been so worthy of him, of resigning dignity and power when he might have done so, who can tell but that his example might have shaped out a course for his successors of future times, as would have protected his unhappy country from revolutions, which have seriously retarded its progress and general prosperity. But it must be admitted, that the Washingtons which have adorned our race, have been few! and also that Washington was never in the same circumstances.

* It will easily be seen, from the strange course pursued by the Senate, that conflicting elements were already at work; nor can there be any doubt that the reasons for a life Presidency were grave and convincing to the parties which carried this measure.

During all this time, the northern power of Christophe was taking deep root; an iron rule was driving on successfully a forced yet real prosperity.

In 1812, the crowned chief of the north manifested an intense desire to reign over the whole island of Hayti, and his decision was, to commence this ambitious design by the conquest of the Western Republic. An army was therefore organized and well equipped; nor was it without discipline; and with the king at their head, all of military power which the monarch had been able to get together, advanced towards Port au Prince.

At first, everything seemed to promise victory. The city on the sea side was blockaded by all the naval power that could be mustered, while Christophe advanced by land with his army, and came up with the Republican forces at a place called Santos, about two leagues and a half from the western capital. Here the royal arms prevailed, and for a time, all on their side seemed to be prosperous. In fact, the presence of the king evidently animated the troops, and their triumph began to appear sure; but during the contest, it was announced to the king that the royal family had arrived at St. Mark's, and he thought proper to return and meet them, not for a moment doubting either the solidity of his system, as to form of government, or the fidelity of his men. This was a false step, and simply proved that this man had been thoroughly blinded by pomp and power, and that the true state of things had, by these deceiving means, been hid from him, as will be seen in the fact, that during his temporary absence, two of his principal officers, one a colonel and the other a general, with the whole of the forces under them, deserted, and went over to the Republicans.

Christophe hearing of this, was soon back; but his eyes were now opened to see that his own army was too much enchanted by the free institutions and the almost unbounded liberty of the Republic, to afford him any hope of success. He had brought despotism too near to liberty. Nor did the latter fail in her charms; and he doubtless felt that the safety of both himself and his kingdom, was in his immediate return to his own capital, which he promptly did, and thus wisely abandoned the whole enterprise. That he would have succeeded, had he remained with his army, is probable, not to say certain. Nothing, however, could more clearly demonstrate the hopeless character of this man, than the fact, that this really humiliating event failed to convince him of the falseness of his position, or of any one of his errors.

Hence the ferocity of Christophe's temper was by no means diminished by this open declaration of hate, both to him and his system. On the contrary, he became fiercer than ever; and the fact of the two deserting officers being men of mixed blood, led him to pour out all his fury upon that class of the community, so much so, that on his arrival at St. Mark's, as he returned to his capital, it is said he ordered a general massacre of the colored people of that town.*

Things, however, soon found their level, and the prosperity of the kingdom, as to general industry and produce, went on rapidly. It is true, all was done by oppression. The king and his nobility were the

* Schelcher.

real masters of the people, and their intense thirst for wealth, together with their power, constituted a strong rural code, and at the same time were the real springs of action; in fact, the power was military.

Amongst many other monuments of the driving energy of this extraordinary man, and of which the remains are still, in part, standing, may be noticed the Royal Palace at Sans Souci, and the great fortress known as "Laferriere," which stands commandingly on a mountain summit of some 2,000 feet high, overlooking and protecting a vast plain beneath.

The palace of "Sans Souci" is thus described by an English traveler, who visited the ruins in 1840, before the great earthquake had completed its general wreck:

"The buildings, though once splendid, were never in good architectural taste. The whole domain, when properly maintained in the days of Christophe, must have been a princely affair, and adds one to the many other proofs he gave, that it was his ambition to be thought, every inch of him, a king! The rooms were lofty and spacious; the floors and side panels were of polished mahogany, or beautifully inlaid with Mosaic. The apartments were said to have been sumptuously furnished, and the gardens and baths for the young princesses, were in keeping with the general splendor.

"The coach-houses and stables were magnificent. A number of royal carriages still remain, the panels of which, gilded and emblazoned with the royal arms, show at how great a cost they must have been constructed—one of which cost in London £700 sterling." *

With regard to the remarkable castle, called "Laferriere," the following is a description of it, from

* J. Candler.

the pen of another English traveler, who visited it about 1826:

"This huge pile of building is said to have three hundred pieces of artillery, and the construction of it, which is said to have occupied several years, must have cost inconceivable labor.

"The materials for the building, and the artillery, were dragged up by human hands, for which, in addition to the troops employed, there were regular levies of the peasantry.

"In looking back upon the precipices to be surmounted, I can easily believe that it cost the labor of an entire regiment a whole day to drag up a single thirty-two pounder. Neither age nor sex were exempt from this duty, and the royal officers were unsparing in their exactions of labor. I saw a woman at Gonaives, whose back was deeply whaled from a cow-skin* applied to it, by the General in command, when employed in carrying stones upon her head. The mortality was very great; and it is said that the severity of the service was one of the causes of the revolution.

"I cannot suppose the citadel was ever intended for anything else than a stronghold, into which, in case of rebellion or invasion, the chief might have retired with all his disposable money, which was there hoarded up, and it is said that at one time, no less than $30,000,000 were collected, some six millions of which found their way into the Republican treasury." †

These great specimens of energy, taste, and enterprise, whatever may have been the motives or causes which originated them, were all demonstrations of Haytian capacity and thought. The same might be said of Marchand, where Dessalines left the traces of his power and wealth. Why, then, should they have been left to perish? Had Boyer turned the palace of Christophe into a National University, he would have immortalized his memory, by turning a great

* A switch of that material. † Mackenzie.

production of the Haytian mind and wealth to good account. The means of doing this were on the spot; but he chose that it should perish, because Christophe was a despot, and the enemy of himself and his republic.

It is stated by an English writer on Hayti,* that Christophe had amassed the immense wealth already referred to, with the hope of ultimately purchasing the Spanish part of the island from the Spanish government. Be this as it may, the castle seemed to be a fitting and sure place for the deposit of any amount of treasure.

From this mountain elevation is seen the immense "Pleine du Nord," having behind the fortification, in a hollow, the well known village of Dondon. This lofty fortress is seen from an immense distance. The climate of the neighborhood, even in summer, is delicious; the winds of December and January being sometimes even uncomfortably cold.

The case of Medina affords another view of the daring character of Christophe.

In 1814, the French government of Louis XVIII. sent out commissioners to Hayti, to endeavor to re-establish its sovereignty in that country. On this occasion an indirect menace was held out.

Medina had served under Toussaint, but had abandoned him for the French. Christophe ordered his arrest, notwithstanding he was the representative of so great and powerful a nation, and on examining his papers, it was found that he was a spy, and that his aim was to excite insurrection, and regain the country for France.

* Franklin.

This man was brought to trial, and found guilty by a military tribunal of the charges made against him, and was thrown into prison. How he died no one knows; no account seems to have been given of him afterwards. *

Christophe's efforts in behalf of education were praiseworthy. With regard, however, to the masses, but little if anything was done. The few schools which he did establish, were worthy of the elevated manner in which he aimed at doing everything. Several English gentlemen of high standing in literature were sent for, one or two of whom were clergymen; and many have believed that it was his intention to supersede the French language by the English. Certain it is, that the English language had begun to be very extensively understood in the northern kingdom. In fact, it is generally admitted that Christophe was quite of English predilection. His schools were furnished with hundreds, if not thousands, of copies of the Scriptures, many of which were printed with one column of English and one of French on each page. The efficiency of these schools was subsequently seen in the fact, that they furnished the country with many well educated and able men, most of whom could express themselves with more or less ease in English, a fact which makes it the more to be regretted that the national plan of education was on so limited a scale.

With regard to religion and the clergy in Christophe's kingdom, it would appear that he had two Archbishops, who both, it is said, fell under his displeasure for a time. He had also in view the cre-

* Franklin, 1828.

ation of a national clergy. Whether he would permanently have placed his church and clergy under the care of the Pope, is perhaps questionable; but whatever difficulty might have arisen in this matter, all would doubtless have been easily overcome, for it would have cost this king but little to assume the position of Henry VIII. of England, in any case of necessity.

In reference to literature generally, it will scarcely be expected that much can be said, either as to Christophe himself, or his kingdom,—a sort routine signature, applied by his own hand to the State documents, was probably the extent of his learning.

A royal Almanac was published once a year. A code of laws was also drawn up, under the title of "Code d'Henri I." A newspaper regularly appeared, in which the system of monarchy was defended. The press, therefore, was introduced into this small kingdom, and notwithstanding there were but comparatively few in the whole country who could read its productions, it is not to be inferred from thence, that intelligence was totally absent; native, although uncultivated talent, abounded, as will be understood from the fact, that that generation had been in close contact with hundreds, if not thousands, of more or less educated Frenchmen, both in the army and otherwise. Still to expect much from the nation generally in this sense, would be even unjust, for the masses had never yet been cared for. They, like most of them in Europe in those days, were simply what circumstances made them.

Years and events rolled on, and this small kingdom increased in wealth, from the fact, that the highest pressure of every kind, except that of avowed slavery, was brought to bear upon the whole nation.

But the iron and clay of tyranny and corruption did never yet combine. The hour of trial has ever brought them down, with all the nation's hopes. Hence Christophe's solemn hour came on. He raved, and stormed, and strutted during his short day, until the memorable year 1820. Towards the autumn of this year, he received what seemed to be the first warning of his fate, by a stroke of apoplexy, which fell upon him as he sat at service in the church at Limonade. The stroke appears to have been a heavy one, not only to himself personally; for the same blow which had thus prostrated him, seemed mysteriously to shake his throne also. During his illness, a mutiny broke out, which no doubt had long been planned. Hence the royal army, which under the "Prince de Limbé," had been sent to St. Mark's to put down the rebellion, which at first appeared there, joined the Republicans of the West, with whom they warmly fraternised.

The unhappy and now afflicted king, hearing this, attempted to mount his horse, but the final knell of his power had now rung, and the attempt was useless. Had he only been able to appear at the head of his army, it is possible he might have recovered all. And yet, even then, he would only have put off the evil day.

The king's household troops were now sent; but the whole kingdom was ripe for revolt; they also strengthened the Republican ranks, by going over to them.

Christophe, informed of this, saw at once that all

hope was now gone, and that his kingdom had fallen. Finding that the Republican army was approaching his capital, and in fact about to enter, he at this moment, being at "Sans Souci," withdrew to his chamber, professedly to meditate on what was to be done, and at the same time requesting not to be disturbed. Soon after this, the report of a pistol was heard in his room, and in a few minutes he was found a corpse, he having evidently retired, simply to end his mortal career. Thus fell the man, who was known often to have reproached Napoleon I. for surviving his misfortunes.

The queen, renowned for her humanity and kindness, coming in at the moment, and finding two of the generals weeping at the dreadful scene, bitterly reproached them, reminding them that their treacherous flatteries had ruined the king.

The Republican army soon entered Cape Haytian. Already the two sons of Christophe were killed, but the quaen was saved, and with her two daughters, was taken under the care of President Boyer, and sent to Port au Prince. Ultimately, the mother and her two daughters were sent to Europe, where the queen lived in Italy many years after the death of her husband.

"Henry Christophe, according to an account sanctioned by him, was born in the island of Grenada, in the year 1769, and came out at an early age to St. Domingue. He was a Sanibo, and the slave of a French gentleman, whose daughter resided at the Cape when I was there, and to whom Christophe was kind and attentive in his prosperity. He afterwards became a waiter at an hotel and gaming house. It does not appear when he entered the army; but in 1801 he was General of Brigade, and Governor of the Cape. He distinguished himself at the arrival of the French expedition: first in his negotiations with Le Clerc, and secondly by filling his house, richly furnished, with combustibles, and setting fire to it, as a signal for the conflagration of the whole city.

"Before Toussaint submitted, Christophe had yielded to French ascendency, and served for some time, but afterwards joined the bands that were roused to revolt, by the unsparing attrocities of Rochambeau, whose memory has an unenviable celebrity in every part of Hayti.

"Christophe was one of the officers that signed the Act of Independence, proclaimed by Dessalines, who afterwards became Emperor Jaques I. The indulgences of Christophe are said to have been of the most abandoned description.

"In the midst of all his brutality, Christophe was intent on exalting the condition of his kingdom, although his personal gratifications were probably the main-spring of his action. He was the principal dealer in the country; and some English merchants, who had extensive transactions with him, have described him to me as singularly well informed on matters connected with his business. To promote the civilization of his subjects, he assembled men of talent even from Europe, and undoubtedly promoted activity and enterprise. As an ignorant man, he may be considered one of those phenomena, that occasionally excite attention, but leave scarcely any beneficial trace behind." *

We now return to the Western Republic, which in 1812 received the submission of the southern part of the island, with the exception of an obscure band under Goman, which occasioned more petty annoyance than real fear.

The important movement which led to the union between the western and southern parts, was under the direction of General Borgella, and was an important accession to the Republic, which was now gradually gaining strength, notwithstanding much internal dissension.

* Mackenzie.

In 1814, the first step in another great movement took place. This was the great question of an indemnity to France for the losses of the former French colonists.

Whatever view may be taken of this question as to the right or wrong of the matter, it is not surprising that the former landed proprietors should have attempted something of the sort. Hence Louis XVIII. was no sooner seated on the throne of France, than he began to think of regaining the old French colony of St. Domingue. The French government, therefore, named three—Lavaise, Draverman, and Madina—not, it would appear, as an avowed and straightforward deputation; but their object was rather to sound the national feeling of the Haytians on this tender point.

With Christophe, as we have already seen in the case of Madina, the question was soon settled. Lavaise also wrote to Christophe, and even proposed to him submission to France, promising at the same time great and flattering things. But his efforts were simply treated with contempt, Christophe refusing all, or any treaty whatever, with France, which did not recognize the independence of Hayti. Petion also demanded the recognition of Haytian independence, but offered at the same time an indemnity, which however was to be given on the ground of such a recognition. Here the matter rested for another year or two.

It must not, however, be lost sight of, that France most certainly never would have renounced what she would have deemed her lawful claims, on any other condition than that of an indemnity in some form or other, and that therefore a blunt refusal on the part of the Republic, would unquestionably have involved a ruinous and exterminating war; for it is not to be supposed that France would have submitted to anything which she might conceive to be incompatible with her dignity as a nation. We shall do well, therefore, to pause, before blaming the prudence of Petion on this really momentous question. All that he did in this matter, was evidently compatible with the highest claims of national honor.*

In 1815, Christophe renewed proposals to the Republican government in the west, to come under his sceptre; but it was well known, that as the monarch advanced in years, he also advanced in ferocity, and his labor, therefore, in this matter, was in vain.

The year 1816 is remarkable in Haytian history, and in fact constitutes an epoch in the events and career of the nation worthy of attention. The remodeling of the Constitution is the case now referred to.

It will be remembered that in 1806, a Constitution was framed by a national assembly, called "l'Assemblée Constituante;" that up to that time, Christophe and Petion had been united; but the difference of character and disposition between the two men, was even at this time well known. Christophe's claims, however, to the chief post of honor were recognized; but it was known that a Constitution which limited and controlled the executive,

* Petion suggested to Lavaise the principle of an indemnity to the colonists, in compensation for private property, from the possession of which they were forever excluded.—*W. Y. G. Smith, M.D.*

would be rejected by him. It is not, however, surprising that the ideas of the educated Haytians of that age should have been even ulta-Republican, and that the Constitution of 1806 should have been incompatible with the despotic notions of Christophe. Even Petion himself found before long that the Constitution to which he had sworn fidelity, left him but little power; hence his ultimate dissolution of his senate, and the formation of another, by which, in 1811, he was without difficulty reëlected. But at the next presidential election in 1816, it was thought time to change the order of things entirely, and the presidency was to be for life. The principle reason assigned being, that the repeated elections for the presidency created aspirants for power and place, and exposed the country to the revolutionary effects of party-feeling and strife.

As has been already intimated, the prudence of this step, however pure and honest the motive which led to it, may be fairly doubted. The question seems rather to be, whether at such a time a periodical presidency did not rather serve as a national safety-valve than otherwise, allowing the heat of spirits, animated with a laudable ambition, to escape through a hope of one day reaching this high and so much desired post of honor. Whether it was right and prudent utterly to cut off such a hope, is at least doubtful; certain it is that revolutions in Hayti have ever since been either feared, attempted, or taking place.

Whatever regrets may mingle with the contemplation of things and events as they present themselves to us about this time in the history of Hayti, let it not be forgotten, that there was also much to approve; for whatever errors of judgment may be apparent in the general measures of those days, it is also quite evident that a great amount of genuine patriotism was the honor and glory of those times. Hence a great and good measure now demands both our notice and applause.

A nearer approach to the representative system, is the question now before us, or the formation of what might be termed a national parliament. This was a fair and honest step in the right direction, and one amongst many others which demonstrates that true independence is at least the right road to true dignity. Error, however, in a young country, is frequent on this great subject of liberty, which is frequently either not sufficiently guarded, or not sufficiently understood. Nevertheless, it must be admitted that the measure in question was a great step in advance towards free institutions; nor would it be just to the memory of Petion not to admit that posterity owes him much.

The system of things now prevailing in the West was entirely republican, and therefore the election of the representatives was understood to be by universal suffrage. It must, nevertheless, be admitted, that for an entirely uneducated mass to be possessed of sovereign power, is an anomally. It is true that in this case, there was an educated class, capable of directing, or doing for the rest. But after all, this is Republicanism, not only in half a sense, but in a dangerous sense; and although upon the whole a right foundation was here laid for the future course and hope of the nation, yet a mass of ignorance in a country is a fearful thing, and the danger of abuse in so free a system, under such circumstances, by unprincipled and designing men, is always great. Hence the withholding the initiative right from the representative body, as a preliminary step, may have been wise and prudent. Still, Republican freedom demands the universal education of the nation; and it must be confessed, that this has ever been the national error of Hayti. There has ever been a much greater eagerness for the free institutions of the age, than for that universal education which fits a people for them.*

During this year, 1816, Fontanges and Esmongart landed in Hayti as a deputation from the French government,—another proof that France was still looking significantly and steadfastly towards their ancient source of wealth, and was still bent on not giving up one iota of what she deemed her rights.

Esmongart, in addressing his despatches to King Christophe, either by design or forgetfulness, neglected to recognise the monarch, naming him simply General. This insult was received as might have been expected by a man to whom boldness and daring were natural. A proclamation was immediately issued by this sovereign, declaring that the Haytians were independent, and would only treat with France as a free and sovereign nation.

All ended here with Christophe in this matter;

* It has been specially gratifying to see in Hayti the engraving of the university building at Monrovia, the capital of the republic of Liberia. It is sincerely to be hoped that an obligatory universal Christian primary education, which should render national ignorance impossible, has preceded and constitutes the foundation of this great and laudable achievement.

what the result might have been, had Petion pursued precisely the same course, is not at all easy to say, except that a struggle more than ever terrible with France, might have resulted, and the independence of the whole of the French part of the island have been seriously threatened; for after all, the bravery and daring of the Haytians, in their former contests with the French, and notwithstanding also the fact, that the climate fought fearfully for them, yet it is scarcely to be supposed that a population of simply seven hundred thousand should be able to keep up a perpetual war, or even a very long one, with a nation of thirty millions, commanding so entirely all the arts of war, with all the means of applying them, as was unquestionably the case with the French.

Petion had evidently considered this important question in all its bearings and in the maturest manner, while the leading minds in the republic, considering that there was more or less justice in the claim as to mere landed property, and that war would simply be ruinous, wisely concluded, that having already done wonders for so small a nation, against one of such superior power, peace would now be perfectly consistent with the national dignity. An indemnity was therefore offered by Petion; but the French deputation, not being authorised to recognize the independence and sovereignty of Hayti, returned to France without any final settlement of the question. Nothing, indeed, had been definitely arranged; but this was at least a first step towards a final understanding between the two nations, which it must be admitted was in every way desirable, for notwithstanding the power of France, her sacrifice of human life, etc., in the Haytian contest, had already been immense, even frightful; and yet she had lost one of the finest colonies she had ever possessed. In fact, the position of so great a nation as that of France, with so comparatively small a one as that of Hayti, is one of the most extraordinary that has ever been recorded in history. Both, however, felt that there was a right position for each in this great matter, and hence there was a disposition on all sides to meet the case in a frank and honest manner.

During the year 1816, the great and celebrated hero of South America, Bolivar, landed in Hayti, and received the warmest sympathies of Petion. Hayti, indeed, could do but little to help on the great plans of Bolivar, yet all she could do in a pecuniary point of view, was done, and it can easily be understood, that two such kindred spirits, having one common aim in view, would deeply and warmly sympathize with each other.

CHAPTER IV.

First Wesleyan Missionaries.—" L'Education eléve l'homne," etc. —Pressoir Persecution.—Stoning, etc.—New Representative Body.—Mackenzie on the Courts, etc.—General Education.—Amount of Exports in 1818.—Fiscals.—Petion's Funeral.—Boyer President.—Christopher Writes to Boyer.—Great Public Fire.—Boyer takes the North.—He Takes the Eastern Part.—The Spelling-Book and the Sword.—The Age blameable, not Hayti.—The News-Papers Published.

The nation's mighty mainspring is its heart,
Oft form'd and ton'd by messengers from heav'n.

If it be a recognized and immutable truth that whatever be the intelligence of a people, or even their civilization and science, without moral principle nothing can be either stable or prosperous;—then we may hail, as one of the most important events of Haytian history, the arrival this year, 1816, of two Protestant Missionaries of the English Wesleyan Methodist Connexion—the Revs. J. Brown and J. Cats.

Roman Catholic Clergymen of sincerity had indeed appeared in Hayti before these worthy men, but the country still needed sincere men;—their arrival was undoubtedly well-timed, and these men of God were welcomed in Hayti by the great founder of the Republic, who had desired their presence.

The fact that Petion had in every way encouraged the sending out of these Missionaries, made everything plain and easy for them on their arrival; hence, they met with neither difficulty nor hinderance in their great and unsparing labors, which were by no means confined to the city of Port-au-Prince; for, like their great founder, they widely extended their labors, and spread the leaven of Christian truth far and near, especially in the neighborhood of the capital, and the effect of their ministrations was evidently great; for, the people feeling themselves entirely free to adopt whatever religious views and principles they might conscientiously become convinced of as truth, did not hesitate to avow that conviction, whenever it was felt; hence, a Protestant Church in this professedly Roman Catholic community, of nearly a hundred members, was soon formed, and the influence of Christian truth, spoken by men, whose aim was rather to change the heart and life, than anything else, became powerful, and all for a time went silently on.*

Among the many aims of these Christian pioneers was that of striking at the root of vice by the formation of a public school, founded on purely Christian principle; hence, according to usage, they, on this great subject, addressed their own special friend, the President of the Republic, and received from him an entirely hearty approval of their benevolent object.

One of the sentences found in the reply of the President to the address of the Wesleyan Missionaries, on the subject of public education, is altogether noble, and deserves special notice, being so

* It is to be borne in mind here, that at that time there was no Concordat with the Church of Rome; Petion had simply in view the diffusion of Christianity.

completely of a piece with all that is known of Petion; it is as follows:

"L' education éleve l'homme, á la dignité de son etre!" *

During the days of Petion, all was well; the prosperity of this Mission was to him altogether agreeable; he evidently wished the advance of plain truth; his thoughts reached beyond the narrow limits of sectarianism; but this happy and peaceful career, as to the Wesleyan Mission, now so evidently the offspring of Petion's own idea, did not long continue; for, on the 18th March, 1818, the illustrious patron and friend of this neuclus of simple, living, Christian truth, terminated by death his mortal career, and the reins of power fell into the hands of General Jean Pierre Boyer.

This painful event—the death of Petion—brought on an entire change of action and policy throughout all the interests and bearing of the nation.

Had the views and feelings of the new President been the same as those of his honorable and distinguished predecessor, his power and influence would unquestionably have been sufficient to protect those honest pastors and their little flocks, at least from insult; but Petion's protecting arm had no sooner fallen under the power of death, than the symptoms of vastly different thoughts and feelings began to develope themselves; religious bigotry had simply been pent up by the power and patronage of the former President, whose views on religious liberty, as well as the real moral wants of his people, had evidently been very much in advance of those of his successor.

* Education raises man to the dignity of his being!

At the death of Petion, therefore, a persecution broke out and continued for some little time.

Wheel-barrows full of stones were wheeled to the places where the meetings were held, and a senseless and enraged populace seemed to be left to their own blind will and fury; stones were hurled, doors and windows broken in, and innocent and honest people, in the name of law, were taken off to prison.

In this age of the world we read these things with humiliation, and yet such has been the history of the introduction of Christian truth, in its simplicity, among all peoples, in all ages.

The Wesleyan Missionaries, at the advice of President Boyer, and also of their own affectionate and devoted people, who, having received the truth into their hearts, could not endure to see their pastors insulted, withdrew and returned to Europe—President Boyer having, in the most honorable manner, guaranteed the Home Committee of the Wesleyan Missions as to all expenses.

In the absence of the Missionaries, now in a sense banished, Mr. J. C. Pressoir came forward as the head of this little Christian band; and, having himself escaped, being put in prison, went to the Palace as the bearer of a letter, which was addressed to the President by one of the thirty-two who had been imprisoned.*

On the appearance of Pressoir before the President, his Excellency accused the Methodists as

* One of the number imprisoned was St. D. Bauduy, who subsequently spent four years in Europe at the request of the Wesleyan Missionary Committee, and then returned to Hayti as one of their ordained Ministers.

"fanatics!" The bearer of the letter replied, "Pardon me, President, they are not!" "Why," said the President, "you have changed your religion!" The letter-bearer again replied: "If I have changed my religion, President, it is the Government which has led me to do so." "How so?" demanded his Excellency. Pressoir's reply was: "It was the late President who sent for the Missionaries; I read the letter and saw the President's signature." "Enough! enough!" replied the President, "I will send an answer!"

The parties in prison were soon released after this interview, but with orders not to assemble any more; they were told that they might worship God individually as they pleased, but that the Government had given orders to disperse all meetings; the meetings, however, were continued, but with every effort to avoid every thing like an air of defiance, by making their assemblies, for a time, as private as possible; yet the stoning and brutal usage continued, until at last a proclamation was issued from "La Place," ordering the people to cease stoning, etc.; and, at the same time, forbidding the Methodists to meet together. By degrees, peace was established; and, by the firmness and unswerving fidelity of these faithful people, whose undaunted sincerity and honest steadfastness, both to God and their own consciences, remained immoveable under every storm, the great boon of religious liberty was ultimately secured. Such has been the cost of religious liberty in all past ages of the world: the future may be wiser!

Painful as this case of persecution was, it is impossible that it should be any matter of surprise; it was simply the clashing of opposing elements, precisely such as has been realized in all countries and in all ages.

That Boyer had the same power as his predecessor, to protect and patronize the Protestant Ministers, is beyond all contradiction, but he evidently differed from Petion; this will appear plainly from his language and style to Pressoir, which were precisely the opposite to anything that Petion would have done or said. Boyer, as a decided Roman Catholic, probably felt it to be his duty to oppose the introduction and progress of Protestantism in the Republic; or, as a statesman, he probably supposed that the presence of such opposing elements in the nation might ultimately engender unhappiness; doubtless his judgment led him to conclusions opposite to those of Petion, and he probably deemed it an error in his predecessor to have brought such an element into the country at all; hence he did not protect, simply because his views were different, not because he could not; posterity, therefore, will judge between Petion and Boyer in this matter.

It is true that religious persecution at any time, or for any reason, is a senseless thing, and always defeats its own purpose; yet, it must be remembered, that this has always been the old routine of things; hence, Wesley's case in England, not so very far back, was much worse than the one under consideration, more brutal, and far more unnatural; the latter being the persecution of Protestants by Protestants.

But Hayti was still marching on in her national

career; and in 1817 the great experiment was tried, of a newly organized House of Representatives, as another branch of the Legislature. Hitherto the country had been governed by a Senatorial body, which was understood to represent and express the mind of the people, that Legislative corps having been elected by them; but the prestige of the Court had, no doubt, suffered from its violent dissolution by President Petion; whatever, or wherever may have been the error which led to a Dictatorship, on the part of the Executive, future times will, doubtless, view the case in its proper light, and give it its proper merits, but the assurance which will ever be felt that Petion in this, as well as every other public affair, was perfectly honest in his motives and ultimate intentions, even though his judgment may have been faulty.

The new branch now added to the Legislature, at least helped to complete the theory of a good system of Government, by bringing in another fair balance against the Executive; it is, however, to be remembered that the initiative of all measures was with the Executive.

It will be remembered that, during the life-time of Petion, the Constitution underwent one or two revisions, and that its last touch took place in 1816, after which it remained the same for many years.

The general Institutions, based upon the Constitution of the last revision, are well described by an English traveler,* who visited Hayti only a few years after the death of the first President, and of which we here give the following extract:

* Mackenzie.

"The affairs of the Government are directed by the President, who holds the office for life; he must have attained his thirty-fifth year before his election to office; he has the right of naming a successor, which is subject to the approval of the Senate; he commands the national forces, and watches over the Tribunals by his Commissaries, whose offices are held during his pleasure; he proposes to the Commons all laws, except those connected with taxation; he makes foreign treaties and war, under the sanction of the Senate; he directs the receipts, and issues the public taxes,—the Senate and the High Court of Justice having the power to demand an account of his administration.

"The details of the administration are carried on in three departments.

"First, that of Secretary-General, whose duties are very extensive and varied.

"Secondly, that of Secretary of State for Finances and the Treasury, and all fiscal matters belonging to this department.

"The third department immediately forming a portion of the Government, is under the 'Grand Juge,' who is the Chief of all the Judicial establishments.

"This High Court of Justice can only be constituted to act by a proclamation from the Senate; it must be held in a place designated for its sittings, which must not be more than twelve leagues from the Senate; it is composed of, at least, fifteen Judges, taken by lot from the different departmental tribunals.

"The Grand Judge presides, except he is then himself under accusation, in which case another is selected by the President.

"There being no appeal from this Court, the accused has the right of rejecting one-third of his judges, and two-thirds only can condemn.

"The Senate consists of twenty-four members; all citizens are elegible, except the actual members of the Chamber of Deputies; the choice is made by the Deputies, out of a list of three names for each vacancy, by private ballot; the sessions are private or public, as may be; each Senator receives a salary.

"The Representatives are chosen by universal suffrage, the

mode of election being by ballot; no law can be effective, of which the project has not originated with the Executive.

"The Court of Cassation revises the decisions of other Courts, and decides on the application of the laws, in the case in which it had been previously made.

"The 'Chambre des Comptes' consists of five members, whose duty it is to examine into, and report on every branch of the expenditure and collection of the revenue to the President, as well as to suggest their views of reform and improvement.

"The internal Government of the Republic is managed in the following manner:

"The whole Island is divided into seventy-six Communes, and thirty-four Parishes; these are classed under twenty-seven Military Arrondissements and six Departments; each Department is generally commanded by a General in the army; he exercises both military and civil authority, and is the medium through which the Government makes known its arrangements.

"Besides the high Court of Justice, and that of Cassation, there are eight Local, Civil and Communal Tribunals; this gradation of inferior Courts is established in the Capitals of the Districts.

"Trial by Jury is established.

"The decisions of the 'Juge de Paix,' without Jury, are final, within the amount of fifty dollars; the functions and powers of the 'Juge de Paix' are necessarily very extensive."*

On the subject of Education, in its widest sense, in the country, about this time, although but little can be said, it must be admitted that provision, at least to some extent, had been made; but it must be remembered that the education of the masses was an idea which, even in the most advanced portions of the human race was, at that time, but just struggling

* Various modifications have since been made, especially in State Secretaryship, etc.; but the general framework of Haytian institutions remains much the same.

into existence. Hayti's model, at this time, was Europe, where the education of the masses was much more feared than sought.

But little, therefore, can be said on the subject of popular Education at this stage of Haytian history.

Nevertheless, Petion founded and established the Lyceum, which, for a number of years, was a good and efficient College, and for a long time furnished good and useful education to many of the youth of the Republic; its range of operation was limited, compared with the wide-spread wants of the nation; yet, it must be admitted, that many men of talent ultimately rose from that institution, and became of great use to their country.

It would, however, be scarcely expected that Hayti should have been in advance of Europe, on the question of the education of the masses; nor, ought it to be lost sight of, that the United States of America was absolutely nothing to Hayti at this time, precisely as Hayti was less than nothing to them, the reasons on each side being very easily understood.

Still, in the general theory of Haytian institutions, schools have always been provided, and it is even supposed, theoretically, that the entire nation is under educational care; the sad fact, however, remains that the great bulk of the people are but little advanced in either reading or writing, from what they ever were; it has, indeed, been the case in Hayti, as it is in the greater part of Europe to this day, that Education, even in its primary department, has never been raised to its proper level of importance and respectability; which painful fact, together with that indifference to education, which is only natural to an ignorant people, constitutes the explanation of the present condition of the masses of Hayti.

That so vital a point as that of an universal education should ever have been lost sight of in a thoroughly free Republic, where every citizen is expected to understand what he is, is deeply painful; nor can such a state of things be justified, whatever may have been the difficulties; real heart and conscience in this great matter would, unquestionably, have overcome anything.

It might, indeed, be said that continual wars, either intestine or foreign, render the instruction of the masses impossible; nor is it to be denied that the difficulties were very great; but in a Republic, where every man that could read ought to have taught him that could not, any obstacle might, and ought to have been overcome; in fact, a determined national aim at and perseverence in such a work, would have overcome every thing, and levelled the highest mountain of difficulty; the masses of Hayti would thus have been saved from being the mere dupes of unprincipled and designing men, who have too frequently tarnished the reputation of their country before the world, and disappointed every hope by revolutionary promises, more hollow than the wind.

It has often been a matter of surprise among the friends of Hayti that the bearing of primary education upon the masses of the people, in relation to general activity, the creation of wants, and its consequent bearing upon general commerce, has never been practically recognized; the interests of every man in business demands that the wants of the people should be increased to the utmost, while stagnation of every kind must necessarily result from settled ignorance; yea, the richest resources of nature must remain closed, while the key of universal education is withheld.

Of Agriculture, much might be said; gigantic plans, at all times and under all circumstances of the country, have been drawn up to sustain and extend this important branch of industry; in fact, the importance of this great national source of wealth has always been largely spoken of in Hayti.

The French Colonists had succeeded in the raising of general produce to a degree which was even astonishing, but it was the effect of slavery in its worst form and highest degree of brutality.

Toussaint L'Ouverture was sufficiently enlightened to see the immense importance of national and agricultural industry; hence, he drove on the culture of the staple exports of the country, but this was done by the most stringent regulations possible, which, doubtless, under all the circumstances of the case, were necessary.

Dessalines also wielded a mighty and terrific power to keep up the agricultural energies of the country; and, although he succeeded in raising produce to a great amount, yet he himself at last sunk under the weight of his own brutalities.

Nor, were General Rigaud's efforts, in the Southern part of the Island, unworthy of notice on this great question of general agriculture.

Christophe's iron rule terrified his unhappy subjects into great activity, and the results were great;

yet the madness of his efforts, even in the cause of industry, quenched ultimately all his hopes of glory and power, and served as a warning lesson to all posterity. All these men, be it remembered, had taken for their industrial standard the forced produce and results of slavery; and, therefore, they could not realize their aims without an undue and unjust force in one form or another.

Later, what were called rural codes were attempted, with a view to bring out more fully the energies of the people; but with regard to these codes, as they are generally understood, no really enlightened people would ever submit to them.

A system which will not allow a free man to come into a town during certain days in the week, etc., etc., is rather childish in its idea, and therefore supposes a degraded people.

The code rural, therefore, should be the Christian school-master; let him temper the mental and moral springs of the nation; let him bring the rising generation up to their right level, and such wants will ultimately be felt as will put all in action; such a "code rural" would need, comparatively, small expense as to military or even civil police.

Petion and his Republic show us the opposite of all that we have now noticed; and, although this doubtless is partly to be accounted for by the mild character of the man, yet the absence of a salutary energy throughout his administration—which the best friends of Petion must admit was the case—was injurious to the true interests of the country; had Petion been more energetical, more, doubtless, might have been done.

Policy was, perhaps, one of the secrets of Petion's mildness; he wished to establish a contrast between the free Republic and the oppressive Northern Monarchy, such as should sap its foundations and bring it down; and, it must be admitted, that the general bearing of the Republic, proved in the end the utter overthrow of Christophe and his tyranny. A bolder aim at doing what was simply right might have made Petion still more popular than he justly was, and have given a healthier tone to his country; yet, notwithstanding the great laxity of the system of that day, it must not be supposed that the culture of the soil was wholly neglected; hence, we are informed that in 1818 the export of coffee amounted to 26,000,000 lbs.; compared with the forced labor of 1789, which produced 76,000,000, this was indeed small, although in fact it was really more; for, it must be remembered that the twenty-six millions of coffee was raised simply within Petion's range of power, which was even less than half the French part of the Island, the Southern part being still more or less unsettled. It is also specially to be noted that a military system, then essentially necessary to the very existence of the nation, weighed upon the entire population.

With these considerations before us, it will soon appear very plainly that the produce of labor under the free Republic was greater than under the iniquitous power of the Colonial system.

In 1818, the export of dye woods amounted to upwards of 6,000,000 lbs., principally from the South, which, although still suffering from past confusion, was now united to the Western Republic.

This, although but a limited view of the exports generally, will at least afford proof that a fair amount of industry was kept up in the country, notwithstanding its general circumstances must have been anything but favorable to national produce.

Christophe had forced on labor and had done much more than his neighbors; but, it is a painful fact, that his whole reign seemed like one unceasing effort to drive both himself and his Monarchy out of existence.

The range of industry now before us, which does not include the Spanish part of the Island, offers, although in fragments, an aggregate of result not unworthy of attention, especially when the great difficulties arising from arms and war are considered.

On the subject of general commerce, it must be remembered that the Haytian people, even at the death of Petion, were only just struggling out of chaos into order; still, their wants were many as to household furniture, clothing, and various articles of consumption, such as flour, salt fish, beef, pork, butter, lard, soap, candles, etc., etc.; hence, the States and Europe soon learnt that the Haytian harbors now offered good markets; thus affording abundant proof that the Haytians, notwithstanding the most paralyzing difficulties, had began the work of financial accumulation in the form of general produce, for the purpose of their national and individual wants; hence, the commercial flags of nearly all nations were soon seen in the Haytian waters, while those also of war acknowledged, by their friendly salutes, the dignity of Haytian Independence.

In fact, the career of the Haytian nation was now

fairly begun. It is true the Haytian people, at this time, existed in two great divisions, one of which was a Republic, and the other a Monarchy; but the great emulation which existed between the parties unquestionably drove them on as a people; for, whatever may have been their divisions, they were, after all, the Haytian people.

With regard to fiscal arrangements, it will easily be understood that an organized system of paid Government functionaries, civil and military, would necessarily require a circulating medium.

The monetary standard was, doubtless, the Spanish dubloon; but, as the whole financial system of those days was rather in embryo than otherwise, the details for the present may not be altogether essential; it will be enough for us to understand for the present that, with a suitable starting point, the force of necessity would do all the rest.*

The military system in those days was, in the most unlimited sense, national; in fact, the whole nation of that day might be viewed as an entire military camp—every Haytian, capable of bearing arms against the French, had been needed; nor, in fact, could the nation have existed at all, in the beginning, but upon this principle. This dreadful and ruinous necessity was continued as a defence against Christophe, whose fury would now and then break forth from the North, while, at the same time, the difficulties in the South had not ceased; nor, indeed, was all yet clear with France.

* A paper currency was early introduced into Hayti, the Haytian dollar being then at par with the Spanish.

Let any impartial mind, from this point of Haytian history, take a fair and honest view of the Haytians as a people.

Like the ancient Britons, the Haytians were originally slaves, but of African hue, and the living property of white French masters. A class of mixed blood was the result, and this class is known in the English West Indies as colored, distinct in color from the Blacks. In Hayti, under the Colonial system, none of the colored people were considered equal to their own white fathers; nor was the case altered in those who had been sent to Europe, and had returned with cultivated and expanded minds, many of them quite superior to their sires. It was enough in this case that the son was darker than the father; this, one would suppose, must have been deemed a crime; hence, on this account, his claims to the honor and rank of a man were spurned with indignation; but educated human nature was not to be trampled under foot in this manner. The instincts of the enlightened mind, in this case, took fire, and the son dared the father in his daring wrong; in fact, all reasoning ended.

The French nation, just at this juncture, proclaimed all men equal and free; the European educated son of Hayti, therefore, on his return to his native land, in defiance of gallows, rack and sword, asserted his claims to all that belonged to him as a man; a claim which posterity will most certainly applaud; in fact, this was already accorded in France; and, notwithstanding all opposing power on the part of the white fathers of colored sons in St. Domingue, the standard of freedom was raised on those shores, and those bloody scenes, in which freedom and slavery met in awful conflict, resulted and continued until the final extirpation of every vestige of slavery. To this great work every Haytian heart beat true; before the monster, Slavery, all was union; one and the same feeling fired every heart while they were engaged in trampling out of existence this foe to human happiness and honor; but, the demon of discord remained among them; and, however unhappy this may have been, it was human; hence, the course pursued by the Haytians themselves was only the old beaten track of envy, hatred and malice; nor was the anarchy, blood-shed and fury of the French Revolution, in any sense less than that of Hayti, to say nothing of other nations, ancient or modern; in fact, order is to be found in the very divisions among the Haytians; hence, Rigaud, who commanded independently in the Southern part of the Island, did not live without even a well-organized state of things, and had succeeded in establishing a high tone of industry.

Petion's Republic, although more spontaneous in all its action, and free from everything despotic, was, nevertheless, a well-arranged and even admirable community; the general elements of an advanced civilization were there; good laws and free institutions constituted the glory of the Republic.

Christophe, also, in the North, as we have seen, was not wanting in high aims, notwithstanding a cruelty and tyranny, which was the grief of his best friends.

It may, indeed, be said that these elements of civilization were left among the Haytians by their superior French masters; but this is simply saying that civilization is transmitted from one nation to another, and from one generation to another; errors, doubtless, abounded on all sides, but without this they scarcely would have been human.

Hayti, therefore, notwithstanding storms without and within, floated, and firmly braved one of the most stormy seas by which any nation was ever tossed; and, although rent by internal discord, she has stood. One thing she has, indeed, ever needed; had her national sinews been strengthened by sound moral culture, her course might have been a giant one; but this was undeniably wanting, and hence the vital springs of her noblest interests were weakened; still, she held on her way, and concentrated her power in the South, while the rule of Christophe, in the North, began to reel before the common sense of Republican liberty.

President Petion was buried on the 31st of March, 1818. On the previous day, Jean Pierre Boyer was elected President of the Haytian Republic, and on the following first of April, his public inauguration to office took place, when he swore fidelity to the constitution and people of Hayti.

To a mind fully and honestly bent on the elevation of the masses, which ought to be the chief aim of the first magistrate of a Republic, a fairer field than that which now opened to President Boyer could not well be imagined, nor can there be any doubt that such an aim, heartily carried out, would have raised both himself and his Republic to that true dignity which ought to be the aim of national existence. Such was the aim of the great North American Republic, nor has it failed in its transcendent effect. This too, should have been the aim of Hayti, and whatever excuse may be found in her difficulties on this subject, her great mission as an African representative nation, demanded this; nor will she ever be fully justified before mankind for the fact that the great mass of her people are ignorant. Yet where shall we look in Haytian history to be convinced and satisfied that an attempt has ever been seriously made to abolish ignorance every where?

Internal and external peace long reigned about this period of Haytian history, and the way for the great work of national education was open. An attempt at such a work, or some sincere expression of desire for its accomplishment, is the least that the present generation could have expected. Nor does it seem possible to avoid the painful conclusion that this neglect was a part even of the policy of the day, upon the principle that it was easier to govern ignorance than knowledge. This unquestionably had long been a ruling thought in Europe, hence the light through the masses was rather feared than sought.

Boyer had indeed been trained in this school; he was intelligent, and was high in the polish of French manners; nor is it astonishing that his model in all things should have been the French nation. France alone, at that time, had broken the chains of slavery; and although treachery had subsequently come in, the source of liberty to Hayti was France, while both England and America still held on to slavery.

But an intelligent man, adopting Republicanism, is supposed to have at heart all that elevates mankind. In fact, he is supposed to mean, with all sincerity, that every member of a nation should be a man, in the full and right sense. Most unquestionably had this been the real spirit of Haytian Republicanism from the beginning, it would have been done; nor can Hayti ever be a nation or a true republic without it.

In the course of June, during 1818, Christophe sent a deputation to the new President of the Western Republic proposing the amalgamation of the two communities, of course under his crown and flag. These men were kindly received, but the effort proved abortive, and was viewed by the Republicans more with contempt than otherwise.

The following year, the insurgents of La Grande Anse, who for many years had given great trouble to the Republic, fraternized with the West; and in fact the past unhappiness of the country began now to subside into ease and peace. In 1820, however, a great calamity befel Port au Prince; an exceedingly destructive fire swept away property to an immense amount. This misfortune was the more deeply felt from the fact that the work of insurance had not yet begun in Hayti, and consequently each one had to support his own ruin as best he could.

We have already seen the ruin and end of Christophe and his kingdom. This, however, we have seen from a northern point of view; it now remains for us to view this important event from the Western Republic.

It was reported to the Western Government that St. Mark's, on Christophe's western frontiers, was in a state of revolt; that Christophe himself was now helpless from apoplexy, and that the Royal troops of that place were ready to join the Republican standard.

Such news was not altogether unexpected; in fact it had been predicted from the beginning that it was only necessary to leave Christophe to himself, and that he alone would bring about his own ruin.

Preparations were soon made by Boyer, and his march to the Cape* was uninterrupted; hence, in a few days the capital of the now fallen and self-murdered monarch was filled with about 20,000 men, commanded by the President of the Republic.

Here the fortunate Boyer was well received, the hated tyranny of Christophe having well-prepared his way. All was joy, and the people of the North felt that a more than iron yoke had been broken by the hand of God himself; hence there was an enthusiastic burst of fraternal congratulation between all parties. The northern kingdom was declared to be extinct, and absorbed into the Western Republic, of which Boyer was President.

A high tone of industry had indeed resulted from Christophe's natural temperament; but that energy had degenerated into cruelty, and his measures became stained with blood, hence the absorption of the monarchy, in this case into the Republic, was a most happy consummation. It is true, that by this means the genuine principles of liberty were spread among the masses, which at this time were but little prepared to comprehend or appreciate them; but even this was better than a murderous monarchy.

Henceforth the entire of the French part of the island constituted the limits of the Republic. This

* A distance of about 200 miles.

was a grand step, and afforded solid ground of hope for future prosperity.

But the good fortune of Boyer did not stop here. The following year, 1821, the Spanish part of the island declared its independence of Spain; but doubtless feeling their weakness, measures were taken by themselves to communicate with the Haytian Republic, which in 1822 were followed up and accomplished by the presence of Boyer in the ancient capital of the great Columbus with upward of 20,000 men.

It must, however, be understood that the Spaniards of the eastern part of the island were not, in this case, a conquered people. The movement which terminated in their union with the Haytian Republic originated with the Spaniards, they themselves having wisely seen, that their own interest and those of the island at large, rendered it desirable that the whole population of Hayti, throughout the entire island, should live under one flag, although there doubtless was a strong opposing party among the Spaniards.

We therefore see here, that there were at least some, in the Spanish part of the island, at this time, who thought more of the whole and general interests of Hayti, as one united nation, than of themselves personally; for they were certainly as capable of defending themselves against Spain as the French Haytians were of defending themselves against France.

The limits, therefore, of the Haytian Republic were now those of the island itself; and a field of nearly a million of minds was now thrown open to, and even called aloud for, the healthy action of the intellectual and moral plough. Had the ruling spirits in the land of that day only had "ears to hear," an increased and widely extended dominion had led to the true dignity of the nation, its unbounded resources had been opened, and unlimited wealth had ultimately resulted; knowledge had taken the place of a standing army, and reason had asserted her power. But this was not understood, hence ere long the complaint was heard, on the part of the French Haytians, that the Spanish part was rather a burden to the republic than otherwise, which will be easily understood was the case, by the fact that arms and troops, more in the sense of rulers than otherwise, were sent among them, which they rather hated than supported.

Men have indeed yet to learn that there is more power in a spelling-book than a sword, and that until the former reigns, we shall ever be in danger of the despotism of the latter.

The Republic of Hayti was now composed of conflicting elements, persons of the most opposite views were now in contact with each other, and the utmost caution and prudence on the part of the Government was doubtless necessary; yet the real interests of the country were one. The main-spring of education, now more than ever, needed a strong and healthy action, and every child in the island should have felt its power; but the grand infatuation prevailed—"There is no time for this!" or, "The time for this had not yet arrived!" Nor will it ever arrive until those who have the power, shall be resolved to do this, whatever else remains undone. The task would indeed be great, but the political as well as the religious soul of the nation, thoroughly strung up to this, it would soon appear that educational parties would be quite as easy as card parties, while they would be far more useful.

It is indeed to be feared that the idea had got into existence of its being more easy to govern a mass of ignorance than an enlightened people. Nor is it strange that the ruling thought and fear of Europe as to making a penman of every individual, should have gained the ascendency in Hayti, for she really never had any other model before her; hence, it must be admitted, that in the infancy of the Haytian nation, the age was more to be blamed for her errors than herself. Europe at this time had not yet risen to the height of this great idea—of teaching every individual to be a man. The United States indeed had, at least so far as the white class was concerned, but in the beginning of the present century all was infancy and experiment on the great question of the education of the masses.

The field of labor now, however, in Hayti, was fully and entirely open. The whole island was now under one government, and the position of President Boyer was elevated and powerful, while at the same time he was himself honored and respected, and his influence was sufficiently great to have carried the whole nation with him in any measure which might have been for the advancement and general welfare of the people, the position was splendid. A man having entirely at his command a country unsurpassed for resources of wealth, with a people naturally mild and well-disposed; with such means and resources what might not have been done? But an utterly false policy reigned, and the sin of the day consisted rather in doing nothing than in dong positive evil.

It might indeed be said that at this period of Haytian history party feeling ran high, and required prudent management, but it might be well replied, that the true safety-valve for party feeling consists in keeping the nation's way open and clear for every kind of progress. Certain it is, that party feeling was never subdued by any course of policy adopted in those days. Party feeling in a nation which knows how to direct its Governors and its Government, is far less dangerous than where the parties are distracted, without properly knowing why.

Nevertheless, about this period of the Haytian history, the press was often heard in tones of thunder. But the ruling power instead of placing itself at the head of an onward movement, which was began by the people, feared and was deaf; hence all was stagnant, but it was a stagnation which consisted in the pent up feelings of the nation. The ruling powers, loving things as they were, were seemingly heedless of the certainty of a national explosion from sheer want of vent, for the great tide which was rising, and which by wise rulers might have been foreseen, should have been directed in its legitimate and natural onward movement, which to check would be simply revolutionary.

We, however, are not to conclude that the silence of death reigned at this time over the Haytian people as to general intelligence. The press was not altogether dumb; hence, before 1807, a career of journalism was commenced in the Republic previous to the above date. "La Gazette Commerciale d'Haïti," made its appearance, and was for sme time directed by a few intelligent gentlemen; also another, named "La Gazette Officielle de l'Etat d'Haïti," which being published at the Cape, became subsequently the Royal Gazette, under King Christophe.

At Port au Prince, was commenced in 1807, L'Abeille Haitienne." In 1818, "Le Parfaite Patriote." In 1819, a paper was commenced at Cayes, dedicated "Au Temps et à la Verité." In 1820, "L'Hermit d'Haïti." In 1821, "La Concorde," and in 1822, at Santo Domingo, "L'Emile Haïtienne."

This list might be very greatly prolonged, for the active and well-developed intelligence of many of the Haytians had been unceasingly at work in this mode of public expression, although frequently shackled by the reigning political ideas of the day.

What has been already noted, although quite limited, will suffice to show that the Haytien mind was already at wotk, and under more auspicious circumstances, had doubtless struggled through every difficulty into full development, but an iron hand seemed already to weigh upon its destiny; not one, indeed, of individual tyranny, but rather one made up of the circumstances of the times, especially on the part of the more intelligent, in crouching before party feeling, fearing to be bold in doing and saying what was purely right and strightforward.

Truth, however, demands the acknowledgment that, as far as we have proceeded in these "historical notes," the independence of Hayti has not been without dignity, and notwithstanding great errors in judgment, and even the miseries of bad faith: the fact remains that the true elements of an honorable nationality are here. That they have never yet been fully brought out is to be regretted. The power and result of education in Hayti, as far as it has been carried out, needs no comment for those who really know this Republic, while at the same time, experience has amply proved, that Christianity in its right sense, well-applied, would work out its elevating effects; but if the living power of Christ is not brought to bear upon the nation, it would be unjust to expect its effects.

CHAPTER V.

The Indemnity.—Arrangements with France.—First American Immigration.—Camp Meetings.—Baudin Returns.—Boyer's good negative.—Code Rural.—The Responsibility.—Blowing up of the Arsenal in 1826.—Question of Population.—All started from Europeans.—Immorality, the ruin of Hayti.

Gold was not here, the price of Liberty,
But simply dust, deep dyed in blood, which now,
The guilty fly.

The indemnification demanded of Hayti by France, was an event which, while it created much anxiety, gave rise to an immense diversity of opinion.

The French Government was doubtless urged to this step, both by the former colonists of this island, which had promised so much wealth, and also by the consideration of the bearing of the whole case upon the national honor and dignity of the French people.

In the loss of St. Dominque, France had doubtless lost one of the brightest gems in her crown, but to be so beaten by an inferior power, with impunity, would have been humiliating. Many opinions, however, both amongst the Haytians and foreigners, have been broached on this subject; some have maintained that Christophe's daring and defying refusal, was the right position of the Haytian people, while others maintained that the course pursued by Petion and Boyer, was the only true one. That France would ever have given up her claim, was scarcely to be supposed, still less, that when once made, she would ever retract; while on the other hand, it would have been impossible for Hayti to have sustained a perpetual war with France; the conclusion, therefore, is tolerably clear, that it was desirable on both sides, that the most honorable arrangements possible should be made; but we will here let the Haytian historian speak for himself:

"In 1825, after a long series of negotiations, the independence of the French part of St. Domingue was recognized by Charles the X. of France, on the ground and condition of an indemnity of one hundred and fifty millions of francs. By this ordinance, the independence of Hayti was but conditionally recognized, and in default of payment, it was understood that things should remain as they were previous to 1825, viz., Hayti independent, but soliciting recognition as such, by its ancient Metropolitan Government.

"The acceptation of this ordinance, drawn up by the Government of Charles the X., on such severe conditions, occasioned much discontent in the country, and in some instances dangerous conspirations, into which even some of the most influential Generals entered.

"But President Boyer found means of surmounting all his dificulties, while at the same time he was deeply convinced of the utter impossibility of paying so enormous an indemnity, and ultimately succeeded in inducing France to treat with Hayti on the supposition of—or assuming—her independence.

"In 1828, Lascases and Baudin arrived in Hayti, as Plenipotentiaries sent by the French Government. On this occasion the independence of Hayti was again solemnly recognized, but apart from all consideration of indemnity by a first treaty.

"Then by a second treaty, simply and purely financial, Hayti engaged to pay to France the sum of sixty millions of francs in thirty years, as an indemnity to the former colonists for their loss of property; hence, the independence of Hayti was recognized, apart from all consideration of indemnification; no conditions or calculations were entered into as a price for her liberty or independence."*

There is truly an honesty and fairness about this transaction on both sides, which perhaps it would be unjust to deny or pass over; the delicacy of France in the whole arrangement is honorable, while the sound principle, on the part of Hayti, in avoiding all definition of the property said to be lost, is commendable; landed property to an immense amount, was doubtless lost in this great political and moral convulsion.

Nor need this debt, although heavy, ever have crippled Hayti in any sense, for her resources are beyond all calculation—agricultural and otherwise—her soil is unsurpassed in richness, while her mines are full of wealth, and notwithstanding the swarming hinderances which indeed have always existed, a right course had undoubtedly realized a far greater development of every kind than has ever yet been seen, and which the age might have expected from a country and people of such unquestionable resources.

Poverty, in the midst of such wealth, cannot exist innocently. Wars and revolutions have indeed been frequent, nor have fires and earthquakes been wanting, but there have been intervals of peace, and breathing time, in which the grand antidote for an uneasy national mind might have been gradually introduced, in the form of national enterprise, of naval, or even land architecture, the construction of public roads, either for ordinary purposes or for rails and steam or both, with innumerable other things, thus drawing off the national mind from military

* Madiou.

pageantry, which the Haytians themselves are beginning to see is but a poor and hollow substitute for sound principles relating to the nation and its general interests.

But the necessity of national action was felt; hence, about 1823, a system of immigration, on a large scale, from the United States, was set on foot, consisting of black and colored free people.

It was proposed that some 20,000 such persons should be induced to come, the Haytian Goverment paying passage expenses, and affording provision for a limited time for such as might really need it. Some came over at their own expense, and even brought property with them to a considerable amount.

It would appear, however, that this difficult undertaking, although well meant and commenced in all good faith on the part of the Boyer Government, upon the whole, was not well managed, for, notwithstanding many respectable people came, with ample means, who were of great use to the country, it must be admitted that many came who were a perfect misfortune to themselves and the community which they had come to join. Some even died of grief, and many returned; the entirely military character and habits of Hayti were unsuitable to the American immigrants; many, however, remained and became respectable and useful in various branches of industry.

Some who persevered in remaining became ministers of the Gospel, and proved to be of sound character, both of the Methodist and Baptist denominations. Small churches therefore soon sprung up, both in the French and Spanish part of the island.

At Port au Prince a neat little edifice was raised by the American colored immigrants which would accommodate some two hundred hearers.

It is an interesting fact, that the religious views and habits of this new community,* tested in a salutary manner the reigning thoughts of Roman Catholic Hayti on the general question of religious liberty, and it must be admitted that this second test was much more satisfactory than the first, when the native Haytians, under Brown and Catts, thought proper to renounce Romanism for Protestantism—in fact Hayti did really receive the Gospel, notwithstanding difficulties.†

But the camp meetings, which were at first allowed, became an interesting test to the reigning thoughts of the day; hence, as might have been expected, they were eventually feared as being likely to be ultimately abused by revolutionists, or other ill-disposed persons, and were therefore disallowed. These fears were perhaps the greater from the fact that all was done in the English language, except that occasionally some of the native Methodists might preach in French.‡

This fear of a revolution at every breath, and that too not without reason, has been the painful peculiarity of Hayti ever since it existed as a nation, and must be, either in Hayti or elsewhere, wherever

* African Episcopal Methodists.

† Dominica, the eastern part of Hayti, fully tolerated Protestantism, but it is doubtful whether even one case of Evangelical conversion ever occurred amongst the Dominican Spaniards of Hayti.

‡ As did frequently G. C. Pressoir.

arms alone are in the ascendency, even though they should be necessary.

Nevertheless, a Methodist camp meeting held in an entirely Roman Catholic country goes far to prove that the Haytian Roman Catholic had already left his European communion behind by his advanced views of religious liberty, for notwithstanding the peculiarities of the case, whether a camp meeting under any of the Roman Catholic Governments of Europe, even under the same circumstances, would have been tolerated, is at least a question.*

This was the first attempt at immigration on the part of the Haytian Government, although not the last, and whatever failure may attach to both, nothing can be more natural, under present altered circumstances, than that Hayti should look favorably towards the colored people of the States, or that they should look with great interest towards Hayti. This mutual interest will doubtless increase; in fact nothing could be more natural. It is not to be supposed that Hayti will always be guilty of military idolatry; sooner or later this must cease, while it is easy to suppose that the colored people of the States, may even yet see many attractions in Hayti, where they themselves might one day be useful in carrying out the wishes and hopes, so plainly expressed by Hayti itself, of working out the great principle which is the glory of Hayti, viz., that independence is the true dignity of the black man. A thousand motives may, at no far distant day, operate in this sense; in fact it is impossible that Hayti should be so near a

* This camp meeting was got up by American colored people recently arrived in Hayti.

neighbor to so great a blaze of civilization as is now lighted up in the United States, without feeling its elevating power throughout the entire ramification of her institutions, so true is it, both with regard to nations and individuals, "none of us liveth to himself!"

Haytian independence is a necessity, it has nothing to fear; let the Haytians therefore develope its dignity; their capacity to do so is incontestable.

About 1827, the Rev. St. D. Bauduy, a Wesleyan native missionary, arrived from England, having spent some four years, principally in the islands of Guernsey and Jersey, under the care of the Wesleyan Methodist Missionary Committee, with the view of preparing him for usefulness on his return to his native land. This native minister, who was ordained in England, on his arrival at Port au Prince, took charge of the Church, which had been kept together during his absence by the faithful and devoted J. C. Pressoir.

By this time, therefore, Protestant Christianity had began to assume a definite form before the people of Hayti, not only by the presence of the English Wesleyan Mission at Port au Prince, but also by the various American churches formed by the colored people from the United States in different parts of the Republic; nor is it to be supposed that their presence was without influence—unadorned truth cannot be powerless—nevertheless, some declared it to be treason to leave the religion of one's ancestors, forgetting that upon this principle, they had remained in the African heathenism of their fathers.

The grand peculiarity of Haytian history about

this time was the ascendency of a sort of negative good, rather than the active and positive; it was nevertheless wise to allow evil to fall of itself. This indeed told well upon the military system; hence, for many years, in the case of the death of a general, his place would not be filled up by the creation of another, but the vacant post would be filled probably by a colonel; a colonel dying, a commandant would fill his place. This wise plan had already greatly reduced the army, and in the end would doubtless have brought it within its desired limits. These negative improvements were unquestionably sound and good, and it is infinitely to be regretted that they were not persevered in, as Boyer meant they should be, until the army was brought within its right bounds.

But there was at this moment a national desire for something more positive and active; hence, now and then a restless spirit would break out in arms and disturb the reigning torpor. Generals Richard, Paul, Roumain, Darfour and others, about this time professing to deplore the national lethargy which seemed to envelope everything, unwisely sought their remedy in the sword, and thereby only aggravated a disease which they assured the world they wished to cure; but the details of these unhappy events must, for the present, be left to the more detailed histories of Hayti.

Let us however here note, that any people or executive power, not having themselves been taught or trained, either by the history of their own past national career, or by sound moral principle, the true principles of government, and knowing no other means of correcting abuses or errors, which will occur and creep in among all fallible beings, but by the sword, are, and in the nature of things must be, in a most unhappy case, for their remedy will prove worse than the disease; nor is there a nation under heaven where this fact has been more fully or more painfully demonstrated than Hayti; and yet, notwithstanding many painful executions, it would be unjust to the memory of Boyer to suppose him cruel or bloodthirsty; most assuredly he was not.

Nevertheless, the blood shed by a perfectly humane man, purely in the interests of his country, and with a view to the public peace and safety, might well serve as a lesson to his successors that such a course utterly fails in the accomplishment of the contemplated purpose.

It should not be lost sight of, that in those days there was more or less liberty of the press; a fact which, while it renders all recourse to arms still less excusable, must raise the Government of the day still higher in general merit and esteem.

Great honor is also due from posterity to Boyer for his successful reduction of the army and the encouragement of a well-organized national guard, a fact attesting the general confidence of the Government of the day in the citizens of the Republic. Nor is it impossible that this well-organized body of poor, wealthy, and respectable citizens might ultimately have superseded the regular army.

Considering, however, the fact already referred to of a great desire for real progress which at this time so evidently animated the nation, it is deeply to be deplored that no means should have been found by so well-meaning a Government to meet the universally expressed feeling and wishes of the nation; certainly such a course was not only possible, but might have been adopted without in the slightest degree infringing upon the dignity of the Government, nor can it be doubted that it was an error for a moment to hesitate, although the error on the part of the people was yet far greater in having recourse to the sword; hence, error here was everywhere, for a war on all sides was resorted to, and reason fled.

Stringent laws were thought needful for the public interest, hence the country people were allowed to come into town only on Saturday morning, to return on a Sunday evening—the Sunday in these days being the great market-day—all the rest of the week, except in cases of holidays, national or religious, they were expected to employ themselves in their various branches of industry, or at least they were not permitted to come to town without a written permission from a suitable authority.

These were measures which may indeed have suited the circumstances of the day. Whether, however, such laws should have been needed at all, is the question. That the ignorance and indolence of the people may have been great might be admitted, but the law-makers themselves told them that they were free, how then could they be coerced!

The true coersion of a free people is, the creation of a sense of want, by a well-adapted mental and moral culture. It is an unhappy thing for a nation where such laws and regulations are deemed needful. The raising of men to a sense of their want and necessities as such, would have been no more expensive than an extensive system of military police, whose example and mode of life would tend more to destroy industry than otherwise.

On the subject of the Rural Code, the following is an extract from a respectable English author, who wrote on Hayti in 1828.*

"The 'Code Rural' was passed by the Chamber of Communes on the 21st of May, and received the President's fiat on the 6th of the next month. All this took place during my residence at Port au Prince. This is the work of General Inginac, aided by one or two of the Chamber and Senate.

"The Chamber of Communes, in its farewell address, tells the people that laws, 'just and severe,' were imperatively necessary for the revival of agriculture.

"It may not be unimportant to give here a few articles from this Code Rural.

"The Purposes of the Rural Police are:

"First. The repressing of idleness.

"Second. The enforcing order and assiduity in agricultural labor.

"Third. The discipline of laborers, collectively or in gangs.

"Fourth. The making and keeping in repair of the public roads, etc.

"Article 180. Every person attached to the country as a cultivator, who shall, on a working day, and during the hours of labor, be found unemployed or lounging in the public roads, shall be considered idle, and be taken before the justice of the peace, who shall commit him to prison for twenty-four hours for the first offence, and shall send him to labor on the public roads on a repetition of the offence.

"Article 183. The field-labor shall commence on Monday morning, and shall not cease until Friday evening. (Legal holidays excepted.)"

All this may be good, but if free Republican institutions are really to exist, then, however great the merit of such a code might be, its full and entire

* J. Franklin.

execution would be simply impossible. Anything like oppressive laws would contradict the great and ruling idea of "liberté, égalité," which now entirely possesses the masses of the Haytian Republic, nor will it be difficult to understand, that in an entirely free nation, there would be men who, either from good or bad motives, would rise up and openly oppose, even well-meant oppression. In fact, whatever good these coercive laws might possess, they did not, and could not, teach industry as a principle; nor would it be surprising if force in any sense should be deemed slavish. But whatever might be the interpretation, it is impossible not to feel that the supposed necessity of such a code, supposes also a degraded people.

Had only the Christian Sabbath been recognized as a suitable day for national moral culture, it had most certainly not been in vain; but the framers of the "Code Rural," doubtless calculated that the public market should be in full and special operation on that day; hence the toils of Saturday and Sunday were even greater than the forced labor of the week. At least a pause in labor should have formed some part of the aim at industry, either as a Christian Sabbath or otherwise. Unceasing labor is simply wild extravagance, human nature being incapable of it.

But little foresight is needed to see the utter impossibility of perpetuating such a system of things. In fact, such measures can only tend, amongst a free people, to revolution. Nor can anything be more astonishing than that good motives and honest aims, should have exacted such breathless toil as not to leave one single hour of repose during the whole year, except the national holidays. Most truly, neither God nor reason have never exacted from man unceasing labor; nor is it surprising that such unwise measures should sink under the weight of their own unreasonableness, while at the same time they remind us of the fearful responsibility of legislators themselves, who by errors both in judgment and principle, become the originators of revolution.*

The course of events, however, went on in Hayti. But the ruling powers of nations are not infallible, and the best intentions frequently fail in their purposes. Meantime a fearful accident took place at Port au Prince; the Arsenal blew up.

An English author on Hayti, then residing at Port au Prince, gives the following account of that event, which is here recorded, as giving some idea of the general habits of the Haytians of that day, and which, in the same class of persons, are not now much altered, if at all.

"The incautious striking an iron hoop with an iron hammer over a barrel of gunpowder, is reported to have produced the explosion. I had, early in the morning of the 3d of February, 1826, received a bag from England, and while busy with its contents, sitting in the gallery of my residence, which overlooked the city, my attention was solicited by a distant explosion, followed by a mass of dense smoke, which on clearing

* At every turn in these "historical notes," the chilling absence of an ameliorating Christianity is felt, all is harsh authority, and yet it is a fact everywhere felt, that neither wise nor ignorant freemen will consent, willingly, to force of any kind, even though it should be to their own interest to do so. Only true Christianity can invest reason with a willing, acting, working power. This will touch the hidden springs of the most enlightened men, but this ever has been and still is, wanting in Hayti.

away, fully explained the nature and extent of the calamity. The French and English sailors in the harbor rendered great service in extinguishing the flames. There was a large assortment of army clothing there at the time, together with a considerable store of ammunition of all sorts, and the whole loss was estimated at a million of dollars (gold).

"But a short time previously, in 1822, a fire had burnt down a considerable portion of Port au Prince; and in fact, considering the great carelessness of the people generally, as to their candles, lamps, and fires, it is even extraordinary that so few accidents of this sort occur; indeed, the want of training and discipline of all sorts, together with the habit of going about their premises, and even the interior of their dwellings, with lighted resinous wood, from which a burning cinder will often fall, exposes the whole city continually to the most frightful disasters. These are things which cannot be corrected by police regulations, but rather by such domestic habits as are rare in Hayti, and can only result from true, genuine, and well-sustained family order. But what can be expected from a general chaos, whether it may refer to the domestic peculiarities of a people or aught else?

"The same remarks apply to the extinguishing of public fires. A more chaotic scene can scarcely be imagined than is presented by the thousands which surround the public fires in Hayti. Either there are no engines, or they are out of repair, or there is no water to be had, or there is no order or organization in the efforts made to extinguish the flames. The presenc of military officers on such occasions, is doubtless useful in keeping order among the people; but the want of suitable judgment and implements will frequently occasion the destruction of property to a fearful amount, which frequently, but for the help of foreign sailors in port, and their well-worked engines, would be greater still."

The question of population, which is of such vast importance, may now perhaps, with propriety, come under our notice, especially as about this date the island, throughout its length and breadth, was entirely under one Government, the seat of which was the city of Port au Prince.

This question will necessarily bring before us the subject of marriage, concubinage, and libertinage—not indeed in any minute or detailed sense, but as the great public sources of vice or virtue to the nation—with the admission, however, that the two latter have fearful sway in Hayti.

Here we must remember, that the starting-point is the European: he it was who laid the foundations of society in Hayti, and was the framer of whatever existed there of domestic life at the declaration of its independence. The importance of this fact will be seen in the difference now existing between the United States and Hayti. The starting-point of the former was unquestionably honorable marriage, while the latter was concubinage. This may have been in both cases the result of circumstances over which neither had had any control, but here we have simply to do with fact, the originating causes in the two cases forming no part of our present reasoning. Divinely instituted marriage cannot be laid aside or departed from—no matter the cause—with impunity, while it must be admitted that the same moral laws which are essential to our well-being, would, if brought into operation, do the same for Hayti that they have ever done wherever they have been fairly brought to bear.

It is not at all intended here to enter into any reasoning as to the difficulties in Hayti of a national conformity to marriage laws, or even the practice of public virtue. Facts, and their infallible consequences, are all that we have to do with in this case.

A departure from any of the fixed laws of God, either as to nature or otherwise, involves inevitable consequences; hence we are now before the fact, that libertinage and general immorality are destructive of population, and even tend to its cessation; nor are difficulties or reasonings of any kind listened to in this case.

Without, therefore, entering into any revolting details on this subject, which it would be very easy to do, as to general immorality, suffice it to say that the statistics of population in this country offer almost insurmountable difficulties, while at the same time the medical faculty as well as the municipal bodies of the Republic, unfold fearful details of the widely extended and ruinous effects of immorality in the nation.

Honorable marriage, in the commencement of this nation's career, was rare, but it is only just to add, that a whole nation under arms for many years together, would inevitably set aside for many years, to a fearful extent, if not altogether, the domestic circle. Nor is it much to be wondered at, that a nation at last loving arms, should become loose in public morals, the more so where the climate, by perpetual heat, gives a laxity of manner to the entire community; in fact, under such circumstances, Christian piety being wanting, even marriage itself is in danger of becoming a cloak for vice. Truly it would be false to suppose that these great evils have been cured in Hayti, while it would be unjust not to admit that great improvement has taken place, or that there are no virtuous marriages in that country; still the great plague of immorality is yet fearful in its extent; nor can it be for a moment doubted that this has told upon the strength and number of its population. Six hundred thousand was probably the amount of the French part of the island at the declaration of Haytian independence.

The question, therefore, now before us is simply, what would have been the result of true Christian morality on such a population during sixty years? This indeed, we will not presume to fix precisely, nor is it needful; it may however fairly be asserted that the increase would have been immense, while its elevating power upon the nation would have been great.

The present population of the Haytian Republic is, probably, little more than 700,000 souls.

This is a matter which truly touches the dignity of any nation, and seriously demands the attention of the Haytian statesman—in its bearing upon the military power, as the defence of the nation, in its power upon the national industry and commerce, as well as upon the future hopes and honor of the Republic.

Is the increase of the population which here appears satisfactory? It will perhaps be impossible to say that it is. Doubtless revolutions, wars, earthquakes, etc., etc., have tended to keep down the Haytian population, but it is at the same time undeniable, that sound national morality, resulting from a universal Christian primary education, notwithstanding all the drawbacks mentioned, would have given to Hayti double its starting population—especially when it is remembered that more or less immigration has been going on from the beginning.

All reasoning on this subject would be useless. Immorality has shorn Hayti of her dignity and strength as to population. And those in Hayti who thought their course to be right on this subject in being, either by concubinage or otherwise, the fathers of thirty or sixty children, simply did not reflect that the women that bore them would, by honorable marriage, have borne a far greater number.

The question, therefore, of national morality, combines with it the true interests and dignity of the nation. It is no sectarian question, notwithstanding its bearing upon religion; it is the source of numbers as to population; it is the source of quality as to the population itself; it is also the mould of the national type, in a moral sense; it is the true bulwark of a nation, as to internal strength. The crime, therefore, of a Government not serving as a model to the nation on this great and paramount question, is incalculably great.

It is perhaps one of the distinguishing glories of the present age, that immorality in courts, whether of kings or presidents, would be insufferable. The past with regard to Hayti on this point has been wanting in too many cases, but it is a growing feeling, that in the present age this cannot be.

CHAPTER VI.

The Executive Sovereign an error.—Periodical Presidency considered.—The People are not the Masses.—Source of Revolutions.—Cayes Revolutionary.—Herard Dumesle and St. Preux.—The House expels them.—Boyer in error.—The expelled Representatives return home.—Rev. J. Tindal arrives.—His health fails.—Revs. W. T. Cardy and W. Touler arrive.—Dr. England.—Gen. Inginac on the Clergy.—Offer to make the Yaqui navigable.—J. Candler.—Representatives on the Code Rurale.—Boyer altogether French.—Freemasonry in Hayti.—Candler on the Military System.—The National Guard.

The rightful sovereign of a people is,
Their God—all other is idolatry.

It will not be surprising that one of the great defects of governing in Hayti has ever been that of attributing sovereignty to the Executive, hence much has always depended upon the temper, character, and intelligence of the governing chief magistrate, who, properly speaking, or in the true Republican sense, is simply bound to execute the will of the people, as expressed through their laws and institutions.

This was evidently Petion's error—few had labored with greater zeal and perseverance, or had fought with greater bravery for Liberty and Republicanism, than this man of deserved fame; yet he was no sooner settled in his position as the presiding magistrate of Hayti, than he pursued such a course as led him to the unenviable elevation of a Dictator: not that he was proclaimed such, probably he had not even such a thought, it is true. Much might be said in justification of this step, and although it would have been wise, and even desirable, to have shunned such a position, yet it must be admitted that he used the power which he had thus assumed with dignity, and perhaps it might even be said, with great benevolence; but the fact remained, that the sovereignty of the nation was absorbed in himself, and that at least for a short time, the institutions and people were laid aside.

It may be said that this was merely a passing event, as indeed it was, and was never intended as a permanent domination; be this as it may, it is certain that one of the fundamental laws and institutions of the country about this time underwent an entire change, hence in 1816 the Presidency, which was originally intended to be periodical, became an office for life.

It is said that circumstances led to this; posterity, however, will judge in this matter: certain it is, that Petion's personal happiness was not increased by this measure, nor will it be difficult to understand, that this change in the Constitution at once closed up a national valve through which ambition might occasionally have escaped, and thus have saved the worthy Petion himself many a pang, for it is not to be concealed that his heart was subsequently wrung by conspiracies against him.

The motive of this change was doubtless to avoid a periodical excitement which a Presidential election every four years would have involved, and which, it was thought, would be dangerous. Whether, however, greater peace or solidity have been secured to the Republic by means of a life Presidency, is at least doubtful.

It has been thought by some that the nation at this time was not prepared for such excessively liberal institutions, and, indeed, it must be remembered that the masses had but just broken the bonds of slavery. But in Hayti, the term people has never yet, really and literally meant the masses, for the simple reason that they have not yet been raised to their proper level by any degree of education.

We must therefore bear in mind that the Republic of Hayti was not formed by the masses, but by the enlightened and educated portion of the nation. The case then is evident, that those who founded the Republic, being themselves its source of existence, had the right to command it; and the chief magistrate, who received power and accepted office from them, unquestionably owed to those who had constituted him what he was, a fair and honest deference, the more so from the fact that genuine Republicanism seemed to animate all parties—the President, in receiving his honors and power from the Senators, and also the Senators in conferring them on him,—all was given and received in this case, on all sides, with the fullest understanding that the government should be literally, and in fact, exclusively Republican. Nor is it possible to read the history of those times without being struck with the amount of decided talent in many who then appeared upon the stage of action in Haytian affairs; hence the great principles of national freedom had been ably and openly developed and discussed by the Senate before the nation, and the enlightened part of the people, who alone were qualified to form a government at all, evidently expected the highest amount of liberty which Republicanism could bestow.

It is remarkable that so many Haytians about this time were men of decided capacity. The fact however reminds us that St. Domingue had rapidly become a place of renown for ease and wealth; in fact "le Paradis des Français" must have been attractive. French society, therefore, was of a superior style both in the army and among the civilians—hence Toussaint L'ouverture, and many others, were what they were. Many, too, of the leading men had already received a good education in Europe.

It must also be borne in mind that an intelligent French white population had long resided in Hayti, and had left the impress of their widely extended civilization; well formed families, even greatly beloved by all parties, had left much that was good behind them. The number, therefore, of the enlightened part of the community must have been something important.

With these facts before us, it will appear evident that the Haytians were more prepared than has been sometimes thought for such institutions as they might choose for themselves, notwithstanding the great mass of the people was in entire ignorance.

The truth, therefore, of the matter seems to be, that those institutions which Petion himself had so strenuously aided in establishing, ought to have reigned, whether he as President stood or fell. But Petion was resolved not to fall, or yield, and his consciousness of great military resources enabled him to accomplish the establishment of his own power, nor is it to be denied that this is the great rock on which so many revolutions have dashed in Hayti, viz., the unyielding and immovable will of the Executive against the national mind.

Motives or reasons here form no part of our consideration; we have simply to do with the fact, that a sovereign Executive in a Republic is an anomaly, and can never be carried out without a revolution, of which the government itself, in such a case, becomes the author.

These reflections lead us to the consideration of some not very dissimilar events, which had long been secretly ripening, but which did not fully develope themselves until 1833, and which took their rise in the city of Cayes.

This important place is situated on the southern side of the great Peninsula, running in rather a westerly direction from Port au Prince, and is considered a second-rate city, with a population of some ten thousand. It is about one hundred and sixty miles from the capital, and is of great commercial importance.

In 1831 this capital of the South was visited by a dreadful hurricane, which nearly destroyed it. About the dates last mentioned, this city of Cayes was the source and centre of such political views and feelings, as ultimately brought on a most unhappy and ruinous train of events.

Two representatives—one from the Arrondissement of Cayes, and the other from that of Acquin—one known as Herard Dumesle, and the other as David St. Preux, were elected in the usual way to represent the two last named places.

Whether these men were of good or bad faith in themselves individually, is not so much the present question, as the fact that they did legitimately represent the feelings and wishes of a great, if not the greater portion, of the enlightened and well disposed part of the nation. We say the enlightened part of the nation, because the best friends of Boyer must admit that the masses had been left to themselves, as to education of any kind, and therefore could not enter into the merits of the case; nor could they be expected to do otherwise than allow themselves to be borne away by any political storm which might occur. Surely there is guilt, which no reasoning can efface, in allowing the masses of a nation, and especially of a Republic, to be the mere dupes of designing men.

Whatever may have been the direct, and really originating cause of the stand taken by these two representatives, certain it is that they did represent a rapidly increasing and already powerful party in the nation, whose feelings and opinions were, that the country did not move on in the path of general progress, either so much or so rapidly as was desirable. This party, evidently supported by the public mind, at last became bold in their declarations that education, arts, sciences, and the general development of the resources of the country, had been comparatively neglected, and in fact, that the whole nation was altogether behind the onward movement and spirit of the age.

Some aver that this party originated in 1825, on the question of the indemnity to the French Government, which so thoroughly agitated the public mind.

It was thought that the payment of this immense sum to the French, looked too much like purchasing the national liberty, which had been bravely and fairly won. That such should have been the views of some Haytians, will be very easily understood, yet it cannot be denied that Boyer's government maintained the national honor in this affair; but the really originating cause of this movement is of comparatively little importance, for whatever that may have been, it is certain that it ultimately assumed for its object and end, the more rapid progress of the nation in all respects, nor can it be denied that this great movement was commenced in an entirely constitutional manner.

The people of the two places named as situated in the southern part of the Island, by a fair and popular election according to the usages and laws of the Republic, sent to the Legislature the men who truly and honestly represented their views and opinions with regard to the general state of this country, on which subject they had an undoubted right to form an opinion.

The course pursued in this case, both by the people and their representatives, was honorable and dignified, and affords proof that the people of Hayti, in this case, understood their duty as Republican citizens. That this ought to have been met with equal dignity on the part of the executive, must be admitted; there was here the fair and open expression of the people's wishes, of whom, according to the spirit of Republicanism, the Chief Magistrate had constituted himself the servant, but the President rather assumed the position of a man attacked, than otherwise, and hence replied by frowns and threats.

In a message from President Boyer to the House of Representatives, in reply to an address to him from that body, he deplores the "blindness of spirit" of the party in question, and speaks of the two representatives as "les coupables,"—guilty men.

The House, however, expelled the two members in question—H. Dumesle, and David St. Preux—and having informed his Excellency of what they had done, his reply, containing the words already quoted, is dated August the 19th, 1833.

The question now is, of what had these men been guilty? Had they done anything more than to represent, in a constitutional manner, the convictions and the wishes of their own constituents, and probably of the majority of the enlightened part of the nation? If so, on which side was the blindness already complained of? If the Executive is charged to see that the laws and institutions of the country work freely, the position of the President in this case gives a fair demonstration of error, with regard to the parties expelled from the House of Representatives, in this affair.

The demand of the people was not only honest and just in itself, but it was constitutionally made; why then should it not have been listened to? The party in power indeed reasoned, that one step yielded would simply lead to another, and so on unceasingly; thus strangely forgetting that legitimate, constitutional demands for improvement, are not only the true order of things among men, but the only safe one. Why should an honest and really progressive government, fear the honest and constitutionally expressed demands of the people? The true and real interests of the nation are not, and cannot be divided.

However good the intentions of the government may have been in this case,—and there is no reason to doubt them—the soundness of its judgment was doubtful, and the evidence here is clear, that the wisdom of a united people was safer and greater than that of a single individual; the former spoke legitimately, and the latter was bound at least to give ear.*

But Boyer succeeded, and the obnoxious men were expelled from the Chamber of Representatives. The legality of this act, or whether there was no better or safer course to adopt, need not now be considered. The fact is now undeniably before us, that this was the starting point for much unhappiness to Hayti; but whether the spring of the revolutions which followed was, in this case, in the government or the people, will be for posterity to judge. Nothing, however, can be more evident, than that a great blow was here inflicted; but whether he who inflicted it, or those on whom it fell, suffered the most, or who were the real victims of this political crisis, is a question fairly open to all parties, and is highly worthy of a fair and candid examination.

The representatives returned to their homes, but it was soon found, that although the President had prostrated his opponents, he had not prostrated their

* The executives in Hayti seem not to remember, that in employing invectives against revolutionary opponents, which perhaps their own errors have created, they lower themselves, and thus bring a shade upon the whole nation. Let them rather watch the public mind, and learn to know when, and how, to stoop!

opinions. On the contrary, during the time which passed over, until the next general election, the attitude of the government was constantly observed by the people, and contemplated, perhaps, with increasing dissatisfaction; the wish for a more rapid movement in the nation's onward course, became the more intense from the very fact that the government seemed to oppose it. Matters thus slept for a time.

In 1834, one of those silent events took place in Hayti, which in the estimation of the world is generally of but little importance; although to the more closely thinking, it would be viewed as one which would tell powerfully upon those imperishable interests of mankind, which the Christian so fully accepts as a reality.

The event now referred to, was the arrival of the Rev. John Tindall, an English Wesleyan Missionary. This gentleman had been appointed by the British Methodist Conference, of the old connection established by the Rev. J. Wesley, to occupy the station of Puerto Plata, in the Spanish part of the Island of Hayti, which at that time was under the Haytian Flag.

Mr. Tindall's mission had special reference to the American colored people, who had emigrated from the United States to Hayti, during a previous great immigration which had been set on foot by the Haytian government in 1824, and from which event we very distinctly learn, that the leading minds of Hayti at that time were convinced that the introduction of a suitable foreign element was needful to this Republic, and that for the Haytians to be shut up in themselves was not to their own interests.

These American immigrants on their arrival located in different parts of the country; some at Samana, towards the eastern end of Hayti; others in the Spanish city of St. Domingo, and Puerto Plata; while some established themselves in the Capital of the French part of the Island.

It would appear that representations had been made to the Wesleyan Methodist Missionary Committee of London, by some American immigrants residing at Puerto Plata, as to their spiritual wants, and the result was that the above named Missionary was sent; this was the introduction of a new moral element into the Spanish part of Hayti. The Spaniards were, and remained inaccessible to Protestantism, but the Protestant missionary was treated with the greatest respect, and the American colored people received their requested minister with great affection.

Mr. Tindall was encouraged and sustained by many influential gentlemen in that part of the country, and before long Mission premises were secured at Puerto Plata, the situation of which, on an eminence, is healthy and beautiful. A neat little Church, capable of containing nearly two hundred, together with a parsonage house, were before long erected by the great activity, perseverance and zeal of the Missionary; in fact as far as the American colored people were concerned, the two stations of Puerto Plata and Samana were soon prosperous and interesting. The distance, however, between the two places, is perhaps nearly two hundred miles, leading over bays, rivers, and roads, which are both dangerous and fatiguing, and therefore the work at first was exhausting.

In 1839 the health of the worthy Missionary failed, and he was under the necessity of retiring from the Mission field, having as his last effort formed a Station at Cape Haytien, in the French part of the Island, from whence he finally embarked for Europe.

Mr. Tindall had been joined in this Mission, by the Rev. W. T. Cardy, whose residence and faithful labors at Samana were highly useful, as they subsequently were, also, at Gonaives & Jérémie, at which places this worthy and laborious Missionary was greatly beloved.

In 1837 this Mission was reinforced by the arrival of the Rev. W. Touler, who remained principally at Puerto Plata, although visiting occasionally the distant station of Samana. The two last Missionaries, as well as the first, were intelligent men, worthy and capable of their great work, and they possessed the confidence and esteem of all parties.

About this time, Dr. England of Charleston in the United States of America, Roman Catholic Bishop, visited Hayti as the Pope's Legate, with a view to establish the supremacy of the Court of Rome over the clergy of Hayti. This Prelate was received with every mark of distinction, but the object of his mission was at that time altogether unpopular, Hayti having hitherto looked with great suspicion, and even dread, on any Papal ascendency in the nation. The whole Roman Catholic clergy had up to that time been entirely under the control of "Le Ministre des Cultes."*

The Roman Catholic clergy, in its then state, without Archiepiscopal control, is described in a printed address to the nation, by the principal Secretary of State, in which is found the following remarkable sentence:

> "What dreadful evils must result from the examples thus set by the priests, who without regard to those who are confided to their Pastoral guidance, give themselves up to all sorts of abominations, who betray both the paternal government which affords them protection, and the Almighty Himself whose ministers they are." †

A more terrible description of an Ecclesiastical body could scarcely be conceived.

In 1838 the Government issued a decree for the establishment of a school of navigation. Such an idea, for an insular people, does indeed appear to be natural, and is one among the innumerable proofs we already have of the design of Providence, that our necessities should promote our civilization and elevation. The number of students in this projected institution was not to exceed twelve.‡

There was indeed nothing at this time worth calling a fleet, commercially or otherwise, as to Haytian constructions; but the carrying out of this measure might ultimately have led to this, while it might also have tended to occupy the national mind, not only by the high character of the enterprise, but it

* The Secretary of State, who is charged with all the interests of public worship, &c., as to the church connected with the State.

† General Inginac.

‡ L'Union, Decem. 1837.

would also have created another elevating branch of industry in the nation. Inconstancy, however, was written on this measure. Still, the idea was good and praiseworthy; the mind which conceived it was doubtless alive to the dignity of true national independence; and the main thing to be deplored is, that a people and country possessing every resource for such an undertaking, should not also have possessed the spirit and energy to carry out and realize what was seen to be so desirable.

In the course of events, during these comparatively quiet days, it was proposed to President Boyer, by an English gentleman, then residing in the Spanish part of the island, whose name will be remembered for many years to come, to render navigable the river Yaqui in that part of the country. It would seem that the idea was to render that fine stream available for steam, which would doubtless have been of incalculable importance in the transport of produce for many miles through the interior; but this hope also went out in disappointment—quenched in sheer timidity—which was in reality prudence pushed to an excess, although it need occasion no surprise that foreign influence in any form should have been deprecated, and even feared at that time.

In fact, notwithstanding the many indications of restlessness and dissatisfaction throughout the nation, the old routine of things, and that only, was deemed safe, and improvements generally appeared to be considered unsafe if not dangerous. Foreign energy seemed to be dreaded as a something, which if allowed full sweep, would soon overwhelm everything that was native; a fear which at that time was not unnatural, and will easily be understood, when it is remembered that while slavery reigned throughout the entire West Indies, the Haytian had reason to be suspicious of a brutal energy which, in the name of slavery, was destroying liberty and life all around her beyond her own shores.

It is true indeed, that the foregoing statements amply justify the Haytians in the policy which they adopted in closing their country. Yet the fact remains, and cannot be changed, that a closed country will ultimately find itself in the case of stagnant waters, so that its very resources will seem to perish. The life-giving stream of full and free intercourse with all mankind must bound and flow through every interest, or the whole nation will become dreamy and inactive. Hayti has now to study the totally new order of things which has come about in the world.

England, France, and America, are now the friends of Liberty. They themselves are open to all, notwithstanding prudential guards placed on their respective nationalities; nor need there any longer be any scruple, hesitation, or delicacy in recognizing the straight-forward duty of the Haytian nation to go onward in the general march of humanity.

It is evident that the eyes of the Haytian people were now opening. The enlightened part of the community saw and felt that as a Republic they were being left far behind the onward movement of the age. The Government seemed to resist improvement from fear of innovation, as though it were really dangerous for a nation to advance otherwise than as its mere instincts might force it on; it was not perceived that stagnation was ruin.

But it soon became evident, that to resist perseveringly the honest and constitutionally expressed wishes of the people was to endanger both those who govern and the governed—so unavailing are the lessons and warnings of history. The great idea was, that the Haytians were an exceptional people, and therefore needed an exceptional Government. Doubtless, as is the case with all nations, there are peculiarities which attach to Hayti only, as a nation; but it was forgotten that there are cardinal principles relating to the Government of nations, which neither Hayti nor any other nation can depart from with impunity.

The next general election came on, and the expelled Representatives were returned, with their party greatly increased and their views and principles more widely extended than ever, and also more matured.

The following extract from "Notes on Hayti," by an observant English traveler, who visited the Haytian Republic about this time, will enable us to form a general idea of the case before us.

"Do the people, who feel this oppression, look to their Representatives for help? They know that all appeal of this sort will be useless. Only four years ago, 1838, in consequence of a bold address to the President, a strife was stirred up between the two Houses of the Legislature, and the House of Representatives was prevailed upon, by a majority, to expel six of its best and most honest members. It is impossible to read the proceedings and notes of this little Parliament without at once seeing on which side the wrong lies. The following sensible and spirited remarks, contained in an address, occasioned the disturbance. But what shall we say of the subserviency of a legislative body that adopted such a resolution by acclamation, one month, and pronounced a vote of expulsion on its supporter the next?

"'The clashing of fundamental principles with the details of the Constitution, is a contradiction which must disappear from the code of rights and duties; experience proclaims this truth. The nation entreats you then, to give it security for the future; you have the power and the genius to do so. At present, peace is undisturbed and secure, it is therefore no time for delay. Express but the wish, and regenerating hands will reconstruct the social system, reanimate our institutions, and save us from decay.'

"The House then goes on to request from the President, the projects of new laws suited to the exigency of the times, among which are enumerated a law to insure the responsibility of public functionaries, to alter the Custom House duties, to fix the rate of interest, and repress usury, to restrict the power now given to the justices of the peace, to determine suits on summary conviction without appeal, and a law to modify the severities of the 'Code Rurale,' which it denounces as at variance with the public feeling, and therefore inoperative to its end; observing also—

"'If we examine at the present moment the instability of certain laws, we shall be astonished to see them stopped suddenly, as if struck with inertia, after having taken a rapid stride; of this number is the 'Rural Code,'—it has fallen, and its fall has crushed Agriculture, although it must be confessed, it has only experienced the fate of all institutions that are opposed to the spirit of an improving age.'

"But the President thought them too much in advance of the age, and requiring more than the public, or the people at large, could bear. He therefore caused the Assembly to be decimated, and made their own votes the executioner of his secret decree. The Government is in fact a military despotism in the hands of one man—mild and merciful, it is true, and desiring the welfare of his country, but mistaken in some of his views—and therefore acting in a manner utterly opposed to the public good."*

* J. Candler.

It will be admitted that the foregoing reasonings from the Representatives fully indicate a class of mind quite equal to the exigencies of the country, and capable of maintaining its dignity. This in fact has ever been the case with Hayti; nor does there seem to have been, on the part of this Haytian Parliament, any want of confidence in the entire capacity and general ability of the President, as a man of intelligence, to understand the great necessity of the moment; why therefore the pleadings, reasonings, and representations of the Representatives, which were so full of sound principle and evident good will, should not have met with due deference from the President, is not easily understood, and seems rather to argue either obliquity of, mind or vanity, or both, than otherwise, such too as posterity will condemn; while the statements and arguments of the Legislative body, as well as the frank, courteous, and constitutional manner in which they are expressed, will ever command the approval of the world, and at the same time remain as a demonstration that Hayti then possessed men who fully understood the wants of their country. Failure indeed followed all, but this has simply demonstrated that mere intelligence, however great, cannot suffice.

Rulers often stoop to conquer.

On the part of the Executive, this whole affair was doubtless considered as a great coup d'Etat, as indeed it really was. It is nevertheless a sad fact, that the force of this great blow ultimately broke the misguided arm which inflicted it, and rendered those on whom it fell miserably triumphant. Up to this day Hayti has been suffering from this error in the ruling judgment.

A faithful adherence to the laws and institutions of the nation would have saved Boyer and his unhappy, although deserving people, many a pang; so truly do governments, ofttimes unconsciously, occasion revolutions.

President Boyer's mind was entirely French. His views of government had been formed principally upon a French model; he was altogether military, from the fact of his career having been entirely under arms, although he gave full proof of his intention ultimately to supersede the military by the civil power. It is true that his distinguished predecessor, Petion, had been trained in the same school, although of enlarged views and principles; but the same education does not always produce the same mind.

Another peculiarity, of a more or less moral bearing upon Haytian society, is the existence, on a large scale, of the Masonic order throughout the Republic.

Whatever be the mysteries of this order, if it has any at all, the continual declaration of that body has been, that the object and end of the institution is, to teach man that there is a great First Cause of all things, and also to inculcate the purest morality. It is evident too, that the Scriptures, which they bear with great formality in their public processions, are considered by them as the ground-work and foundation of the Masonic structure, and that these same sacred oracles are freely open to the examination of all. This, at least, is freedom of religious thought, leading to an independence of all ecclesiastical tribunals. Whether such an independence is right or wrong, we will not now discuss; but it cannot be doubted that this institution has had its effect upon the Roman Catholic community of Hayti, and possibly may have tended to produce that love of religious liberty which, it must be admitted, has long distinguished this Republic. This will become the more apparent when it is remembered that another cardinal point in this order is, that all religious opinions are entirely free, and that religious liberty should be entire; and to add to all which has now been advanced, it should be noted, that the Chief Magistrate of the nation, has almost, if not quite, invariably been the protector of Free Masonry in Hayti.

It is not at all extraordinary at Port au Prince to see a Protestant minister conducting to his church the remains of one of his communion, followed by a respectable concourse of Masonic Roman Catholics, and joining with great solemnity in the sublime burial-service of the Church of England.

Nothing more is intended, in what is here said of the Order of Freemasons, than to show that this institution is so widely extended in Hayti that it has become a distinct feature in Haytian society, and may possibly have given more or less stimulus to the general question of religious liberty in that Republic.

It is supposed that there are about a thousand Freemasons in the city of Port au Prince; and in all the second and third rate towns, as well as even in some of the villages, their numbers are in similar proportion with the communities in which they exist.

But the prominent and distinguishing peculiarity of the Haytian nation is its military system, which, as it originated under extraordinary circumstances, will now for a moment engage our special attention. The well-authenticated notes of the English traveler, already referred to,* will greatly help us in this matter.

"The last account in detail, placed in my hands by the Government, gives the following enumeration:

"Under the head of Military Commanders of Districts, there are nine generals, fifteen brigadier-generals, sixty-three colonels, forty-eight lieutenant-colonels, nine captains, and twenty medical men, whose united pay amounted to 188,407 dollars, or 15,700 pounds sterling. The pay of a general is £225 per annum, that of a brigadier-general £170, that of a colonel £125.

"The Standing Army consists, in addition, of 33 colonels, 95 lieutenant-colonels, 825 captains, 654 lieutenants, 377 sub-lieutenants, 6,815 non-commissioned officers, 25 medical men, and 19,129 rank and file. Total, 28,151. The pay of a common soldier is £3 per annum, for one week on duty out of every three, being at the rate of three shillings (English) per week, for every week that each soldier musters on parade. The total cost of the army, in 1838, including the arsenals, hospitals, marines, was, in Haytian dollars, $1,418,557, or £118,213. A small sum for the maintenance of such an immense standing army, but a much larger sum than Hayti can afford to pay.

The army is in a state of gradual reduction; its numerical force in 1840 was 25,000.

By the present arrangements, the common soldier attends one week on duty in the muster-field, and is left at liberty to go to his own home, or to procure work where he can the two succeeding weeks, hence there is but little time for agriculture, especially if the distance from home is considered."

With regard to military discipline, although but little can be said, yet it must not be imagined that

* J. Candler.

there is none; and notwithstanding much has been said on this subject that is unfavorable to the Haytian nation, we have only to remember that the arms of Hayti won, and have maintained their independence, against forces and discipline far superior to their own; nor let it be for a moment supposed that life and liberty would be less sternly defended in the present day than in former times, were any such emergency, in any sense or manner, to occur.

Happy, indeed, would it be for the world, if all arms were beaten into ploughshares; but in the present state of human nature, this is perhaps too much to expect, not to say impossible.

About this time also existed a national guard in Hayti, of some 40,000 men, which, with the regular army, made an armed body of 65,000 soldiers, out of much less than a million of people, constituting the population of the entire island; for it must be remembered that at the date last mentioned the Spanish part of the island was united with the Haytian Republic; in fact, it must be admitted, that the Haytian, nation present the most singular organization of things that can well be conceived of, but it must be borne in mind that this singular state of things has resulted from the peculiar circumstances which gave birth to the nation. In the commencement of their existence as an independent people, the Haytians, as will be understood, were all soldiers, and like the Jews under Nehemiah, labored with their arms at hand; in fact, in some cases even the women have been engaged in some of the great struggles for national independence; a fact which, while it marks the history of this extraordinary little country, at the same time does away with all surprise at its deeply-rooted military character.

Had the Haytians had nothing to fear, when once their national victory was complete, it might have been vastly different with them at the present moment; but for a long time their affairs with France remained in the greatest uncertainty, and required the utmost vigilance, for the former masters of St. Domingue were anxious to re-rivet its ancient chains. Deep plans, in the name of liberty, were laid for this; the Haytians, therefore, could not lay aside their arms; and even when peace and security began at last to dawn upon the nation, and its institutions seemed to assume organization and form, pride and jealousy, those fearful inmates of the human heart, began their dreadful work; hence, those who had bravely fought side by side before the common enemy, now turned their swords against each other, and their arms were mutually stained with fratricidal blood. Alas! they fell upon each other, and by this unhappy means, became yet more emphatically a military people, and the whole country was in the end a military camp. This is indeed deplorable, but it is man; hence, few nations are more deeply stained with fratricidal blood than the three great nations of the age—England, France, and the great Republic of North America. This is no justification for Hayti; nevertheless, it is man.

It cannot, therefore, be wondered at that love of military life and display should be the result of all this, especially with an ignorant mass, such as the great body of Haytians must have been when they first became free; moreover, in addition to all else which has been noted, the yet greater explicative must be remembered: Hayti had been cast in a French military mould. Indeed it is far more wonderful that agriculture and commerce should so soon have become so extensive as they were than that there should have been so little; and considering how the military system has ever prevailed in this country, as the natural result of things and circumstances, it ought not to and cannot fairly be wondered at that the general progress of the nation has been slow, or that the views of true liberty, under military rule, should have been erroneous.

Certain however it is, that under Christophe and Petion, although in arms against each other, much was done in the way of general industry; nor would it be just or fair to taunt such a people, under such circumstances, with indolence, for it cannot be denied that there are but few communities, if any, under similar difficulties, and in such a climate, that would be either disposed, or even capable of, such a general amount of industry and labor. Yet, that inaction and sluggishness, even to an unhappy degree, must necessarily have been engendered by so many thousands of men throughout the nation so perpetually under arms, and consequently drawn away from their homes, their fields, their commerce, and their trades can easily be conceived.

In fact, there is much to be said on this subject for a Haytian soldier on garrison duty, notwithstanding the degrading indolence of such a life, where there is neither the taste nor ability for reading, is compelled to attend to some branch of industry, his pay not being sufficient to support him; still the system is the most unhappy that can well be imagined in its effects upon the morals and general civilization of the nation.

Yet the amount of industry which, under the most disadvantageous circumstances, has from the commencement been brought out in Hayti, leads fairly to the conclusion that such a country, and such a people, under civil, and in the right sense of the word, Christian liberal institutions, would rise rapidly in prosperity of every kind.

In fact, it must be admitted, that with every kind of hindrance, and even discouragement, arising from unsoundness of view and principle in national rule, both on the part of the governing and the governed, the Haytian people have proved themselves capable of a high degree of agricultural and commercial activity. The moral maladies of the nation have indeed crippled her in every way, and it is devoutly to be hoped that the leading minds in this Republic will at last become religiously convinced that their only hope is in the practical working of those principles which were preached by the Son of God on earth.

CHAPTER VII.

Arrival of M. B. Bird at the Cape.—Arrival of J. T. Hartwell at Port au Prince.—Clergy responsible to the "Minister des Cultes."—J. Candler and the Priest.—Different classes of Funerals.—Atheism in Hayti.—A National University desirable.—School for Medicine.—The Earthquake of 1842.—No foreign sympathy for Hayti.—Opening of the Wesleyan Church at Port au Prince.—Journey through the Spanish part.

Temples of Truth, and Halls of Science, spring
From Love, and knowledge of the Great First Cause.

In January, 1840, another English Wesleyan Missionary—M. B. Bird, with his wife and infant son—landed at Cape Haytien.

This missionary was well received by the Protestants of the rather handsome city of the Cape. From the Roman Catholics, also, he received every mark of respect and kindness; but ina moral and religious point of view, all around appeared to be sterile.

With regard to evangelical Protestantism, a few American colored immigrants constituted a small band of less than a dozen individuals, who were united together in church fellowship.

In the French department of the Wesleyan Mission at Cape Haytien, no Protestant Church as yet existed. Public services in the French language had been held, but the number of hearers was rarely more than a dozen—and frequently not so many—

while the prospects, as might be expected in a Roman Catholic community, were not encouraging.

The newly-arrived missionary soon felt the peculiar difficulties of his post. He, however, promptly visited the people generally, irrespective of creed. A fine development of feeling was the result; for although an entire stranger, he was everywhere very kindly received.

The following year, 1841, the Rev. J. T. Hartwell, another English Wesleyan Missionary, landed at Port au Prince.

It will be remembered that a small church, of the Wesleyan Methodist communion, had been formed at the capital during the years 1816 to 1818.

On the arrival of the last-named missionary, this interesting little church still existed, consisting of French Haytians; some of the colored Americans had also united themselves to the English branch of this Mission, so that the field was here more or less prepared. All had indeed been sustained and carried on in comparative obscurity, yet much had been done. Land—although not quite central as to the population, yet in many respects well suited, and of good dimensions, being about 200 feet in length and some 90 feet in breadth—had already been secured; and some few of the natives had received and submitted to the Word of God, as their sole guide.

Mr. Hartwell, and his truly estimable wife, were well received and deservedly esteemed by all parties in the capital; and before long, this zealous and laborious missionary laid the foundation stone of a commodious place of worship. Some few funds had been long in hand for this purpose, and the undertaking was greatly encouraged by the foreign merchants, who were joined in their praiseworthy liberality by the public at large.

During the following year, it pleased Divine providence to remove by death the beloved wife of this esteemed missionary; and her mortal remains still repose in peace at a place called Post Marchand, in the immediate neighborhood of Port au Prince.

It is pleasing to record the appearance of such men in such a country; and it is also pleasing to attest the fact, that in all cases they have invariably been well received on their arrival, notwithstanding the Haytian community is attached to the Roman Catholic communion.

In the case of the two first missionaries in 1816, persecution did indeed take place; but their reception was good, and their success greatly encouraging, until a change of Government took place; nor should it be lost sight of, that the Haytians of themselves are not persecuting, either in temper or character; in such cases, there is generally another element besides the native.

Men whose only business and whose only aim is to do good of every kind, have ever been appreciated by the Haytians themselves; yet a country where education and enlightened piety are wanting as national elements, may be expected to offer peculiar difficulties, especially when the idea of a national and ancestral religion prevails.

With regard to the national ecclesiastical establishment, it is a remarkable fact that for many years after the independence of Hayti, the court of Rome was never able to gain a permanent footing there.

On the part of the Haytians, this was evidently the result of much well calculated thought and principle; hence the Roman Catholic clergy of Hayti, for many years, was without the presence of any controlling bishop over them, or even any connection with the court of Rome, and consisted of Frenchmen, Corsicans, Italians, or whoever else might happen to come—their credentials being examined by "le Ministre des Cultes," to whom they were in every way amenable.

The Romish clergy in Hayti, for a long time, derived its revenue from the fixed prices attached to funerals, masses, etc. etc., a considerable portion of which was claimed by the State, in consideration of church repairs and other expenses, which it binds itself to afford in all cases of necessity.

The income of the clergy, therefore, consisted principally of their share in the fees, when the claims of the State had been met—a functionary being appointed to see what was due to both parties. This individual bore the title of "Marguiller," or Church Warden. The country clergyman, who was diligent in visiting the outposts of his parish, and collecting the fees for baptisms, masses, and all sorts of funerals—that is to say, the first, second, and third classes, into which they are divided, each one varying in price, and consequently in the amount of prayers, chants, etc.—frequently returned to Europe in the end, well recompensed.

The following quotation from the English traveler already mentioned,* may throw some light on this subject. This gentleman relates that on one occa-

* J. Candler.

sion, in conversation with an ecclesiastic, the following remarks took place :—

"I ventured to remind him that sixty Haytian dollars were allowed by law, for a funeral of the first-class; and a dollar for every baptism. 'These dollars,' said the priest, 'are the sweat of our brows, but the Government impounds a large amount of them, and applies it to other purposes. We only obtain twenty dollars for a funeral, and half a dollar for a baptism. What is half a dollar for a baptism?'"

It is indeed most unhappy that by such a system, religion should seem to be an affair of merchandize, especially while other means and plans might with so much ease be resorted to for church support.

From the remarks of the Abbé just quoted, it will appear that all funerals in Hayti, although a Republic, are not upon an entire equality; rather Republican aristocracy is practised in death. Hence, here there are three gradations of honor; in the superior class, there is much more ceremony than in the inferior—more prayers, more chanting, more everything—all of which, in such a case, commands more money. A golden cross is borne before the corpse which represents wealth; while the honors of the church for a poor man are poor indeed. There is, it must be admitted, something exceedingly revolting in the idea that a poor man's soul should command much less attention from the Church of Christ than that of a rich man. It is indeed true that riches and poverty will in all cases have their effect upon society; but when this becomes avowedly a part of a religious system, so that even the ministers of Christ refuse to act without it, then it is done in the name of God, who is no respecter of persons, and seems to be a violation of one of the first principles of Christianity.

It is to be lamented that the punctual and exact performance of mere ceremonies in religion has too much sufficed, while the regeneration of the heart by the power of God—that grand aim of true religion, and only real corrective for the vices of our nature—has been wholly unthought of, or looked upon as a mere sectarian idea.

Will it be for a moment pretended, that if real Christianity, in all its power and simplicity, had been really brought to bear upon the Haytian people, they would, as a mass, have been what they now are? Christianity, as revealed and taught by Christ himself, and fairly brought to bear upon the nation, would doubtless have elevated it, changed its character, and set it on the track of truth and prosperity.

A national or native clergy would unquestionably be very much in the interests of Hayti, by saving much of its wealth from exportation, which on the part of a foreign priesthood, would only be natural. Whether, however, Roman celibacy would ever be a prudent system for the Haytian youth, is more than doubtful.

In fact, the religious question in Hayti, in the form of a State religion, must, in the nature of things, be complicated; for it must be admitted that the atheistic element of France has not been without its effect upon the educated classes of the Haytian community; and this fact, perhaps, constitutes the only explanation to be given for that indifference to moral culture, by means of a really Christian education, or to religion in its real and positive sense, in Hayti. Certain it is, that the reigning spirit and element, in a moral point of view, which laid the foundation of the Haytian Republic, was vastly different from that which directed the foundation of the great Republic of the United States of North America. In the latter case, the people themselves organized their own churches, from a deep and genuine sense of their need of them; but in the former, there was no such deep sense of need, as to religion, except as a political engine, to rule man in deep ignorance. Nor indeed is it to be expected that it should have been otherwise; for the masses were sunk in ignorance, while the intelligent part of the nation was tainted, not to say swayed, by infidelity; hence, no such element was present as was necessary to originate a sense of the indispensable necessity of an honest, sincere, and evangelical native clergy. Yet the advantages arising from independence in this department of the national interests, is as striking and important as in any other, as will be seen in the fact that Hayti's only failure is in her moral element, which is confessedly too weak to stem the torrent of moral corruption which has ever threatened her.

A national university, possessing an architectural style worthy of the grandeur of its purpose, and also well qualified and suitable men of every nation to support its literary and scientific dignity, by a fair development of every branch of human knowledge, would have been such a powerful leaven in the Republic, as would have been felt throughout every ramification of society. The power and worth of such an institution, would have been beyond all human calculation, especially with sound religious principle, such as Divine inspiration has revealed to us as its soul; for history has now long demonstrated to mankind, that whatever may be the intellectual capacity of either an individual or a people, sound moral principle must not be absent; and if it is, it will be at the peril of the nation, whatever be its amount of intelligence.

An attempt towards the formation of a national clergy, was indeed made under President Boyer; but the effort was so feeble, and on so poor a scale, as to be unworthy of notice; hence, like the attempt at a School for Navigation, it was soon forgotten.

But the School for Medicine and Surgery was more happy. This institution, although on a limited scale, was nevertheless seriously undertaken, and really encouraged, as will appear from the following extract, which may be found in a work on Hayti by an English Consul once residing in the country. Speaking of Port au Prince, he observes:

"There is an hospital. The President confers Degrees in Medicine, of which the Professor is a Frenchman.

"The building which serves the Institution, is well situated, although low and mean. A botanical garden was attempted, and many useful plants are there, with also a few models in surgery. The grounds, although not extensive, are well watered; and the establishment might be easily placed on such a footing, as to be an honor to the country, as well as highly useful. In fact, this important establishment has, from the beginning, been both interesting and useful. The only thing to be regretted concerning it is, that it has not been carried out with greater spirit, and that its whole plan has not been on such an elevation, as its importance both merited and demanded. This, however, appears to be one of the inherent defects of Hayti.

Vast sums ill applied in arms, impoverishes the resources for all else; hence, whatever is done, must be stinted, or merely provisional, until something better can be realized. The result, therefore, is that the national mind becomes stinted and contracted—the habit being established of doing nothing fully, completely, and boldly. It is, however, only fair to admit that there are at present signs of improvement in this respect."

We now come to the grand event of 1842, which on the 7th of May of that year, overwhelmed by earthquake the city of Cape Haytien, as well as several other places on the Island. The Cape, it is true, suffered most, being a comparatively large and populous city, and particularly from the fact that the houses were nearly all of stone or brick.

The devastation of this dreadful visitation extended more or less throughout the entire island. Port de Paix, an important and ancient town, situated between Cape Haytien and Mole St. Nicholas, in the north-west part of Hayti, was not only severely shattered by the shock, but was also overwhelmed by the sea, which unnaturally rushed from its limits, deluged the yet smoking ruins, and instantly engulfed many, not only of the wounded and the dying, but also many in full strength.

The scene at this place appears to have been fearful. Boats and small vessels were borne up the streets of the town, some of which were left stranded. The victims were many, considering the smallness of the town—the population of which, at that time, was probably not more than 3,000.

At St. Jago, in the Spanish part, towards the northeast, the shock was exceedingly powerful. This old city, situated between Puerto Plata and the Spanish capital, Santo Domingo, was very strongly built. The walls of its church were more like fortifications than otherwise; and although the houses were mostly low, having nothing more than the ground floor, yet they were all—including even their strongly built church—utterly prostrated, and many of this small population were killed.

From Puerto Plata the Rev. W. Towler, Wesleyan Missionary, thus writes to his Committee in London on this subject:

"You will most likely have learned, by a more direct conveyance than I can avail myself, of the awful visitation which this Island has just experienced.

"On Saturday, May the 7th, about five o'clock in the afternoon, we had three violent shocks of an earthquake, the two last of which were the most powerful; the surrounding mountains and trees, and the houses of this city, reeled to and fro like a drunken man!

"'The earth trembled at the presence of the Lord, at the presence of the God of Jacob!'

"Even while thinking and writing about it I feel dizzy. The Mission-house rolled so much as to throw over the chairs and water jars; the books and bottles of medicine in my study were cast down from the shelves to the floor, and most of the houses in the city were affected in some manner. A range of stone and brick buildings, consisting of dwelling houses and stores, were, in a moment, laid in ruins; but the greater part of the houses, and all our lives have been mercifully spared. Glory be to God for his great goodness towards us.

"It has not been thus with some of our neighboring cities. St. Jago, sixty miles in the interior, is in ruins; many were killed at the time, and many are now suffering from want of the necessaries of life.

"Cape Haytien, built of stone, was overtaken with sudden destruction; whilst all were occupied with their usual business their houses shook and fell, burying many of their inhabitants in the ruins, maiming some, and, in a moment, sending others into eternity. In a wonderful manner, (for such it must have been) our Brother Bird and his family have been saved. I have not had any letter from him, but I have received a verbal message from a friend.

"'God is our refuge and strength, a very present help in trouble.'

"We have heard that some of the smaller towns are sunk and overwhelmed with water.

"How terrible is He in his doings towards the children of men!"

The Rev. M. B. Bird, another Wesleyan Missionary, with his whole family, was in the midst of the falling Cape, at the moment of this dreadful visitation; but, escaping, he also writes to his Committee in London on this extraordinary occasion.

The following is an extract from the description given by the last named Missionary, of this dreadful scene, of which himself and family formed a part in that fearful moment:

"At the moment of this awful catastrophe, I was sitting reading in the balcony of our house, which projected into the street; Mrs. Bird was in a belvedere, two stories from the ground floor, with two of our children, the youngest and the eldest; the former being only nineteen days old, the latter nearly three years of age. A young person who was living with us was, at the moment of the shock, in the act of walking from one part of the house to another, while our second little son, just able to walk, was under the care of a servant in the kitchen, on the ground floor. Mrs. B., who had not left the house since her confinement, had, with the two children, withdrawn to the belvedere for the enjoyment of the cool breeze, which was generally to be found there, and which she, in her then state of weakness, so much needed.

"The instant I felt the shock, I started from my chair, and soon became confounded, not knowing whether to run backward or forward. A glance through the house showed everything to be in full swing; and, as I held the balustrade of the balcony, at the same time leaning over and looking right and left, I, before falling, caught a glimpse of the whole street, as the clouds of dust suddenly burst forth from the breaking walls. In this moment of inconceivable agitation, the entire wall from which the balcony on which I was standing was projected, fell, and I was precipitated with it into the general ruins; the height from which I was thrown might have been some twelve feet, but I scarcely felt the fall, nor could I ever call to mind how I fell out of the balcony, or even remember the sensations of falling. For some seconds after the fall I was perfectly unconscious, until at last I was astonished to find myself in existence, and recognized that I was sitting upon the ruins, with my head leaning upon my hand, almost suffocated with the dust which arose from this general and fearful crash. In this position I remained a few moments, during which time the earth continued to tremble. I had no other idea than that a beam, or some falling wall, would send me into eternity; and, as I waited in breathless suspense the final moment, I commended my spirit to God my Saviour; but his great mercy suffered me to live. When the dense cloud of dust had passed over, I rose, beheld nothing but one vast scene of ruin and desolation, which extended to the utmost limits of the now fallen Cape, with here and there one emerging from the ruins, which I could compare to nothing but a resurrection from the dead, especially as all had a ghastly appearance, being covered with the white dust which had started from the falling walls.

"Finding myself really living and safe, which, for a moment, I could scarcely believe, an intense anxiety seized me for my wife and children, whom I remembered I had left in the belvedere of the house, previous to the event. I therefore rushed to the place, in doubt whether they were still living; on my way, I heard the voice of our servant from the kitchen, crying out, 'Here we are, safe and well!' She was standing in the doorway of the kitchen, with our second son in her arms, both being unharmed! I kissed the dear little fellow, and went on.

"My ascent to my dear wife and the two children was partly

over the ruins of the house; the two stair-cases which led to the belvedere, one of which was built of brick and the other of wood, had both been dreadfully shattered, and were quite unsafe; but my intense anxiety overcame all sense or thought of danger, and I soon reached the memorable spot; there I found Mrs. B. and the two children sitting on the floor, having been violently thrown there by the shock; my joy at finding them safe was inexpressible. My next anxiety was for the young person living with us, but of whose position I knew nothing at the moment when the house fell; not seeing her, I concluded she must be dead; but we afterwards found her safe, she having leaped from a window at the time of the shock, and, alighting on her feet, was saved. Thus, by divine mercy, our whole household had been sheltered from one of the most painful visitations of God, perhaps, on record.

"To give you anything like an adequate idea or description of this awful calamity, would be utterly impossible; it is one of those events which overwhelms and baffles all imagination.

"Picture to yourselves, dear sirs, the suddenness of this visitation, literally 'as a thief in the night;' the groans of the dying, and the cries of those imploring help from under the ruins, without even the possibility of being rescued; the continuance of the shocks; the rush of the sea towards the devoted city; in fact, think of one of the finest and most strongly built cities in the West Indies, with a population of about nine thousand, at least, cast down in a moment by Omnipotence, and two-thirds of its population buried, in one instant, in one common grave, and you will have some faint idea of a scene which it wrings my heart to think of.

"In the night which succeeded the earthquake, the fallen timbers among the ruins took fire, caused, no doubt, by the fires of the different kitchens, which had been lighted for the last repast of the day, and which must have been an awful addition to the agonies of those whose death was not instantaneous."

This Missionary also describes how himself and wife, with one servant and three children, had to climb over the ruins of this fallen city to reach the sea-shore:

"Our descent from the belvedere was exceedingly dangerous and difficult, both the brick and wooden stair-cases being everywhere fractured, so that every effort and movement were entirely unsafe: we, however, at last reached the ground without accident, and at once, fearing the standing, though shattered walls, might come down upon us, proceeded to climb those dreadful ruins.

"Mrs. B., myself, and servant, carried each a little one. The mother, in this case, carried her infant son of only nineteen days' old; and, after crossing this frightful scene, by climbing and crawling over the dying and the dead, amid expiring groans, which we could now and then hear, we at last reached the sea side, and took refuge on board ship, where, for a few days, with scores of others, we literally suffered want."

Bloody struggles for wealth, which now lay flung in all directions, soon ensued, as may be seen by the following extract from a journal, quite in favor of the Government of that day:

"Even man himself did not respect these misfortunes. Beings without pity came in from the country—we are informed—and pillaged what they could snatch from the ruins, instead of rather helping their fellow-citizens in their distressing misfortunes. Strange effects of cupidity and ignorance."

The Church at Cape Haytien was a noble structure, and, but a few months previous to the earthquake, had been beautifully restored from its former dilapidated condition, by General Bottex, a man of great discipline and order, then Commanding that city; it, however, fell in this dreadful moment, and many who were inside when it yielded to the shock, although not an hour of public worship, met with instant death.

It was sad, and deeply humiliating to the foreign resident in the Haytian Republic at this time, that little or no sympathy was shown to Hayti, in her great affliction, by any of the neighboring Islands; nor was this unfelt by the Haytians themselves, although they were nobly silent! In fact, it is much to the honor of Hayti that she has always been able to look after herself; this, too, is one of the secrets of her just pride—which it is true may have been pushed to an extreme—never has she sought help from any one, notwithstanding her fearful debt to France of 60,000,000 of francs, which is now nearly paid! In fact, it is worthy of notice that latterly Hayti has aided her neighbors in their great calamities.*

Immediately after the earthquake, a Court of Inquiry was instituted by the Boyer Government into the conduct of some of the authorities in certain parts of the Island, with regard to their seeming toleration of the disgraceful and inhuman pillaging which immediately followed the dreadful catastrophe, but the all-absorbing Revolution of the following year broke up this Court.

The earthquake confounded many plans and enterprises; many were at a loss to know what course to pursue; some, too, for several days after the event,

* The great principle of overcoming evil with good, at least in this case, falls to the honor of Hayti; hence, on the 4th of November, 1866, collections were made in two Protestant Churches of Port-au-Prince, in behalf of the distressed population of Turk's Island, which had been visited by a hurricane of such violence as had swept away nearly everything from the Island, leaving nearly all the buildings a total wreck, many with their families being thus exposed and left destitute of both food and shelter.

were in want of the necessaries of life; this was the case of the Wesleyan Mission family, which had lost nearly all but life; their sorrows, however, were relieved in a few weeks, by their arrival at Port-au-Prince, where they were received with the warmest affection by the Rev. J. T. Hartwell, who was at this time the residing Wesleyan Missionary at the capital. Arriving here, the Mission family from the Cape were soon surrounded by many kind and sympathizing friends; but the seeds of disease had been deeply lodged in them all, from want of suitable food and clothing, and also by great exposure to both the sun and rain, having been obliged to remain for many days without home or dwelling after the earthquake, it was not therefore, surprising that the two youngest of the family, after having been saved from all the horrors of this dreadful event, should have escaped to heaven in peace, soon after their arrival at Port-au-Prince.

Towards the latter end of this memorable year a highly important event, of a purely moral and religious bearing, took place in the capital of this Republic, which was the opening of the Wesleyan Church; the foundation stone of which had been laid a year or two before, by the Rev. J. T. Hartwell.

The opening and dedication of this neat and commodious little building, the walls of which are of brick and stone, and which will hold nearly four hundred persons, took place on the 4th of December, 1842, which, being a Sabbath day, was entirely devoted to the great and solemn duties of this deeply interesting occasion. Four public services were held during the day, two of which were in French and two in English; each of the Ministers—Bird and Hartwell—taking an equal share in the work in both languages. The attendance at the services on this extraordinary occasion was altogether interesting and encouraging, the place being comfortably filled at nearly all the services, and the liberality of the people altogether praiseworthy, especially when it is remembered that on this occasion the majority of the largest congregations were Roman Catholics.

It may be considered that from this time Protestant Christianity took a bolder and more elevated stand, and acquired a more commanding influence upon the public mind of Hayti.

It is not intended to say anything in this production, otherwise than incidentally, of the Spanish part of this splendid Island. The following sketch of a journey by land from Port-au-Prince to Porerto Plata, extracted from the journal of the Rev. M. B. Bird, may perhaps now be in place, especially as the French and Spanish parts separated almost immediately after the performance of this journey, while it may enable the reader to form some faint idea of the people now forming the Dominican Republic:

"MONDAY, January 9th, 1843.—Left Port-au-Prince at 4 A. M., accompanied by Rev. J. T. Hartwell, my colleague, and a guide, all three on horse-back, the object of the journey being to attend an annual District Meeting, which it was decided should be held that year at Pererto Plata.

"Towards noon we halted, and took a very rural repast near by a clear rivulet, which afforded us all the wine we needed; towards evening we reached the neighborhood of Arcahaie, about forty miles from the capital, where we were entertained for the night by some kind colored Americans, who had, by persevering industry, surrounded themselves by many comforts.

"TUESDAY, 10th.—We reached St. Mark's in the evening, having crossed the large Artibonite river in a barque constructed for passengers and horses; our route had been through a rather dreary and but little cultivated country.

"The town of St. Mark is quite of historical renown. In the time of French rule and power, it was important and prosperous; and, during the great Revolution, it was the scene of the massacre of several hundred French Colonists by Dessalines. Here we left copies of the Scriptures, etc.

"WEDNESDAY, 11th.—We arrived at Gonaïves, where we were informed a great fire had taken place at Port-au-Prince; but our informant having received a rough map of the fire, we were assured that our Mission premises were quite safe, and resolved, therefore, to continue our course.

"THURSDAY, 12th.—This morning we walked through the town, and found that the great earthquake of the previous year had left severe marks of destruction in many places.

"The town of Gonaïves is remarkable as the place where Dessalines declared the Independence of Hayti! It is now a place of great commercial importance, with a population of some six thousand. We held a public service here this evening, and had a small company of hearers.

"FRIDAY, 13th.—Soon after mid-day we continued our course towards Cape Haytien.

"The country between Gonaïves and the Cape is exceedingly picturesque, being mountainous, yet open and fertile. The place called 'Les Escalliers,' or Steps, is of great celebrity; it is a steep pass between two mountains; the road is paved with pebbles, and is, therefore, dangerous for cattle; it is perfectly zig-zag, so that at each turn in ascending, the turn left is seen below, and the one to be reached is seen still above; which, perhaps, accounts for the name given to this rather romantic pass. In this neighborhood there is considerable cultivation, and the general scenery is rich and grand, the great mountains of the neighborhood being luxuriantly verdant.

"SATURDAY, 14th.—At two A. M., we were again on horseback, and reached the neighborhood of the Cape towards night, through a great deal of mud and rain.

"SUNDAY, 15th.—This morning we visited the Cape, our lodgings being on a small estate about four miles outside the town.* On reaching the city, it looked more like an assemblage of ruined tombs than otherwise, and I found it exceedingly difficult to recognize the different spots which had once been so familiar to me. The general scene brought on old sensations, and it was deeply affecting to me to remember that the hand of God had so signally saved both me and mine in the overthrow of that city. On re-examining the touching past in this case, as I again stood on these ruins, I was more than ever amazed and struck with the conviction of a minute and particular Providence. The public market was, at the time of this visit, held on the Sabbath day; hence, there was no opportunity for any religious meeting, and we returned, in every sense sad, in the evening, to our distant lodgings, where we held a meeting for the few that were about the place.

"MONDAY, 16th.—This morning we again rode into the Cape; and, seemingly by accident, we met with two Spaniards, whom we engaged to travel with us as guides on the rest of the journey through the Spanish part.

"TUESDAY, 17th.—About five A. M., we were on our horses, and on our way for the Spanish country, with our two Spanish guides, who spoke a little French. After traveling through a level region of country, not much cultivated, we arrived, towards evening, at Terriere Rouge, where we halted, and were very hospitably received by a military man, who soon informed us that his wife had gone on a pilgrimage to Higuey, a place of great Roman Catholic fame, at the Eastern extremity of the Island; where, it is said, there is an image of the Virgin possessing extraordinary virtue. The man evidently saw the absurdity of the thing; but, like many others, he loved darkness rather than light. We left a French Testament with him, which he gladly accepted.

* The town being still in ruins, it was difficult to find accommodation among its still suffering inhabitants; these travelers, therefore, remained outside at a friend's house.

"WEDNESDAY, 18th.—Left Terriere Rouge about four A. M., and, on our way, called at Fort Dauphin, which had evidently been once a neat place, but, at the time of our visit, was little better than a heap of ruins, wearing the melancholy aspect which seems to attach to every place where the earthquake was violent. Continuing our course we soon reached Ouanaminthe, where again the saddening traces of last year's earthquake were very visible. From thence we shortly reached Laxavon, a neat little Spanish town. The Church of this place, which had been built of stone, was entirely in ruins, from the dreadful visitation of the previous year.

"The whole neighborhood here has an open, beautiful, and healthy appearance, not unlike, although far richer than Salisbury Plain in England; but, we continued our route a little further until we came to a Spanish cottage, where we were kindly received according to the Spanish rural habit; our hammocks were at once swung by our kind host, and we were soon at ease in them. The room assigned to our use for the night was shared with us by three or four strong fighting cocks—the Haytian Spaniards delighting in cock-fighting—an amusement which seems to constitute the sum total of Spanish earthly bliss! The hearty crowing of these feathered warriors, and the boisterous clapping of their wings during the night would, no doubt, have been most deplorable for light sleepers, but we were heavy with fatigue, and our sleep was consequently such that they might crow altogether, and storm to any amount in the clapping of their wings, etc., in this case, with entire impunity!

"THURSDAY, 19th.—In the morning, about four, we were off, and passed through a beautiful country, more like an ancient English Park than otherwise. At mid-day we halted at another Spanish cottage, and refreshed both ourselves and our horses, which was very greatly needed. After two or three hours' rest we continued our way until evening, traveling slowly, frequently not more than three miles an hour, especially when the roads were difficult; at times, however, our movements would be quicker. Our journey, this day, ended on the banks of the Mao, where we slept in one of the worst hovels I ever saw occupied by human beings; the place was without doors or windows, and on one side of this wretched hovel there was little standing besides the posts, which supported a miserable and broken roof; as to a seat, that was out of the question. We found the miserable inmates squatted round a fire, either on the ground or on blocks of wood, with their chins between their hands, and their elbows on their knees; they, however, made us welcome to the place, and did what they could for us; worn down by fatigue, we took a hasty meal, and were soon cradled in our hammocks. The dew and air, to which we were thoroughly exposed, were cold, but our sleep, though short, was sweet.*

Friday, 20th.—We forded the Mayo at daylight, and soon reached the river Yague, which is a noble stream, and with a little trouble might be made navigable for many miles. We crossed this fine stream in a canoe, our horses swimming by the side.

"With regard to the country through which we were now traveling all was richness, fertility and splendor. Towards the middle of the afternoon we arrived at the cottage of a white Spanish family, of rather Donish bearing; the house was scarcely a shelter from either sun or rain; but the airs of the inmates were very significant, not to say imposing, especially on the part of the young ladies, whose lofty style seemed to indicate a supposed, or real descent from ancient nobility; but who, certainly in these poor modern times, had nothing more than a cow-hide and the ground to serve as couch. We, nevertheless, gladly availed ourselves of the kind hospitality which was, with right good feeling, offered to us for the night. Before retiring to rest something was cooked for us, but everything was so entirely uninviting as to cleanliness, that, though we were literally in want, yet we ate with little or no enjoyment; fatigue, however, soon sent us to our hammocks, where we very gladly underwent the needed preparation of rest for the next day, which we knew would be one of hard work.

* The scene here represented consisted of men who were much more attached to the Dons of Spain than to Africa.

"SATURDAY, 21st.—At day-light we were again on the road, and resolved to reach Puerto Plata that evening, if possible. Our path, for some time, was through a thick wood, continuing for a good distance along the side of a steep hill, where, now and then, there would be scarcely space enough, as a road, for our horses' hoofs. About ten A. M. we halted and breakfasted; up to this hour this morning we had rain, and were wet, but after our repast by the road-side, we went on until mid-day, when we reached the romantic village of Altimera; continuing our journey, we had to encounter and struggle with such mud as rendered our traveling perfectly distressing; the more so, as we now began to be thoroughly fatigued; at last, however, we reached the long-desired city of Puerto Plata, and were kindly and heartily welcomed by our Brethren Eacott, Towler and Cardy, who had all been anxiously waiting for us. Mrs. Towler was, unhappily, an invalid. Our journey from Port-au-Prince to this place had cost us—including rests—eleven days' toil. We were, indeed, thoroughly fatigued; yet we had, upon the whole, greatly enjoyed our long and hard labor on horseback, and a little rest soon brought us round again, while the remembrance of the country and people with which we had now become somewhat acquainted, reminded us that Christianity alone can bless mankind, and that without it indolence can live amidst the unbounded wealth of nature, and be still in wretchedness; while the glories and luxuriance of the most imposing scenery, even of the tropics, fails to purify the heart, or of itself even to elevate the mind: some other elements and power must evidently be brought to bear upon the human race to raise them to their right level, as moral and immortal beings.

"The object of this visit being purely of an official character, with regard to the annual District Meeting usually held in the Methodist Connection, it will not be necessary here to enter into its details. Several public services were held during our stay, all of which were deeply interesting, and well attended by the American immigrants. Some of the services were held in the French language, but most of them were held in English, none in Spanish.

"Puerto Plata is situated by the sea side; its population

makes it quite a second-rate town in the Haytian Republic.* At the time of our visit this Spanish city had quite an air of respectability. The Wesleyan Mission was situated on a beautiful elevation, commanding a good view of both the town and the sea; but the Spaniards have in no case submitted to the influence of Protestantism, as to this city. The Mission property consisted, at that time, of a good little Church, holding about a hundred and fifty, and a comfortable Parsonage, to which has since been added a School-house.†

"MONDAY, 30th.—Left Puerto Plata this morning for Port-au-Prince; the Brethren, Cardy and Towler, accompanying us for a considerable distance outside. We reached Altimera a little before dark, and halted for the night. This somewhat singular village stands on a good elevation; the climate in these mountains is exceedingly agreeable; in fact, during the night we found it to be quite sufficiently cold.

"TUESDAY, 31st.—Left Altimera about day-light, and traveled through an interesting country until about mid-day, when we rested at a Spaniard's house on the road. In the afternoon, about four, we arrived at the ancient town of Santiago. This interior city is beautifully situated; fertility and grandeur are round about it; in fact, the whole neighborhood is highly picturesque and healthy. Before sun-set we took a stroll round the place and saw, by its ruins, that it once had been a well-built place. The houses were low, with thick walls, and the Church, which was a low building, was remarkable for solidity. But everything, at the time of our visit, presented a more fearful spectacle than even Cape Haytien; for, although the town was small and the buildings low, and of remarkably strong mason-work, the general ruin seemed here to be more decided and complete; from whence it seems natural to infer that the shock must have been more powerful in the Eastern part of the Island than towards the West. After contemplating this sad

* It will be borne in mind that at this time the entire Island was under one flag, which was that of the Haytian Republic, of which Boyer was, at that time, President.

† At the present time Puerto Plata is little better than a heap of ruins, as the result of the late war with the European Spaniards.

scene we returned to our lodgings, which had been kindly afforded us by a Haytian Colonel, then commanding the place, and whose hospitality was very hearty.

"WEDNESDAY, February 1st.—After an early breakfast, we left Santiago and directed our course towards the Mao, near the banks of which we again rested for the night.

"THURSDAY, 2d.—About three A. M. we commenced the labor of the day, and continued our traveling until between eight and nine, when we paused at a Spaniard's house and breakfasted. Here was something like a productive garden, but the dwelling or hut was the picture of wretchedness; the man, however, made us heartily welcome; and, having refreshed ourselves, we continued our course; but, our guide not being thoroughly acquainted with the country, we missed our path, and took one which led us through a wood where we saw many wild pigs and a good many wild horned cattle. Continuing our course, we at last came out upon a fine open country; the richness and splendor of the scene was really enchanting, which was the more interesting to us from the fact that we had just come out of a thick wood; a more fairy-like aspect of a country could not be imagined; all was nature, pure, rich, and beautiful; no traces of the hand of man were anywhere to be seen, in the way of cultivation, buildings, or otherwise. The thought, however, was sad that we should have toiled so long, and gone so far, to no purpose. Having entirely missed our way, however, we alighted in this splendid wilderness; there was, indeed, nothing but the ground for us as a resting place, but with this charming view before us we took our rural meal, for which we were well prepared; and, notwithstanding the assurance that we had lost our way, we enjoyed the moment. Having finished our repast, we now returned, and slept that night where we had breakfasted in the morning.

"FRIDAY, 3d.—Our horses needing rest, we did not leave this place till mid-day; but, before leaving, we gave our hospitable host a Spanish Testament, for which he appeared to be very grateful. With this man we had conversed much, and found him quite open to religious instruction, as was the case in most places which we had visited. Wherever we halted for the night we introduced prayer; but if the idea of our being heretics had occurred to these poor people, it is probable that, from Christians, we should, in their estimation, have been changed into demons.

"My horse having been bitten previous to this journey by a poisonous insect, had shown signs of weakness for a day or two past, but as we were now riding along the poor animal literally sunk down with me, and could not rise again. At this moment we were on a road leading through a large Savanna, where we were compelled to leave him. It was well for us that we were just approaching houses, which we soon reached; and were really thankful we had not further to travel, for we were wet, fatigued, and benighted. The first house we came to happened to be one of a man holding office; he made us welcome; we refreshed, called all together for prayer, swung our hammocks, and were soon soundly asleep.

"Saturday, 4th.—Early this morning our man rode back for the horse, and brought him up; we were soon again on our way; but before we arrived at the place which we had in view, as the end of this day's journey, this poor animal utterly failed, and there was now no alternative but to leave him on the road. We were, however, again fortunate in being near the first Spanish cottage of cock-fighting notoriety, in which we had slept in our outward bound course.

"Sunday, 5th.—Spent the Sabbath day at this Spanish cottage, which, notwithstanding fighting-cocks, dissipation, etc., etc., we endeavored to turn to good account by reading the Scriptures, both in French and Spanish, and by religious conversation.

"Monday, 6th.—Having made arrangements with this man to get my horse up, which we had left two or three miles behind us, on the savanna, and to keep him for me until I should return, which I told him I might do in some three or four months' time,* we left at daylight for the town of Laxavon, which was not far on, and where we soon arrived. Our pass-

* Some three or four months after, I again visited this neighborhood, and found my horse in good condition; nor would this kind man accept of the slightest recompense.

port served us as an introduction to the commandant of the place, by whom we were very kindly entertained.

"Here I was necessitated to purchase another horse, and we continued our way through a tolerably well populated country, evidently very rich, but not much cultivated. Towards evening we arrived at a cottage, where fighting children, confusion and misery seemed to abound. We were, however, made welcome, and the people did the best they could for us.

"TUESDAY, 7th.—About daylight we were en route. A military post, however, on the road, ordered us to halt, and our passports were examined. This was a special military guard, in consequence of rumors of revolt and revolution in the southern part of the island. The commandant of Laxavon, our last place, had indeed sent a man on with us, to avoid all difficulty at this post; but he had only a verbal message, and was therefore not believed. We were told we must return to Laxavon (some twenty-six miles behind). This we refused to do, knowing that our passports were correct, and doubting whether any one there could read them. At this they shouldered arms and surrounded us. This brought straw hats and ragged coats a little nearer to us; but finding that we were resolved not to move, they sent one of their own men back with our passports, who probably before long met with some one on the road that could read, and was therefore soon back again, assuring the officer of the guard that all was right. However this might have been, our papers were returned, and we were rather sheepishly told we might go. Putting incompetent men in office, must in the nature of things be attended with many inconveniences, and indeed evils.

"Towards evening, after traveling through an undulated and very woody country, where the rich pitch-pine very much abounded, we arrived at a Spanish cottage, where misery really seemed to preside, but where we nevertheless were made heartily welcome, and our fatigue soon sent us into sweet forgetfulness.

"WEDNESDAY, 8th.—About daylight we were again on our saddles, and traveled through a country still undulated, and full of splendid pitch-pine.

"Rather late in the evening we reached Banica, and were very kindly received by the commandant, who provided lodging for us.

"THURSDAY, 9th.—We were very courteously invited to dine with the commandant, whom we found to be intelligent, gentlemanly and agreeable. In religious matters, he like many others in the country, was a Protestant, without the courage to avow it.

"Here we were informed that the excitement which had taken place in the south, was entirely over, and that all was now quiet.

"In the afternoon we left for L'Ascahoba, and towards evening we arrived at a hut, where we halted for the night, and slept in a miserable shed. But by this time we had become inured to this sort of life.

"FRIDAY, 10th.—Left about four A. M., and reached L'Ascahoba in about six hours, where we rested till the afternoon. My horse which I had bought at Laxavon, now began to show signs of weakness, and we thought it best to leave him here, to be sent on to Port au Prince in a day or two. I therefore mounted the pack mule, and we reached Mircbalais in the evening, where we were kindly received and entertained by a member of the House of Representatives.

"SATURDAY, 11th.—About one A. M., we were on our way to the capital. After fifteen miles' traveling, we arrived at the settlement of Fond Cheval,* which is about thirty miles from Port au Prince. Here we have a little chapel built, and a society of some thirty members, all of whom are Haytians. This small place of worship was built by our own people, and at their own expense, the ground having been given by one of them for that purpose. We remained at this place amongst the kind members of our church until about mid-day, and then

* The Methodist church at this place was of wattled walls and a thatched roof. At the time of this visit, this rustic place of worship, built entirely by natives, had been burnt to the ground by the commanding general of those quarters, doubtless by superior orders; such meetings in the mountains having been forbidden. In fact, the Boyer Government was not hearty on the question of religious liberty.

commenced the last stage of this long journey, to Port au Prince. This last effort was painful, men and horses being now thoroughly tired. For my own part, I had been somewhat fatigued by the failure of my horses; but my worthy companion and fellow-traveler had been more fortunate, his horse having gone through the entire journey.

"We reached home about eight o'clock in the evening, and found all in good health; but a devastating fire had laid a great part of the city in ruins; and we found that the excitement in the south was beginning to assume a serious aspect. The Government labored hard to conceal everything, but their efforts were entirely useless.

"The results and general impressions of this journey upon our minds were various, but powerful. We had ranged through an immense field, where, in every sense, much was to be learnt and seen.

"Our outward course not having been direct, it is probable, according to the route we had pursued to and fro from Puerto Plata, we had gone through the labor of little less than a thousand miles on the saddle, and in many cases, over fearful roads. The physical labor was great; and yet even this laborious mode of traveling has much to interest. At least, by this means, the country and people become more intimately known to the traveler.

"The sight of such a country, under the circumstances in which we found it, morally and intellectually, as well as in reference to general agriculture and industry, would naturally awaken much thought, and in fact become deeply afflicting, not only to the missionary, but to the merchant, the man of science, and the general philanthropist.

"A land unsurpassed in either beauty or wealth, as to nature, occupied, as to the Spanish part, by a widely scattered population, from which we had received every mark of respect and hospitality, and of whom we had had every proof of good will. But all was stagnant. Want of knowledge had shut up everything. The power, or even thought, of developing the boundless resources around them, were absent; the very consciousness of the existence of such wealth close at hand, did not exist. Ignorance, inaction and poverty seemed to reign everywhere, whilst even amongst the more enlightened, rising from nothing into wealth, seemed either to be considered as impossible, or was unthought of altogether. The cry for capital was much more thought of than its creation by the strong mind and arm of industry.

"In a moral point of view, we had before us at every step a full and afflicting demonstration of the utter madness of leaving the masses of a country to themselves, to become a prey to their own ignorance, and consequently unprofitable to the world. Wherever we went nature was glorious; but man we found sunk, wretched, and ignorant, and frequently without the means, although never without the heart, to refresh the weary traveler; in fact, an almost universal destitution of the commonest comforts of life. And yet all this amongst a people with whom the love of gain is strong, and who only need to be set upon the right track for everything good, by greater contact with enlightened men of all classes, and especially with the enlightened laborer and mechanic who fears and loves God.

"Who shall be blamed for all this? Had it been the same with Hayti as with the various tribes of Africa, where chiefs and people are all alike sunk in ignorance, all might be left to the silence of regret. But what shall we say when an enlightened community in a nation, with an enlightened government at its head, for more than sixty years suffer the great masses of their brethren to remain in ignorance? Thousands of apologies are made for this in Hayti. But the time is come when no reasoning can be accepted in justification for the entire ignorance of the great masses of a Republic. Under such free institutions as those of true republicanism, the great fact of human equality must not be made an absurdity by the utter inability of two-thirds of the citizens to be Republicans, they themselves knowing nothing of the difference in principle between Christophe and Petion.

"With every citizen in a Republic, capable of understanding and fulfilling his duties as such, even a weak people would become rich and strong.

"It is particularly worthy of remark, and especially for the information of those who are disposed to think meanly of the

African race, that in the population of the Spanish part of Hayti, the blacks are in the minority, a large proportion being entirely white, and many of mixed blood; the whites are principally descendants of the European Spaniards, and are not, evidently, without the remembrance of ancient Spanish nobility. Whether, however, this supposed superior race have really left the French black Haytians far behind, in general progress and civilization, is most certainly no difficult problem. We will not enter into this matter at present; but it is perhaps more than probable, that Black Hayti would suffer nothing from comparison, commercially, intellectually, or politically, with her higher and prouder brethren, of either Mexico or Dominica."

CHAPTER VIII.

The nation in movement.—Herard Riviere revolts.—The Government without the means of transport.—"Liberté ou la Mort!"—Boyer sends forces.—They fraternize.—The alarm gun.—Port au Prince in great confusion.—Boyer abdicates.—Reviere enters the Capital.—He forbids all ceremonies.—Ten thousand troops in Port au Prince.—No disorder.—The new Government inaugurated.—Reviere marches on the Spaniards.—"L'Assemblée Constituante."—National Guard demands pay. Riviere threatens "L'Assemblée Constituante."—Bad elements creeping in.—The government Provisoire deserving.—M. B. Bird's journey to the South.—He preaches in a Catholic Church.

A People seizing on the Nation's reins,
Draw oft opposingly, till madness seizes
On their steed, and all is lost.

THE events of 1843, constitute one of the great national epochs in the history of Hayti.

From the statements already made, it will easily be seen that for many years previous to the last date, feelings of dissatisfaction, whether founded or unfounded, had been generally and gradually increasing, but about the beginning of this year all the unhappy feelings of the nation came to a crisis, the result of which was such an overwhelming torrent of revolutionary passion, that a government in many respects wise, but never rightly, or enough so, to know when and how to yield with dignity to the honest wishes of the people, now found itself under the imperative necessity of precipitately abandoning all.

During the first three months of this year, the whole nation had been in a most intense state of excitement, and the Government, instead of enlisting the good feelings of the people by an honest and open declaration of the real state of things, issued orders and proclamations which either concealed everything, or gave a wrong view of the case. Conversations on politics were regarded as a crime, and in fact, the free and sovereign people of the Republic, seemed rather to be considered by the Government as having nothing whatever to do in their own affairs. The fact however of the case was, that the entire nation was rising, and the orders of the Government to be silent operated more like sparks on gunpowder than otherwise.

All this had long been foreseen by many; that it was not foreseen by Boyer himself, is not to be wondered at. He was doubtless tied up to his own special views of politics, and especially to his own views of the Haytian people, whom he thought he perfectly knew, and whose servant, according to his own Republican principles, he was; but he evidently belonged to an age in which he would be considered as its master, rather than its servant.

In the early part of this year, Riviere Herard, an officer in the artillery, with several other leading characters, raised the standard of revolt against the Government of Boyer, on an estate called Praslin, near the city of Cayes, in the southern part of the Island. This estate, it would appear, was the property of Riviere himself.

General Borgella, who at that time commanded the city of Cayes, took so decided a stand against the insurgents, who had invited him to join them, that they found it necessary to withdraw to the other side of that part of the Island, and they therefore soon established their head-quarters at Jéremie.

Just at this time, it would appear that the revolting party had well nigh lost courage, and there is no doubt but if the Government of Boyer had been in possession of only one ordinary steamer, so as promptly to have despatched a few well decided troops to that spot, this great revolt would no doubt have been nipped in its bud. This, however, was not the case, as the leaders in this revolt well knew, and this must be regarded as one proof that Hayti was not driving on with the age.

It is worthy of note that about this time, or rather a little before, an American merchant had solicited permission of the Boyer Government to ply two steamers round the Island, with the understanding that they should be at the disposal of the Government in any case of necessity; this, however, had been refused. The Government, from sheer want of a spirit of enterprise—not of means—or purely from imaginary fears as to the general bearing of the solicited permission, was now without any suitable means of transport, and therefore had compelled itself to allow this revolt to spread, notwithstanding in its first movements it reeled with weakness and uncertainty, and might have been put down with ease, had the Government only had the energy to have furnished itself with the ordinary means of self-preservation; but it had been strangely preferred to have a million of dollars in the treasury, and thus leave the country defenceless.

Great military movements now began throughout the country. Divisions of troops, of four, five, and more thousand strong, under different Generals, were now marching from different directions, while in the meantime the revolters were organizing their plans, gaining strength, and forming a committee of public safety. By the Government, however, they were looked upon as a mere faction.

Riviere was now named by the Committee of public safety, as the "Executor of the sovereign will of the people!" This Committee distributed military grades and honors, and the fearful motto of its standard was "Liberté ou la mort!"*

General Borgella and some others, showed a noble front of fidelity to the old Government; all, however was useless. Boyer, not recognizing the feeling of the nation in what was going on, and had been for several years past, but treating all with disdain, as the work of a mere refractory party of jealous and ambitious men, extinguished by this means his own star, and thus rapidly drew on the moment of its fall.

When the hour is come, a nation will roar, and the people will be heard, even though it should be to their own destruction. Happy are the rulers who know how, and when, to stoop; such deservedly become the lights of history, serving to many a future generation.

Some of the troops sent out by Boyer, may have been disposed to be faithful to him, while at the same time it is not to be concealed, that many were already predisposed to fraternize with the revolting arms.

* "Liberty or Death."

The tide of this great Revolution rose and rolled on rapidly, until towards the end of February, when the President made a final effort. Orders were now given, and some 1,500 men were sent under confidential officers, to meet the approaching forces under the new standard, which now were nearing the town of Leogane. Riviere's column is said to have consisted of some 4,000 men.

The officers in command of the Government forces, were the devoted friends of Boyer, and therefore were resolved to strike a blow for the still existing power. The armies met at Leogane, and as soon as the attack was commenced, the Rivierists returned the blank fire of a cannon; in fact had it not been for the humanity of Reviere's troops there might have been a dreadful slaughter, but a second attack on the part of the Government forces was responded to, by a deadly charge from one of the heavy pieces of Reviere's army, which killed some and wounded others; the result was, an open manifestation of decision. As many had expected, Boyer's army dispersed, leaving the officers principally to return to the Capital.

The President might possibly have made another attempt, but some of the mothers of those who had been killed in the Leogane affair just related, assembled before the Palace, and besides bitterly reproaching the President, gave vent to their feelings of hatred to his Government, &c., &c.; this led him to desist, and probably to conclude that all was lost.

The alarm gun was now fired three times, and the drum beat to arms; the country was now considered to be in danger, and now the voice of the people seemed to be heard with terror! The completest confusion followed in a few moments. Men were seen stalking about the city in all directions, some with pistols at their belts, others with swords at their sides, or muskets on their shoulders; in fact it was a terrific military sight, half savage. Each one, heedless of superior orders, pursued his own course, as though every man's hand was turned against his fellow, without any previous thought, or distinct understanding anywhere, or of any kind. It was the confusion of an unhappy dream, for none seemed to have the sligthest idea as to who these arms were to be raised against, or whether they were to be used at all.

The terrors of a plundering horde, driving in upon the city in the midst of this confusion, now seized the more enlightened portions of the people, hence it was not astonishing to see loads of goods going in all directions, on donkeys, men's heads, &c., &c.; some were to be lodged on board ships in the harbor, and others to be taken to the neighboring plains and mountains. In fact all was consternation, although it was generally and confidently believed that there was nothing to fear in the approaching army, which certainly was looked upon at that moment as patriotic, and having only in view the honor and welfare of the country.

The Army of the South was now powerful, and rapidly approaching the Capital. The crisis of the moment was intense, and only ended on the 13th of March 1843, when President Boyer, with his family, went on board an English man-of-war then lying off the harbor of Port au Prince, and the responses to all the military challenges of "qui vive!" at all points, were "Patriote!" or "l'ame populaire!"

The excitement and suspense of this night, although all was calm, were painful. A man who had held the reins of power, and ruled the destinies of Hayti for a quarter of a century, had now decided on throwing up all, and leaving a people by many of whom he was still greatly esteemed. A solemn stillness seemed to prevail over the whole city. Neither voice nor sound of joy was anywhere heard, although it was generally known that President Jean Pierre Boyer and his family were embarking for a foreign shore.

On the 4th of March following, the President's abdication was read at the Senate, of which the following is a brief translated extract; its simplicity and truth are not unworthy of notice:

"CITOYENS SENATEURS,

"The efforts of my administration have ever been to economise the public funds. At the present moment there are nearly a million of piastres in the national Treasury, besides certain sums in France, held in deposit for the Republic.

By submitting myself to a voluntary exile, I hope to annihilate all pretext for a civil war on my account."

In fact, in a financial point of view, President Boyer left the Republic in comparatively prosperous circumstances, as will appear from the following brief financial statement, furnished by a friend for this volume:

"A little before the Revolution of 1843 there had been in circulation, besides two millions and a half of one and two dollar notes, a considerable number of ten dollar notes, which the President had withdrawn from circulation, at the rate of forty dollars to the doubloon; at the commencement of this same year, (1843) the Republic having a surplus amount of one million two hundred thousand piastres deposited in the particular vaults, besides a considerable sum at the 'Administration' at Port au Prince, both of gold and silver, as well as paper currency, as it was certified on the 'Exposé.'

President Boyer had decided on redeeming with a part of this surplus capital, the amount of paper money still in circulation; to effectuate which, he assembled a committee of well chosen men to take into consideration this important project, with a view to its speedy realization, at the rate of forty dollars to the doubloon." *

These facts are truly to the honor of Boyer, nor would it be generous or just to slight his memory, not only in these, but also many other matters. Defects doubtless existed in his Government, but they consisted rather in not doing the good which might have been done, than in doing evil; had he but have stooped, he doubtless might have conquered, but he wrecked on the rock of unyielding pride, which has overthrown many a mighty one. Happy had it been for Hayti, if the evils which he feared had been shunned by his successors, and if they had only done the good which they accused him of neglecting to do.

Among the exports of 1840, are found the following:

Coffee,	46,000,000	lbs.
Cocao,	442,365	"
Tobacco,	1,725,389	"
Various Woods,	39,283,205	"
Mahogany,	4,072,641	ft.

* W. G. Smith, M. D.

In a Haytian journal called the "Manifeste, dated April 2, 1843, is found a Manifesto addressed "A nos Amis à nos Enemies."* This piece is an appeal to the nation. It is rather long, and enters fully into what the parties considered the various grievances of the people, such as a defective Legislature, want of national education, want of freedom of the Press, the expulsion of the Representatives, &c. &c.

This appeal bears date September 1st, 1842, and is followed in the same Journal from which it is taken, by an oath, taken by those who were disposed to unite themselves to the party, in supporting the general aims and bearings of the piece, of which the following is an extract:

> "I swear before God and man, upon my faith in my country and my reputation, to be faithful and devoted to this association, formed for the regeneration and salvation of Hayti."

The rest of this oath is much to the same purpose, in connection with the manifesto in question, and the secret organization of the Revolution, which broke out on the following year. These pieces, however, are followed by a proclamation to the nation, in which the entire system of Boyer is denounced as hypocritical and tyrannical, directed by an organization of spies; and the whole concludes with the following outburst of military passion:

> "Haytians, to arms! The country looks to its Citizens, and we are sure you will show yourselves worthy of its confidence."

* To our friends and our enemies.

In this appeal are to be found many resolutions and decrees, among which it may be seen that a provisional Government was to be formed, composed both of military men and civilians. This seems to have constituted the platform and ground-work of this great movement, the grand and leading idea of which was, that true liberty had been trampled under foot, and that now the Sovereignty of the people was to be gloriously maintained; while the ardor and decision of the insurgents was to be seen in their motto, as already given, "Liberté ou la mort!"

It will be evident in these proceedings, that those who projected this movement, were not sufficiently advanced themselves, to see that the means by which they proposed to reform abuses, were themselves the greatest and most ruinous of abuses. Attempting to annihilate a military system, by the creation of a yet far greater military power, is, to say the least of it, a most strange and dangerous course.

Notwithstanding, therefore, this great national effort in the name of patriotism and reform, combined the greater part of the intelligence of the Republic, a resort to arms in such a case was a fundamental error, and simply demonstrated that great intelligence may exist, without a sound knowledge of the real principles of true liberty; the same number of intelligent men which in this Revolution flew to arms, publicly declaring their opinions and wishes in a reasonable manner, unarmed, would have been utterly irresistible to any Government. Hayti, however, is not the only nation of the age which has to learn this lesson; better for the errors of a mild

Government to be left to die out, than for them to be indefinitely increased by false and pernicious measures of reform.

On the 20th of March of this memorable year, 1843, the newly chosen Chief, Herard Riviere, was within a league of the Capital at a place called Marquissant, with the advanced guard of his army, which consisted of nearly 5,000 men. The excitement in town rose as he approached; the joy, however, was intense. A sudden dream of brighter days, having their source in bayonets, was now deluding the people.

On the 21st of March, 1843, Charles Herard Riviere entered the Capital of the Republic, amidst such bursts of exultation as have seldom been heard in Hayti.

The popular committee, which had already been formed by delegates of the Revierist army, had ordered a great display and roar of cannon, and other manifestations of the high satisfaction which seemed to fill all hearts, but all was forbidden by the new Chief, who wished as little show and parade as possible; a course which seemed to produce the happiest impressions.

Never was a man more idolized for a time, than was this successful and triumphant General, nor ever perhaps was a Revolution more hopeful in its first movements; in fact, never could any man have had a more splendid opportunity of immortalizing himself in the right sense of the word, or of raising a nation to dignity, honor and prosperity, than had this successful and apparently deserving man on this great and important event.

Indeed it cannot be denied that this Revolution was for a time an exceedingly popular one; many, with highest hopes, had made immense sacrifices, and in good faith patriotically helped forward, as they imagined and meant, the welfare and best interests of their country.

Proclamations, addresses, and appeals of all sorts, were now poured forth by the new Rulers, in which the past state of things was denounced as a system of tyranny and oppression, and in which promises of the most brilliant character were made to the country, assuring a glorious career for the future. In fact all was hopeful and dazzling, and the whole nation seemed to bound with joy at the prospect of the future, which now was lighted up with the most glowing expectations.

The Capital was now full of soldiers, the whole army having come in with General Riviere, and notwithstanding they were without barracks, or nearly so, some ten thousand men without shelter, lodged principally under piazzas in the open streets, and not abundantly supplied either as to clothing or food, yet the most perfect order reigned everywhere, nor was ever an army received by a people more in the character of friends, than was the case in this great national event.

On the 4th of April the Provisional Government was inaugurated; this was done in the open air on the large square before the Palace, on what is called "l'Autel de la Patrie."* The ceremony, although not pompous, was imposing.

* A national stand, from which the people and troops are harrangued on great occasions.

On this national stand were to be seen many of the leading men of the nation, military and otherwise. The foreign Consuls for various nations, in full costume, were in the group, indicating by their presence the sanction of foreign powers to the proceedings of the day. The sight itself was gratifying, but it was the hope that all was genuine and sound in principle, which gave it grandeur.

The ceremonies at "l'Autel de la Patrie" being terminated, a procession was formed and marched to the national Church, where all was wound up with the ceremonies of Rome.

The new organization of things was now so far provisionally arranged, as to give full hope of something more permanent in due time.

The Provisional Government deemed it necessary that the new Chief Magistrate should visit the Spanish part of the Island. Herard Riviere himself, it must be remembered, was a member of the Provisional Government.

The object of this mission, was to establish the new order of things everywhere. With this view, General Charles H. Riviere was invested with an unlimited power to do or to undo whatever he pleased, but at the same time, according to the different decrees issued by the Provisional Government, he was not only to render to them an account of all his proceedings on his return, but also to resign to them the immense power with which he had been entrusted, for the execution of his great mission.

The date of the decrees of this military tour, is the 7th of April, 1843, and on the following 16th, which was a Sunday, the advanced guard moved out of the

Capital, and was followed by General Herard himself the same night.

Port au Prince was now therefore emptied of soldiers, and the protection of the city was left to the National guard; it would seem, however, that this militia being now called into active service, demanded the usual military pay, and addressed themselves to the Committee of safety, which had been organized by delegates sent for that purpose from "l'Armée Populaire." At this appeal of the National Guard, the Committee resigned its powers to the Provisional Government on the 22d of April, but on the 24th a meeting took place of the officers of the National Guard at the Palace, with the Committee, by request of the Provisional Government, and a good understanding was re-established between the parties, after which the Committee of public safety resumed its functions.

But it was now necessary to carry out the great purposes of the Revolution, the leading one of which was, to draw up such a Constitution as should secure to the nation all it desired, and at the same time be more in harmony with the spirit of the age. This was felt to be, as indeed it was, an important step, and the great point was to secure right and capable men.

This great Assembly was called "l'Assemblée Constituante," and was composed of representatives of Arrondissements, chosen by electors who themselves were elected by universal suffrage.

"L'Assemblée Constituante" met on the 15th of April, 1843, and formed themselves to order.

The nation was anxious. All felt it to be an

undertaking, which in the most serious manner involved the interests and hopes of the Republic.

The various articles of the Constitution were very fully and amply discussed in detail, by thoroughly argumentative and well reasoned speeches, which brought out an interesting display of tact and talent. In fact a fair proportion of the elite of the country was evidently present, and the indications were clear and strong that the real intelligence of the country had decidedly advanced, and was struggling to meet the exigencies of the age.

At the beginning of these discussions, great spirit and animation were displayed, and all promised well. More than three months were taken up in this great work, but cross elements crept in at last. Each one did indeed express himself freely, yet it must be remembered that a great military Chief was at hand, a fact which in the nature of things, would more or less restrain the general spirit of this Body, especially as one dominant idea of the House appeared to be, that the ruling power of the country must be partly military; the sword being the servant of the nation, was an idea which seemed to be limited to but few minds, doubtless upon the old and oft-repeated principle that Hayti is an exceptional country, which has long been a starting point for much reasoning in this Republic, both on civil and political subjects, but which, however true, has led to much error and stagnation.

The great task of framing a new Constitution, was at last accomplished on the eve of 1844, and General Charles Herard Riviere was on the following 4th of January proclaimed President of Hayti.

It is to be deplored that this great Reformer and Regenerator of his country, should have been so impatient with the Constituant Assembly for their lengthy discussions, as to draw up two pieces of artillery by way of driving them to a close with their work; still worse that he should, as a military chief, possessing at that moment the power and affection of the people, have forced that Assembly to name a President at all, notwithstanding they were perhaps competent to do so.

But the elements were already becoming conflicting; even conspiracies, jealousies, &c., &c., were giving fearful sings of hidden fires, the details of which it would be impossible to enter into at present, but they will doubtless be brought out by other pens.

With regard to the Provisional Government, it must be admitted, that during its brief existence, which was less than a year, Hayti was truly, and in the right sense of the word, free. Every one felt that he breathed the real and genuine element of liberty!

The following extract from the journal of M. B. Bird, Wesleyan Missionary, who, during the reign of the Provisional Government, traveled on a missionary tour through the southern part of the island, where this great movement originated, will give some idea of the really free and unshackled state of the country, under this entirely new political dispensation, while it will show how fully prepared this whole nation was at that time, for all that the missionary and philanthropist might have done; or rather, it will show that the moral soil of Hayti is prepared for all that the Gospel could do for it.

At the time of which we now speak, the Church of Rome was indeed the national Church, but its hold was then comparatively weak; no Concordat bonds at this time existed, while every parish and cottage were open to any and every man who might wish to enter with the word of God in his hand. This was indeed a golden moment for the diffusion of pure Christianity, whether by means of education, the public ministry, or otherwise; these facts too were fully and anxiously represented to British Christians, but utterly in vain. It will be seen, that in some cases, during this remarkable journey, even Roman Catholic churches were placed at the disposal of "le ministre Protestant;" in fact, the simple peasant, as well as the educated man, felt that a happy moment had come on for Hayti.

The views which will be afforded by the details of the journey in question, will also show, in some degree, the contrast which exists in all respects between the Haytian, French, and Spanish communities, as to habits, circumstances, etc.

"DECEMBER 12, 1843.—Left Port au Prince with simply a guide, about day-light, both of us being on horseback—the only present mode of traveling in Hayti, and in a hot climate, sufficiently laborious. Our way led through a rather populated and cultivated country, and in the afternoon we reached the town of Leogane, the population of which may reach some 3,000. On my arrival, I without delay sent a circular round to announce that a meeting would be held at such an hour in the evening, at such a place; nor was this in vain. The attendance and the attention were good, and both tracts and conversation were sought after the service.

"WEDNESDAY, 13th.—Left Leogane this morning about daylight for Jacmel, a distance of some fifteen leagues, through a mountainous and exceedingly picturesque country, well watered. We reached our destination about dark, and were kindly entertained by a friend to whom I had a letter of introduction. We were tired and wet, having had to cross a serpentine stream of water on the road some eighty times.

"THURSDAY, 14th.—This morning I presented my passport to the Mayor of the town. Such a civil officer, it is right to observe, is the result of the revolution which has just taken place, everything of this nature having been previously done by military men.

"Jacmel is a clean, neat, and healthy town, on the southern shore of Hayti, with a population of some 7,000, and of considerable commercial importance. At this date there was no Protestant missionary establishment in this town. By the call of a circular, we had a large congregation this evening, all listening with profoundest attention, notwithstanding all were Roman Catholics. I was allowed to use the National Schoolroom, and some two hundred may have been present.

"FRIDAY, 15th.—This morning about four, we were on the road to Baynet. Our course was over a bad road, through a woody country, with very little to be seen, either as to population or cultivation, or indeed anything else. After eight leagues of slow traveling, we reached our journey's end for the day at noon.

"As there are no places of accommodation in Hayti, as a general thing, the traveler gets hospitality how and where he can. It must, however, be said of the Haytians, that they are even remarkable for hospitality. In this case we were allowed an empty room for our use, and in the evening we had a good attendance at a public service, which had been announced to the village during the afternoon.

"SATURDAY, 16th.—This morning about four o'clock, we left Baynet for "Côte de Fer," another small, but important and singularly situated village, standing by the sea-side, about ten leagues from Baynet. Our road to this place was distressingly bad, and through a very dreary country. On entering this strange-looking little village, about mid-day, I inquired for the Mayor of the place, whom I soon found, and was very well received by him. He made me welcome to his house, and during my stay in the village I lodged with him.

"The object of my journey being explained to this worthy magistrate, he forthwith procured for me a suitable place for the preaching of the Gospel that evening, and the attendance was quite encouraging. Probably the Gospel had never been preached in this village before; certainly not by any Wesleyan Missionary. The following day being the Sabbath, an announcement was made for another meeting the following evening.

"SUNDAY, 17th.—To-day being the Sabbath, I remained at Côte de Fer. Nothing was to be seen or heard here during the whole day, but arms, drums, and traffic; the Sabbath being at this time the great market-day throughout Hayti. The Mayor did his best to get a good attendance for this evening, and particularly requested me to speak to the people on the general subject of industry, which I unhesitatingly did, and we had quite a numerous meeting.

"This is one of the most singular places that I have ever seen. One has here the idea of being shut out of the Republic, a most isolated place, seemingly cut off from everywhere else. Crime of any kind, one might suppose, might be practiced here, with even impunity, and yet the people are evidently of a mild and interesting character.

"MONDAY, 18th.—This morning it was difficult to catch our horses, and therefore we did not start early; at last, however, all was ready, and the Mayor with the Vice-Mayor, accompanied us a couple of leagues outside the village on our way to the Vieux Bourg d'Aquin, some twelve or fourteen leagues distance.

"The greater part of our journey between Le Vieux Bourg and Côte de Fer, was through a hot, sandy, and rather desert country; the heat and monotony of which made it quite fatiguing. On this sandy road we halted in the course of the morning and partook of what we had with us; then proceeding, we soon reached the fertile plains of Aquin, and entered the old Bourg* about 5 P. M.

* Village.

"This small but well-known village, was commanded by a military officer, to whom I presented myself and passport. This colored gentleman received me with politeness, and gave me a hearty welcome to his house. I told him that, notwithstanding I was fatigued, I should like to preach the Gospel in the village that evening; and inquired of him if he could procure me a place. His reply was:

"'Your passport announces you as a "Ministre de l'Evangile," and I think the Gospel should be preached in the church. Will you preach in our church?'

"I replied that I should be sorry to pain the mind of the parish priest or any one else.

"'I will then see and get you a place.'

"He went, but was soon back, and observed:

"'It is now getting late, and there is difficulty in getting a place. The parish church does not belong to the priest but to the Republic and its citizens. If you will preach in our church I will take all responsibility upon myself, for there is but one Gospel, and that Gospel ought to be preached in the church!'

"I therefore consented, and about 7 P. M. the commandant got the little church lighted up, and ordered the bell to be rung. Nearly the whole village must have come together, for the meeting was very large.

"On entering the church, I took my stand by the side of the Virgin Mary; she seemed to be nearly my own height, was well-dressed, but said not a word! 'A mouth but they speak not!' All was deep attention, and in the midst of the sermon the priest, who had attended a funeral in the plain, came up; he listened silently at the door, and when all was over, the commandant presented me to Monsieur l'Abbé le ——, who received me with great blandness, and we spent some little time in conversation. Before leaving he invited me to take coffee with him the next morning, which I promised to do.

"TUESDAY, 19th.—Left this singular, and to me ever memorable old village. Before day-light the next morning, as I rode along the road, it appeared to me amazing, not only that I should have preached in a Roman Catholic church, but that a Roman Catholic country, so evidently open to truth, should be so little thought of, or sought as a mission-field.

"Continuing our journey, we soon arrived at the large town of Aquin, and, en passant, I according to promise, took café with the Abbé, who resided here, the distance from the Vieux Bourg being about a league. Our course was now through a pleasant country, and on leaving the town of Aquin, we soon arrived at the very neat little village of St. Louis du Sud, which in the time of the French appears to have been an important place. Here we could do nothing more than leave a few tracts, and then went on till we arrived at the rather large village of Cavaillon, about seven leagues from Aquin.

"We arrived at Cavaillon about mid-day, and I immediately presented myself to the Mayor, to whom I explained that the object of my visit was simply to preach the Gospel, and at the same time begged hospitality and a place to preach in that evening, both of which were very promptly assured. We soon made everything known through the place, and about seven in the evening, a large congregation came together at the place appointed, consisting of respectable and intelligent people; in fact, there seemed to me to be something specially interesting in the general bearing and character of the people of this neighborhood as though it was a special centre of intelligence.

"WEDNESDAY, 20th.—Arrived at the city of Cayes, about 11 A. M., and was kindly received by an American friend, who was a member of the municipality of the city. The same evening we held a meeting, and although the notice was very short, we had a good congregation.

"THURSDAY, 21st.—To-day presented myself at the municipality, where I was heartily welcomed by the Mayor and the rest of the members of this corporate body, most of whom appeared to be educated and intelligent men. Having stated the object of my visit to the Mayor, he very kindly offered me the use of one of his own houses, which was just finished and which had in it a very spacious room on the ground-floor. But the funeral of the parish priest was to take place that evening, and I therefore desisted from doing anything until the next evening. Being thus at liberty, I attended this funeral service myself; the crowd present was very great; but of all the intolerable bawling I ever heard, in the name of divine worship, never did I hear anything to be compared to this. The chanting was literally vociferous, and the responses on the part of the people amounted, at times, to a perfect scream. Never was I so thoroughly fatigued and disgusted, for I knew that the people were roaring out from the top of their throats words of which they knew nothing. At the end of this dreadful storm, which was called chanting the praises of God, it was a great relief to hear an intelligent and rather eloquent funeral oration from a French priest, with whom I had the pleasure of supping afterwards at a friend's house, which afforded us the opportunity of a good deal of very pleasant conversation.

"FRIDAY, 22d.—This morning sent a circular round the city inviting the inhabitants of Cayes to a public service that evening, and at 7 o'clock we had a numerous and attentive congregation. The novelty of a Protestant service was doubtless powerful, for, with the exception of a visit many years before from a member of the Society of Friends, no such meeting had ever been previously held in this city.

"SATURDAY, 23d.—Spent the day in visiting the people, accompanied by my kind host. Wherever we went we were kindly received. In the evening we held another public service, which was very numerously attended.

"SUNDAY, 24th.—The usual sound of arms and commerce during the greater part of the day, there being then no observance of the Sabbath day in Hayti. In the evening held another public service, which was well attended.

"MONDAY, 25th.—This afternoon, in company with Mr. D., called upon a colonel in command here, who, finding I was resolved to cross the island by way of Plymouth Mountain, offered to send some military men with me, both as guides and guards, which offer I gladly accepted.

"In the evening I held my last meeting at Cayes during this visit, and had a good attendance. At the first of these meetings there may have been upwards of two hundred persons listening and looking on from all directions, for in the tropics, it will be remembered, that all dwelling-houses are as open as possible.

"TUESDAY, 26th.—This morning left Cayes at day-light for Jérémie. We were accompanied by an individual who was sent with us by the colonel at Cayes, already referred to, as far as the military post called Camperan, with orders to the colonel commanding there to send men on with us over the far-famed Plymouth Mountain. We arrived at Camperan early in the evening, it being only about six leagues from Cayes. The colonel here received us in the kindest manner possible, and after some refreshment, and examining some specimens of coal found in that neighborhood, he accompanied us two leagues on to another military post, where he left orders for men to be sent across the mountain with us. Here we remained for the night in one of the most wilderness-looking places I ever saw anywhere. The people in this elevated region were exceedingly rough, but not unkind. We attempted prayer, but order was out of the question, still we did the best we could.

"WEDNESDAY, 27th.—Left this post about day-light, accompanied by three soldiers, armed with broadswords, who were under orders to accompany and see us safe across this terrible mountain, which we began to ascend immediately on leaving this last military post. Before long we discovered the nature of our case, and the entire correctness of all that had been told us of this frightful mountain-pass. In many places the mountain was so steep, and the rocks so nearly perpendicular and rugged, that it was necessary to dismount and set ourselves heartily to work at climbing, while our poor horses, even without their riders, were also at times in the greatest difficulty to keep upon their feet. After a great deal of such toiling, as in all my experience in traveling I had never gone through before, we at last reached the summit of this great elevation, but before we could find a suitable place where we might pause, as it was now about mid-day, we had to wade through mud up to our horses' bellies. This, however, did not continue long, and we soon found a place where grass was growing which was green and inviting. Here we halted, to the great satisfaction of exhausted horses and men.

"From this lofty summit, the view stretching over the rich outspread plains below on either side, reaching to the ocean, which was now before us, both on the north and south side was grand beyond description. What the precise altitudinal measurement of this mountain may be, I will not pretend to say; it may be however, some 4,000 feet above the level of the sea; but the fact of seeing the ocean on both sides from the same point will give some idea of its height. The sight was perfectly splendid, the climate also was salubrious, and even bracing, although it was noon when we ceased ascending.

Our much-needed and refreshing meal being over, we commenced our descent. This I preferred to do on foot, in this cold and invigorating region. Our downward course, although not rocky, was at times very rough; but we at last reached 'la Riviere glacée,' where our guards left us in charge of three others, who had orders to go on with us to the village of Coraail, which was quite at the bottom of the north side of this great mountain, on the sea-shore. About 5 o'clock P. M. we arrived at a cottage by the road-side, where feeling quite fatigued, I begged and obtained hospitality for the night. This poor fellow urged me to go on, assigning as his reason, that I should get comforts at the village of Corail, which he could not afford me. I however remained, and we were quite comfortable. Our water, and all else needful, was found. No small solace to a weary traveler.

"THURSDAY, 28th.—About daylight this morning we were on our way for the village of Corail, which we reached in a couple of hours. On arriving at this village, I was very civilly received by the military officer to whom I had to present my passport. But to my great dismay, on seaching for it, I found that I had left it at Cayes; this was really mortifying. I remembered that I had left it in the hands of the Mayor of the last-named city. The officer observed that he had no doubt of my honesty, but he did not see how, according to law, I could continue my future course without a passport; he however sent for the Mayor, who, on hearing the case, shook his head quite significantly, as though it was a most serious affair, although we had military men with us who could not have come without special orders; but he left us, requesting us at the same time to remain where we were.

"I therefore was now rather in the position of a prisoner than otherwise. But I was soon cited to appear before the municipal board of Corail. These gentlemen received me very politely, and begged me to be seated. One of the members inquired of me, quite officially, if I had a passport? I replied that I had left Port au Prince with one, but had left it by mere forgetfulness in the hands of the Mayor of Cayes, from which place I had just arrived. I was then asked if I could show my ordination credentials. I replied that they were buried in the ruins of Cape Haytien. It was then demanded what countryman I was, and having answered that I was from England, one of the Board, in broken English, and with no small difficulty, put me to the test, by speaking to me in my own language, and I had no sooner replied than he pronounced me to be an Englishman.

"I was told, however, that I must remain at Corail until I got my passport from Cayes. This would have cost me such a loss of time as would have defeated all my plans and arrangements, and I therefore protested against this delay, proposing at the same time that they should send me on to Jérémie—my journey's outward terminus—under military guard. This being assented to, I invited this municipal corps to a public service that evening, which I told them I hoped to hold somewhere; upon which one of them immediately offered me the use of his house, which I gladly accepted; and at the hour appointed, we had quite a large company.

"Friday, 29th.—This morning, about three o'clock, left this memorable place for Jérémie. My military guard was of course to have gone with me; but he told me that he had no shoes; that the road was very bad; that it was dark, cold, etc.; to all which I replied that I could do very well without him, and went on, leaving him to follow when he pleased. The morning was very dewy, and on the hills which we had to cross, it was even cold, so that the sun was welcome when it rose.

"We traveled through a picturesque country, pretty well populated, and not without cultivation. About mid-day, we entered Jérémie, where we were heartily welcomed by brother Bauduy, our missionary, who was at this time residing at this place. In the evening, I preached to an interesting and rather numerous company.

"The town of Jérémie has a population of five or six thousand, and is remarkable for its salubrious climate, being open to the sea. It was here that the Revolution which has just been accomplished took its starting strength. The Gospel here has its open course; much has already been done, and our hopes are good.

"Fever now laid hold of me, and I suffered severely for about a week: but on the 10th of January, 1844, I left Jérémie, being now accompanied by brother Bauduy, who left with me for our annual District Meeting, which was to be held at Port au Prince. Our whole company, therefore, consisted of four men, and four horses. We left Jérémie towards evening, simply to cross the river, which runs near by Jérémie, and thus be ready for a fair start in the morning.

"THURSDAY, 11th.—About 2 A. M., we left the banks of this river, on our way to Corail. The moon was in full splendor, and the morning air was invigorating. I was indeed weak, and scarcely fit for the journey, but was resolved to do the best I could. We reached Corail before mid-day, and this time our passports were at hand. We held a public service in the evening, and had a good attendance.

"FRIDAY, 12th.—This morning, about 7 o'clock, we left by sea in a canoe for Pestel, to which place we sent our horses on before over the mountains, which route might probably have been too great a trial for my weakness, in my invalid state. We soon arrived at this very singular little village, which is situated on the side of a very steep and rugged mountain, running down to the sea, without leaving any level land. In the evening we held a public service, which made no small stir in this really isolated place. In all probability, it was the first time that a Protestant pastor had ever preached the Gospel here. The attendance was numerous, and the attention profound.

"SATURDAY, 13th.—Left Pestel this morning, about two o'clock, for Baradere—a journey of about nine leagues. The road we found to be both bad and dangerous; our traveling was therefore slow, and we did not reach Baradere until about mid-day. This village stands in a nicely watered dale, a little in from the sea. It is surrounded by very fertile hills, and the general appearance of nature here is rich and beautiful. We had a letter to the Preposé, who received us very kindly, and made us welcome. In the afternoon, we called upon the priest, whom we found to be an intelligent man. The public service which we held in the evening was well attended.

"SUNDAY, 14th.—During the former part of the day, nothing but traffic, drums and arms. The market was held in front of the church; many therefore profited, leaving their merchandize outside, and running in to say a prayer, bow, cross, and then fly out again to their gains.

"In the evening we held a public service. In the course of what was said, I declared that there was but one Mediator between God and man, and that neither the Virgin nor any one else could take his place; on which the priest, whom we had visited in the course of the afternoon, being outside, *incog.*, broke out with fury, and in a defiant tone, demanded where I had found my religion. I made no reply, and the police ordered him to be quiet, on which he walked quietly away.

"MONDAY, 15th.—Left Baradere about 8 A. M., in an open boat, for Petit Trou, sending our horses on by land to meet us at that place. The men that rowed us, having a bottle of taffia (rum) with them, our safety was soon endangered, and we were really glad to land at Petit Trou. We were kindly received by the Colonel commanding there, to whom we had a letter of introduction, and who, on hearing our wishes, soon found us a suitable place for an evening service, which having been announced, was well attended.

"TUESDAY, 16th.—About 3 o'clock this morning, we left Petit Trou for l'Anse à'Veau, and arrived there in about four hours by land. Here we were received with great hospitality by a private citizen, to whom we at once made known the object of our visit; on which our kind host immediately made us the offer of his own house, for a public service that evening. The priest, on hearing our intention, opposed us in every way; but we nevertheless had a large and respectable assembly in the evening, all manifesting even an eagerness to hear the word of truth.

"WEDNESDAY, 17th.—This morning, about 2 o'clock, we were on our way from l'Anse à'Veau to Miragoane, a distance of about nine leagues. We arrived there between 9 and 10 A. M. The country through which we passed, although fertile, was but poorly cultivated. In fact, we scarcely look for extensive cultivation in a country where there are so few capitalists, and the population so small.

"At Miragoane, we were welcomed by a black gentleman whose career is specially worthy of note. By birth he was African. With many others, he was stolen from his country when young; but he was rescued from the slaver by a British man-of-war, and left free at Sierra Leone, from which place he was sent to the Borough Road School, in London, where he received an English education, and ultimately was allowed to choose where he would be sent to—whether back to his own native land or elsewhere. He chose Hayti, and was sent there. At the time we saw him at Miragoane, he was an influential man, and since that time has occupied various posts of high importance in the Republic.

"In the evening, notwithstanding the utmost opposition of the priest, we had a good attendance at the service, which had been publicly announced.

"THURSDAY, 18th.—Left this busy, active little place, which is a seaport, about 3 A. M., and after about seven leagues' traveling, we reached Petit Goave, during the morning, where we were very kindly received by a member of the municipality of that place, who, at our request, soon found us a suitable place for a public service in the evening, which was very well attended. This nation evidently desires the Gospel.

"Petit Goave is a beautifully situated village by the seaside; well watered, and surrounded by a rich and fertile country; yet it has the reputation of being unhealthy.

"FRIDAY, 19th.—This morning, about four o'clock, we started for Grand Goave, about three leagues on, and arrived there soon after daylight. Here we were kindly received by a military man, who immediately placed his house at our disposal for public service, etc.; but his wife and the priest together were too powerful for him, and he was therefore obliged to retract. We at once proceeded to the house of the Mayor, where, unexpectedly, we met with the priest, who without hesitation gave us to understand that he was opposed to our intentions as to public service; but brother Bauduy reminded him that he was in his own country, and declared that he would not give up his liberty to him. The Mayor, who was present, allowed us the use of the National School-room; and the violent opposition of the priest procured us a good congregation.

"SATURDAY, 20th.—Left Grand Goave this morning about three o'clock, for Leogane. We traveled through a very rich and not badly cultivated country. Our day's work this time was heavy, and we arrived at the town of Leogane towards evening, quite fatigued. We nevertheless attempted a service in the evening, at the house of a friend, who had very kindly received us; but an African dance close by rendered it impossible.

"These heathenish assemblies usually take place either at the death of some one, or on the occasion of prayer for the dead some time afterwards; in fact the occasions for dancing and feasting in Hayti are many. Wakes, house warmings, baptisms, etc., are all times of dissipation, especially with certain classes; and in some cases, even property has been sold to furnish the extravagance of these thoroughly heathenish occasions.

"SUNDAY, 21st.—This morning, President Riviere rode into Leogane, from Port au Prince. He was on horseback, and his suite was quite modest and unassuming. Soon after his arrival, he reviewed a regiment, and announced that the Government had decided on rewarding every soldier of that corps with twelve acres of land each, for the very active part they took in the late great struggle.

"In the evening, we held another public service; but the same heathenish dance was repeated, and we therefore had but few hearers.

"MONDAY, 22d.—Left Leogane about 1 A. M., and arrived at our journey's end, Port au Prince, at an early hour, where we found all well, and were glad of rest.

"With regard to the country through which this long journey led, much might be said, both as to general cultivation, as well as the character and condition of the people. As to nature, all was rich and beautiful; but for want of the order which results from cultivation, all was more or less wild. The roads, as usual, indicated want of public spirit and judgment, although not entirely neglected; and although this great peninsula is more populated than perhaps any other part of the Republic, yet the want of population was very apparent. Farms and properties are wide apart, and poorly, if at all, fenced in; hence the general appearance, from the various hills and elevations over which we passed, would rather represent a rich wilderness than otherwise. Coffee plantations were numerous, but greatly, and perhaps inevitably, neglected; for it must be remembered that military duties had hitherto absorbed every other. The cottages also, although in some cases neat, both as to the exterior and also the interior, would generally have a slovenly appearance, which by many travelers would doubtless be attributed to mere indolence and sloth. Unquestionably this to too great an extent would be true. Let, however, the facts of the case be fairly weighed.

"First, we have here to do with an uneducated mass, whose views and wants would necessarily be, in all respects, limited, and who had been left, for more than a quarter of a century, entirely to themselves.

"Secondly, a military system, which was ever draining away the farmer and the laborer from their work, and in fact, which rendered it impossible for anything really continuous to be perseveringly kept up. The condition of the people, therefore, in any respect, was not simply the result of indolence.

"It will be evident from these notes, that we frequently met with highly intelligent people, of all shades of color. Forty years of independence had given to the people, the majority of whom were blacks, such an air and gait of manliness, as can belong only to men who are fully conscious of the rights and dignity of freedom, and who also feel that they are living in their own free country, under their own institutions, with their laws administered by themselves, apart from all foreign influence or power. In fact, independence has fully stamped its impress upon the Haytian character, needing, no doubt, such modifications as can only result from greater national experience, and yet greater contact with the foreign element; for it can never be supposed, not even for a moment, that independence, which is the life and glory of any people, can be in any sense exclusive.

"In fact, the hope of general good, as the result of the great Revolution which had just been accomplished, was evidently very great; and it is quite true that every way was now fully thrown open for this; but it was little thought of, and yet less understood, that the moral element of a people constitutes one of its main and vital springs—so much so, that, this corrupt and unsound, leaves but little to hope for, whatever may be the amount of general intelligence.

CHAPTER IX.

Remarks on the Journey.—Provisional Government attempts the Education of the Masses.—Riviere takes Azua.—Gurrier proclaimed President.—Postal Arrangements.—Riviere attempts to land.—Death of Guerrier.—Pierrot President.—He enters Port au Prince.—A strange sight at Port au Prince.—Baptist Mission founded at Jacmel.—Riché proclaimed President.—Wesleyan School opened at Port au Prince.

The postal messenger, o'er hill and dale,
Char'g with the people's written thoughts, proclaims
Another onward step.

THE notes of the journey which terminated the preceding chapter, afford good ground for reflection in reference to Hayti and its general social features, etc., at that time. The views of religious liberty which then prevailed, will be seen in the fact that the Missionaries, as in this case, were traveling through a Roman Catholic country, which was under the care of a Roman Catholic clergy, were Evangelical Protestants. These individuals, too, were going through the country for the avowed purpose of publicly preaching the Gospel according to their own religious views and convictions, and wherever they went, they openly and fully made known their object, at the same time inviting both the authorities and people to their meetings, who all patronized, encouraged, and even helped them in every way. These Missionaries also, it will be observed, were at perfect liberty to converse, either controvertially or otherwise, with the people, or to distribute the Scriptures among them in their own language. No restrictions are placed upon them, as to the distribution of tracts, attacking the national Church, or anything else they pleased. In fact, notwithstanding the entire bearing of this journey was unfavorable to the national creed, not the slightest restraint is put upon them. It is a singular fact, also, that the Missionaries wrote out their own passports, giving themselves liberty to preach wherever they went, and had only to send them to be signed by the proper authorities of their place of residence. This was such liberty as had never existed in Hayti since the days of Petion; and the Provisional Government, then reigning, was its source. Perhaps it might even be asserted, that such full and entire religious liberty did not exist, and never had, in any Roman Catholic country in the world.

It must also be borne in mind, that revolutionary feelings, at that time, animated the entire mass of the people, and that there was even a spirit of emulation, each one seeming to aim at surpassing the other in liberal views. Under such remarkable circumstances, it will be easily understood that the true and genuine character of the Haytian people, not to say human nature, would be fully brought out before the world. Such was the case, nor did ever people give greater proof of the existence among them of a deep, profound, and universal desire for every kind of progress and improvement than was shown by the Haytians during this "Gouvernement Provisoire."

With regard to the Missionary, it was not simply that he was allowed to pass on unmolested in the name of toleration and freedom, but he was eagerly received. There was a burning desire for the truths which he was known to preach; the people confessed and deplored their darkness.

About this time, one of the leading members of the Government then in power, in a conversation with one of the Wesleyan Missionaries, made the following remarks: "Sir, if I could have it so, every man in Hayti should have a Missionary!" In the same conversation, the same functionary observed, on the subject of religious liberty: "It is not merely toleration that I wish of our Government, but I wish it to be understood that religious liberty, like every other, is a right to which every man is heir!"

In fact, this was a glorious moment in Hayti, for everything relating to the best interests of the nation.

These facts were fully made known to the friends of missions in England, but up to that time, all, since the death of Petion, had been dead and uninteresting.

President Boyer had left the Missionaries unprotected, and had even advised them to leave the country; a fact which had for years past thrown a gloom on every missionary effort in Hayti. Hence, with regard to the present bright moment, the fear was, that it was simply the flashing meteor of a revolution, which would soon disappear. All the entreaties, therefore, were in vain, and to the cry of "Come over and help us!" all ears were stopped; * an indifference ever to be deplored, as will be seen in the fact that what had been done by the two first Missionaries stood firm, notwithstanding every element was at last against them, and that the present spirit of the nation was so changed as to give every assurance that the work accomplished would not only have been now immovable, but highly aggressive upon error and vice, whatever after difficulties might have occurred.

Another characteristic, which was even prominent under the Provisional Government, was an attempt at the education of the masses, an attempt truly laudable in itself, but it brought out the fearful fact that the means for an universal Christian education were wanting. Where find the men of heart and soul for such a work? Yet the need of it was felt, and the attempt was made; but the deep moral sleep into which the country had been plunged during the last quarter of a century had almost withered its energies; and, notwithstanding much was done, yet the unhappy masses sunk at last to their former level.

The parents of the new rising generation, as well as their ancestors, had done, to a very great extent,

* It is not meant here, that absolutely nothing was done for Hayti, but when a whole Roman Catholic nation suddenly starts open, and even calls upon Protestants Churches for help, as was the case in this instance, could any discouragement be more icy to a Missionary in such a case, than that not one single extra effort of any kind should be made in reply to such a call? Well might the Roman Catholic clergy express their amazement at Protestant indifference to so extraordinary a call. Truly such an opening for Rome would not have been so lost.

without education, and had even won their liberty; and the cry in many cases was, why should not things go on in the same way? Nor was it surprising that the untutored masses should be wrong, deeming, as they did, the labor of their children to be needful for the support of their families.

Doubtless these difficulties might have been overcome by dint of untiring perseverance, but the infidel element of the French Revolution had not been without its influence upon Hayti, and a Christian education for the masses was therefore scarcely to be expected, however much its need might be felt.

The case in hand will be explained by the remarks of a Secretary of State about this time to an English merchant: "Why do you not," inquired the merchant, "put such and such policemen, for such and such posts?" The Secretary of State simply replied, "Because, sir, there are no such men to be found!" This was the case with the education in question. Had the education needed been simply literary, there would have been no difficulty. Nor need this be any matter of surprise, for we are not, in the nature of things, to expect fruit anywhere, the seed of which has not been first sown. Such was the position of Hayti. Its starting-point of national existence cannot be said to have been the Word of God: notwithstanding its struggles were righteous, the elements of its birth were not those of the "Pilgrim Fathers!" whose first object of solicitude was the education of every child among them. The circumstances, indeed, of Hayti were altogether different; nor are we seeking here so much to blame as to explain.

It is not to be wondered at that such a commencement of national existence should have engendered not only a love of arms, but a swarm of other evils, which in after days it would not be easy to root out, or even gradually to correct. It must, however, be admitted, that the tendency of the Boyer Government was unfavorable to African usages; its heathenish dances were frowned upon; but with this there was a moral vacuum, evil was sought to be abolished, without filling up its place with positive good.

One great and important event which resulted from the Revolution by Riviere was the establishment of a Wesleyan Primary Day School for boys and girls. The founding of this institution at Port au Prince, was the result of a proposition on the part of the municipality of that capital to the Wesleyan Missionaries then residing there. It was proposed to them, that if they would undertake the direction of a primary school, which should be open to the children of both sexes, the corporate body of the city would meet the expenses, leaving the Missionaries at liberty as to its management in all respects.

This offer was promptly accepted, and in the course of the year it fell to the lot of the Rev. J. T. Hartwell to conduct the opening of th school, the Mayor of Port au Prince presiding on the occasion.

This school was for a long time held in the Wesleyan church, and it soon became prosperous and encouraging.

Here also we have full proof of the liberal spirit which pervaded the nation about the time of this extraordinary Revolution. In all probability, there was not at that time one Protestant member of the municipality. They were, nevertheless, not indifferent to religious creeds, but they were free from religious bigotry; they had seen and known the Wesleyan Missionaries for some time, and they doubtless had watched their lives and labors, and were convinced of the soundness of their general principles, and of the entire honesty of their motives.

These gentlemen of the municipality of the day, were of nearly all shades except really and fully white, and of good education, their sole object in this remarkable movement being the public good; in fact it it is evident that the noblest feelings animated a great many of the Haytians in this great national Revolutionary movement,—we say a great many, for it is a deplorable fact that a great many tares ultimately appeared in this great event. The grand idea of the movement was national "regeneration!" but it was forgotten that God only can regenerate human nature.

Towards the beginning of 1844, rumors began to be heard of movements and dissafection among the Spaniards in the eastern part of the Island, who, it will be remembered, had for some time past lived under the Haytian flag.

Two or three executions had already taken place since Riviere's accession to power, the offences of the guilty ones being purely political; here is one of the strange things which stares out ludicrously in these ephemeral and hollow Revolutions. A man, or a party, get into power through an armed and military Revolution, and they immediately consider that they at once have a right to put to death the man who does precisely the same thing; which is simply a confession that they themselves deserve the same penalty. What can result from this but bitterness, mutual hate, and party feeling? while the universal demand would naturally be, who are these who thus assume over their brothers? notwithstanding these very same brothers assume in their turn, even unto death. In fact, Hayti ought long ago to have known, above all other countries, that executions for political offences are the most impolitic of all acts.

Certain tendencies too of the Government, now began to appear, of a most unhappy nature. It became gradually apparent that the civil Institutions of the country, which had been the result of the Revolution, were becoming distasteful to the powers that were, hence the cry was soon heard that Riviere had proved false to his pledges. For a short time this was only muttered, but these thoughts and feelings gradually acquired strength.

News now poured in from the Spaniards. It was known that they were in arms against the Haytian Government; and on the 9th of March, 1844, Riviere left the Capital again, with an army of considerable force, to subdue the Spaniards and reduce them to submission; here was indeed the beginning of grief. Many who had been looking for peace, prosperity and happiness, as the result of the new state of things, were now torn from their families to go on a long and exhausting march of perhaps three hundred miles out, over rivers and mountains, against the Spaniards, their neighbors and their brothers!

News of the advance of the Haytians was continually coming in, until at last it was known that a contest between the two forces had taken place, and that Riviere had taken Azua; but the heart of the nation was already sick. Party feeling now ran high. Riviere's egregious errors, in seeking to put down the civil Institutions which had sprung up from his own Revolution, became the support of his most violent enemies. For a time all seemed uncertainty and suspense, until the morning of the 3rd of May, when General Guerrier was publicly nominated to the Presidency at Port au Prince, on the Place Petion; the reason assigned being, that Riviere had violated his oath to support the Constitution; and on the 9th of May, only six days later, Philip Guerrier was proclaimed President of Hayti!

Thus fell the man who had taken up arms to regenerate his country. Civil Institutions had risen up at his beck, but they were no sooner established than he sought to destroy the work of his own hands, that he might reign by the power of the sword; hence he fell, covered with shame, nor did he ever re-enter that Capital which but a few short months before he had entered so triumphantly. His army, which gradually learnt the truth of things, abandoned their General to his fate, and returned to Port au Prince by small bands.

Meanwhile the newly constituted authorities, not knowing how either Reviere or the army might take these things, put the Capital in a state of defence. The whole population of the city, capable of bearing arms, was enrolled and formed into a temporary sort of militia force; the ramparts and forts were manned, sometimes by soldiers in uniform, sometimes by plain citizens without. In fact, the reactionary feeling of indignation was decided and intense,—on the part of the friends of the old Government, because they considered the Revolution against Boyer to have been unjust,—and on the part of the former friends of Riviere, because they now considered him to be a traitor to his own cause. But Riviere understood his position, and he did not therefore attempt to re-enter the Capital; in fact, as we have seen, his army disbanded, while he himself embarked for Jamaica, with those whose counsels had probably ruined him. Riviere died in Jamaica, after residing there peaceably a few years.

Throughout the Southern part of the Island, where the Revolution had commenced, great dissatisfaction now prevailed. This, however, had been greatly calmed by a prudent and conciliatory deputation which had been sent for that purpose, by those who had been left in charge of the Government during the absence of the President; but peace was no sooner settled in this judicious manner, than Riviere himself deranged the whole affair through the medium of a Commission of his own, formed while he was in the Eastern part, and meaning to apply fearful severity to certain political offenders, (as he deemed them.) By this means he embittered the entire of the Southern part of the Island against himself, and originated a rebellion which ultimately was headed by an obscure individual named Acaau, who was finally named General, and for a time became powerful and exceedingly troublesome to the Government. In fact, it is easy to conceive from these statements that the general element of things was now conflicting; but General Guerrier's Government gradually acquired strength, and more or less of an onward movement seemed to be the order of the day.

A new and highly important national institution, which came into existence about this time, is worthy of special notice—we now refer to a well organized system of Postage. It is, indeed, a singular fact that a nation so long under the direction of an intelligent man, with a gradually increasing commerce, should, up to this time, have been without the means of a sure and safe postal intercourse and correspondence. Up to this date letters, etc., in the merchants' service, had been transmitted by men hired for that purpose, or by any other accidental opportunity which might occur, and was attended with more or less risk and inconvenience; but the value of the new institution, so long needed, was soon felt, and its necessity and advantage soon became its security.

In fact, all was again hopeful; the spirit of those who had been of good faith in this Revolution, now began to develope itself, as will be seen by the following extracts from one or two official Circulars, sent out this year, 1844, by "Le Ministre des Cultes et de l'Instruction Publique."

The first of these remarkable Circulars is addressed to all Judicial, Educational and Ecclesiastical functionaries, whether Roman Catholic or otherwise:

"Gentlemen,—The influence of Religion on public Education, and on the happiness of a people, is now no longer a matter of dispute.

"Napoleon the First felt the necessity of re-establishing a

public faith; his powerful legislative instinct revealed to him the fact of, no Altar! no People! No more than there could be a People without laws and magistrates.

"At the present time, smitten as we are with this great internal plague, and honestly wishing to apply the needful remedy, we, on looking into the source and cause of the disease, find ourselves compelled to see it in the neglect and indifference of our former Government, which never adopted any effectual measures for keeping out of the country evilly disposed and unworthy ministers, rejected by their own Bishops, mere intruders, whose papers no one took the trouble to examine; coming rather to cultivate our vices than to expel them; much more eager for gain than to gain souls to God; who, with impunity before an indifferent authority, have made a merchandize of Religion, adding to their scandalous simonies the scandal of a wicked life, and thus misleading a people who would have followed better examples.

"You, Ministers of the Protestant worship, continue to exercise with perfect liberty your religious rites; our creeds may be different, but our hopes are in the same God; and let all our subordinate authorities bear in mind that intolerance is a monstrous thing.

"It is worthy of the Christian pulpit publicly to preach the duty of industry, as one of the great pillars of society; and also as one of the conservative powers of our nationality. Let the sacred Word recall from their errors any who through ignorance, depravity, or any other cause, have been led to attach any importance to the color of the skin; let it be remembered that He who created our bodies, and gave them different hues, also created the soul, that nobler part of man, which is without color.

"I beg all the members of Judicial and Municipal Bodies, with the entire Clergy, Catholic or otherwise, to accept my most distinguished consideration."

The next extract is from an official Circular, sent out from the same Department of State, on the subject of Education:

PUBLIC INSTRUCTION.

"The whole system of Education is now to be reconstructed; it existed only in name under the late Government. Hence, what do we see as the result of what was done in the way of Education during the last quarter of a century? How truly is this lost time to be regretted!

"It is now evident that if, during the past prosperity of the country, there had been any real effort, on a large and becoming scale, to spread light and knowledge throughout the Republic, Hayti would, at the present time, have presented a splendid spectacle to the world; she would now have taken an honorable stand among the civilized nations of the age. Society with us has retrograded; it is, indeed, now stirred from its deepest depths.

"It is desirable that in every place, where a Municipal Body exists, some of the public funds should be devoted to the establishment of a Primary School; there can be no doubt but Government would help.

"In my judgment, it would be better that the Schools should be upon the plan of the Protestant School of the Capital, viz., for both sexes.

"I would not conclude this Circular without calling upon all Educational Committees to send me a note of all such public School Masters as render themselves especially worthy of notice, that they may receive the encouragement which is due to them. Those who devote themselves with energy to the work of banishing ignorance from society, deserve well of their country."

Another extract from a public Oration, made by the same distinguished individual, will also show the earnestness of the spirit of that day on the subject of Education. The occasion of this oration was the public distribution of prizes at the National Lyceum, after the annual examination of 1844.

On this occasion great preparations were made; the object being, not only to encourage the students to the utmost, but also to prove to the world, in the most practicable manner possible, the views and feelings of the then existing Government, on the great and important subject of Education.

It has long been customary in Hayti, at these public examinations, for the successful students to be crowned with a laurel wreath, and also to receive, occasionally, other handsome tokens of encouragement.

On this occasion the President of the Republic was present, with the Ministers of State, as well as the Foreign Consuls. A special tent was erected and decorated for this brilliant and numerous assemblage, and the intervals were cheered by military music.

Soon after the arrival of the President, Mons. H. Fery, the Secretary of State, Ministre des Cultes, etc., came forward and pronounced an Oration, from which the following is an extract:

"Jeunes Eleves *—This Educational Fête, established to demonstrate before your own families your own progress, and to distribute among you those crowns of approbation which your assiduity and ardor have merited, etc., is the patriotic joy of the authorities, by whom you are now surrounded; in fact, this touching scene reminds us all that Education effaces national distinctions and brings all hearts into unity; the spread of light abolishes prejudice, unites peoples, polishes man, and introduces into Commerce the charms of urbanity and honor.

"The youth of Hayti thirst for knowledge; they wish to drink at the fountain of truth, and seem to be impelled forward by an irresistible instinct towards the great object of their being; and we hope, therefore, that henceforth the competition will be great.

"The present Government hails this intellectual movement with delight; and, without pride, wishes to identify itself with

* Young Students.

it, and to encourage it to the utmost; knowing, as it does, that love of knowledge is the distinguishing feature of the present age; which, founded in, and ruled by religion, lights up the hopeful future of a nation.

"Perhaps, before long, you, young students, will be called by your country to bring into action the talents which you are now acquiring; therefore, under the shield of an enlightened faith and a pure morality, resist unceasingly every evil passion; amass the precious treasure; your country demands, not only enlightened men, but men whose knowledge shall be found to be of a sound and honorable character.

"May that Divine Providence, which has ever watched over Hayti, make you better than your fathers.

"Vive le President Guerrier!"

More was, indeed, said on this occasion, but perhaps the preceding extracts will suffice to show the laudable feelings which animated, not only the Secretary himself, but the nation at large.

In fact, it is impossible to read these addresses without being deeply impressed with the thoroughly liberal and noble spirit which breathes in almost every sentence of them; and the pleasure of these statements is even increased by the fact, that Mons. H. Fery was a conscientious Roman Catholic; a man of good education, great intelligence, and well worthy of his distinguished position. Indeed, it will easily be seen that the reigning spirit of the day was liberal and stirring: but alas! the Revolution, while it brought many an honest man upon the stage of action, opened at the same time the flood-gates of iniquity, and lighted up the fierce fires of party feeling, jealousy and hate.

But Divine Providence was again about to change the scene; the days of President Guerrier were now nearly numbered; he was drawing near the borders of mortality.

About this time also, Riviere made a great attempt to regain his lost seat; he hovered about his native shores, and the alarm of his approach soon ran through the nation; anxiety was, for a moment, intense; but this man had utterly lost the affections of his country.

A proclamation was issued by the Government that Riviere deserved no further compassion from the nation; there was, however, no danger; his case was lost with the people; but another wave of national sorrow, which had been feared, was coming on.

President Guerrier expired on the 15th day of April, 1845, and his death was a great grief to the whole Republic.

On the following day, General Pierrot was proclaimed President of Hayti. The residence of this Military Chief was in the Northern part of the Island, near Cape Haytien.

An idea will be formed of one of the national weaknesses, which was now prevailing, by the following simple anecdote of Pierrot, who was more a sort of military farmer than otherwise:

> "Do you observe that the chickens of the hen, all vary in color, etc., yet they all come from one source!"

It may seem inexplicable to all who are not acquainted with Hayti, as indeed it really is, that such a thing as prejudice of color should even be possible, especially where men of all hues and shades have resided, and been in such close intercourse for so many generations. It is not, however, to be concealed, that this great and unpardonable absurdity has had sufficient power in Hayti to create party-feeling. The thing itself has always been felt to be too great an outrage on common sense to be openly avowed; still President Pierrot, knowing the feelings of his country in this significant, although simple manner, openly repudiated the idea of such a thing.

But the tares of the Riviere Revolution were becoming stronger than the wheat. Good had indeed been done, as will be seen by the preceding pages. But it will not be difficult to perceive, that only one evil, thoroughly dominant, in any form, will soon generate countless others. Such was the case in this instance; the sword once drawn, is not always easily put down.

On the 8th of May, President Pierrot made his official and formal entry into Port au Prince, amidst great firing of cannon, and every other display that was considered becoming such an occasion. Still there was great uneasiness in the present state of things, as will appear from a small incident related in the journal of the Wesleyan missionary, then residing at Port au Prince.

"SUNDAY, *May* 18.—While reclining after the morning service, I heard a great bustle in the street. On looking out, I found that the whole town was in confusion—generals, colonels, officers of all grades, together with private soldiers and simple citizens, were all running together, pell mell, some on horseback, others on foot, and all in excessive haste; some falling down with their horses, others buckling on their swords, as they scampered hurriedly along. In fact, to crown the whole business, the alarm-drum was sounded, and although but few knew why, yet such a note being so well known in Hayti, all was soon confusion worse confounded.

"The history of this whole affair at last turned out to be, that the National Guard being ordered to the frontiers, instead of going forthwith, demanded time to prepare, and were therefore considered by the President to be in a state of rebellion. Hence the alarm-drum, and all the ludicrous scene that followed. For a few moments all was terror and confusion, but everything soon subsided, and all was peace."

The fact was, that the general state of things just at this moment, was very excitable. The Western part of the Republic was not pleased at the course pursued by the people of the North; but party-feeling would have a northern man, however unfit.

Towards the latter end of this year, a few misguided men attempted a stir in the town of Leogane, not far from Port au Prince; but some of them, in their struggles with the authorities, were shot, and the thing was put down.

During this year the English Baptist mission was commenced at Jacmel, by the Rev. E. Francis, who landed at Jacmel December 10, 1845. His urbanity soon won upon the people; but to the grief of that entire community, he was soon called away by death. He died July 26, 1846.

The very prompt manner in which this first English Baptist Missionary had gained upon the public at large, afforded the strongest hope of success, had his valuable life been spared. He was, however, soon well and effectively succeeded by the Rev. W. H. Webley, who landed at Jacmel from England on the 14th of February, 1847, and by whose intelligent and untiring zeal an interesting church of several members was soon formed. Before long a suitable place of worship was erected, the entire frame-work of which, with the workmen, came out from the United States, which the Missionary himself had visited for the direction of this important undertaking.

The whole of this building is well planned, and combines under the same roof both the church and dwelling. The hall, serving as church on the ground floor, is spacious, and might accommodate about two hundred and fifty hearers. Two rows of Corinthian pillars, while they give an air of elegance to the interior of the church, support at the same time the dwelling above. The pulpit is of American style, with a commodious sofa in it; in the communion stands a powerful, but sweet American melodeon, the gift of the deservedly beloved Mrs. Webley, whose mortal remains were committed to the earth in the graveyard at Jacmel, by the Wesleyan Missionary, M. B. Bird, of Port au Prince, on the 30th of October, 1852.

The front of this building facing the street, with its bold Corinthian columns outside, although of wood, as is the whole structure, has a somewhat imposing appearance, especially for such a town as Jacmel, and to one of Protestant feelings, is exceedingly gratifying.

On the 13th of March, 1853, this handsome hall, serving as church, was as such opened and dedicated to the public worship of God by the same Wesleyan Missionary, who but a few months previous had performed the mournful duties above referred to.

The openings and dedications of such buildings for such high purposes justly form important and deeply interesting epochs in the annals of Haytian Protestantism:

Temples where truth stand, naked and uncarved,
Bold as eternity, nor veiled, nor marr'd!

The congregations at these opening services, morning and evening, consisted mostly of Roman Catholics, the greater part of whom were of good education, and of the highest respectability. In fact, the hearty welcome given to this event by the Roman Catholics as well as Protestants of Jacmel was evident, marked, and hopeful; and it is gratifying to add, that truth has long silently told upon error in this great work.

This important mission was now, therefore, finally established. But the friends of missions have to remember, that in all such cases, it is simply the nursery that is completed, the main work still remaining to be done.

The great work of education was well and earnestly commenced at this station, and the good that was done by means of a prosperous school, in a comparatively short time, by two devoted English ladies, was incalculable in worth, and in some cases, will doubtless be everlasting in duration. But circumstances ultimately came on, which withdrew these ladies from this institution, and their loss may be considered to have been a calamity to the Mission, and to the town of Jacmel. Had this institution continued, the good that would have been realized—if we may judge by its success during the few years of its existence—would doubtless have been incalculable. It is, therefore, to be deplored, that needful means were not furnished to this Mission for this purpose: the support and continuance of such a school, in such a community, would have been worthy of any and every sacrifice.

Pierrot's Government soon became unsatisfactory; the utter unsuitableness of the man seemed to be the universal conviction of the nation. This gradually increased, until the 28th February, when the alarm-gun was again fired from the national fort of Port au Prince. There seemed, however, to have been so general an expectation of this, that the effect was not very terrific; and on the 1st of March, 1846, the public was informed that General Riché had been named President of Hayti. But for some ten or eleven days after this announcement, the whole country was in suspense, not knowing how the southern part of the island, which was still in a state of excitement and agitation, might view this singularly rapid change. Nor could it be known at the moment how the people in the North would submit to such a dismissal of the President, who was principally of their choice, and who was living amongst them. In fact, it was uncertain whether peace or war would be the result of these seemingly hurried steps of putting Pierrot aside for Riché. But the entire unfitness of the man dismissed, seemed to overcome every other consideration throughout the country; and on the 12th of March, 1846, General Riché, with all due formality, was proclaimed President of Hayti, on which day he himself appeared on l'Autel de la Patrie, at Port au Prince, where, with an uplifted sword in one hand, and a recently remodeled Constitution in the other, in the presence of a great multitude, he swore fidelity to the nation, which was followed by loud vivas, and firing of cannon. In fact, there were very hearty and general demonstrations of joy. The national feeling on this occasion, and in favor of the change, being unanimous, or nearly so.

All being over here, the whole procession moved solemnly on to the cathedral church, attended with every possible display of music. At the church the usual ceremonies were performed, to which was added an eloquent oration from the priest.

On the 24th of March, 1846, President Riché took the oath of fidelity to the nation, officially, and with all due formality.

Things now were tranquil, and the country once more seemed to have the hope of better days; in this, there can be no doubt, that both the President and his ministers were entirely sincere.

The President now chosen, although not a man of education, was doubtless of good faith with the people, and being surrounded as to his cabinet, etc., by well-educated and intelligent men, in whom he had entire confidence, the general impression seemed to be in all respects favorable.

It will be remembered that in 1843, the municipal body of Port au Prince proposed to the Wesleyan Missionaries then residing in that city, that they should commence a public school, to be gratuitously open to both sexes, and that the institution should be sustained by the municipality; but the various changes which subsequently took place, had proved unfavorable to this establishment. Up to 1847, it had received more or less encouragement from the different Governments which had succeeded the days of Riviere. The municipality which gave it birth having changed its form of existence, and lost many of its pecuniary resources;—in fact, circumstances had so changed, and the means of supporting this important institution were now so completely embarrassing, that it became a question whether it should stand or fall. The great difficulty was the creation of funds. The Mission funds of England, it was said, were raised purely for the preaching of the Gospel; hence there was no hope from that quarter. The Missionary, therefore, was compelled to appeal to the public, or cease this now important department of his work.

To allow such a school to disappear was impossible, numbering as it did at that time some three hundred scholars, of both sexes, to whom the Word of God was taught, and so preached as unquestionably to have justified the appropriation of Mission funds for that purpose.

The appeal for monthly subscribers was promptly and liberally responded to by many Haytians, and especially by the foreign merchants, who most of them understood this trying case. The labor of thus sustaining this Protestant institution was great; but the importance of the work was also great, and all was compensated by abundant prosperity.

A building expressly for this institution had long been desirable, the Wesleyan church having been hitherto occupied during the week for educational purposes; but the want of funds was the great difficulty. All, as to public instruction, was now dependent upon the liberality of Port au Prince. A special effort, therefore, in the way of public subscriptions, was undertaken, apart from the monthly contributions which were still going on; and the good will of the public of all classes crowned this extra effort with success. A building, fifty feet square, fifteen feet from the floor to the ceiling, having large openings, with a house for the head master attached to it, were soon completed—all being on the Wesleyan church premises.

This large school house was opened and dedicated to the great purpose of Christian education, on the 1st of July, 1846. At half-past eight o'clock on the morning of this day, Mons. Larochel, Secretary of State for Public Instruction, etc., appeared, and presided on the occasion. The whole Board of Education, with the Council des Notables, were all officially present.

The proceedings were commenced by singing, according to the usages of the school, which on this occasion was accompanied by various instruments of music, several amateurs of the capital having volunteered their services, as an expression of good-will towards the institution. At the conclusion of this sacred but hearty song, prayer was offered by the Missionary.

The chairman then explained to a numerous and respectable meeting the object in view, warmly congratulating, at the same time, the friends and supporters of this institution, on their success. The chairman in his remarks also spoke feelingly and encouragingly of those who had left their homes for the good of humanity.

This esteemed Secretary of State, having concluded a speech which was an honor both to himself and his position, and yet more so, considering him a true representative of the progeny of Ham, as he really and literally was, the edifice was formally dedicated to its great purpose by the pastor of the Methodist Church of Port au Prince, in the name of the Father, and of the Son, and of the Holy Ghost.

The principles, aims, and object of the institution were then explained by the Missionary then residing at the capital. Several others spoke on the occasion, some of whom were members of the bar, all showing great warmth and animation. One, a distinguished lawyer, declared that he felt himself bound by love to his country to be present on that occasion. He was convinced that education, founded upon genuine Christianity, was vital to the prosperity of Hayti.*

It was then announced to the meeting by the Missionary, that a small debt remained, which he had no doubt would soon be effaced. The National Hymn which had been composed for the institution, was then sung to the national air of England, all being terminated by prayer.

It should not be forgotten that the speakers on this occasion, as well as the meeting itself, consisted principally of members of the Roman Catholic communion; nor should it be overlooked that the Wesleyan school was not proposed and thus encouraged, because of any dearth of schools of the above-named communion; in fact, their aim was the education of the masses, and certainly great efforts were made for it. This institution, therefore, was patronized and encouraged from purely liberal principles and motives, as well as from an entire confidence, both on the part of the Government and people, in the Wes-

* Dumai L'Espinasse.

leyan Mission. It was doubtless a national feeling at this time, peculiar probably to Roman Catholic Hayti, to give free scope to evangelical churches, both of America and Europe; and yet indifference, on both sides of the Atlantic, to a Roman Catholic country thus entirely open to the truth of Christ, is an astonishing fact. An utter indifference seems everywhere to have reigned at this time towards Hayti.

It is true we shall have to speak of dark imperial days in Hayti; but the fact referred to will ever be a reproach to all who have ever professed a sincere Christian desire for the real welfare of Hayti, and who unquestionably at that time had it in their power to place her in the way to all they might themselves have wished—but they did not.

With regard, however, to this school, it became ultimately necessary to make it partly paying, meeting its deficiencies by voluntary subscriptions, wherever they could be obtained. In fact, it was finally thrown open to the entire Republic, as a boarding school, giving up for the present the girl's department, with the hope of undertaking the great work of female education at a future day, upon a scale and in a style which should be worthy of its vast importance; and it is worthy of notice here that a special effort for this great purpose was finally made, in the United States, and also in Europe; but it is to be deplored that neither American nor English Christians, although both called upon in behalf of this deeply interesting and important undertaking, by both public and private appeals, came up to complete this great work.

It is only due to the feelings and motives in which the public Wesleyan School at Port au Prince originated, to record here that moral culture was the thing in view, on the part of the Haytian officials who had proposed it, and that the conviction of its great and indispensable necessity was certainly one of the peculiar features in the great movement of 1843; nor is this fact at all lessened by the unhappy contrary one of its utter failure, in a national sense. In fact, there have ever been Haytians who have seen and felt the truth that it was the moral element of their country which was at fault, and although they have been overwhelmed by the great tide of human depravity, these convictions still exist, and must ultimately prevail.

CHAPTER X

Riché arrives at Cayes.—His proclamation.—He returns to the Capital.—The half-pay measure.—Death of Riché.—Soulouque President.—16th of April, 1848.—Soulouque leaves for the Spanish part.—J. T. Hartwell builds at the Cape.—Faustian the I.—M. B. Bird's memento to the Government.—Jeremiè Wesleyan Church finished by C. H. Bishop.—Opened by M. B. Bird.—A. Folsom, Esq.,—Final Coronation.—Cannibalism.—Another march to the East.—Midnight Imperial entry to Port au Prince. Dr. Smith's Pamphlet.—Science needful in Education.

Th' ancient Hebrews, daring heav'n, chose a crown,
And found the warnings of its despotism
True.

PRESIDENT Riché entered the city of Cayes on the 4th of July, 1840, and from this Southern part o fthe Republic he issued a proclamation, in which he speaks freely of the object of his official tour, which was nothing less than to subdue a revolt which had been occasioned by a few misguided individuals.

The ringleader of this unhappy affair is said to have shot himself; a miserable event, which probably put an end to further blood-shed.

A passage in the proclamation referred to, will show the spirit of the Government ruling the nation at that time, and is specially worthy of attention:

"Financial reforms will not suffice; we must have more than this. It is now time to make the foundation of our Institutions sure and solid; I shall not therefore delay revising the Constitution of 1816, in order that we may be in harmony with the leading ideas of the present age; by which means we shall be able to labor unitedly, in bringing our unhappy country out of the difficulties into which it has been plunged, by various tumults and divisions which have distracted it.

Soldiers! and companions in arms, be faithful to your standards; the moment is not far off when peace shall be the reward of our toils."

It is true this was not a civilian speech to the nation, nor has it either the air or tone of genuine Republicanism; but it is the national address of a man whom circumstances had raised to military power, but who is disposed to use it in promoting, to the best of his knowledge, the real interests of his country.

At this time, the country was indeed alternating between hope and fear, in all its interests and Institutions; but there were well meaning men at the helm of affairs, during this time of trial, and the President had at heart to show himself worthy of his high responsibility, as Chief Magistrate of the nation.

The official circulars were, about this time, singularly mild and prudent; but by the side of the greatest good, is not unfrequently found lurking evil, a truth strangely applicable to all Haytian political affairs. Hence, with all the good intentions, good theories, and good principles which may be seen even to abound in the Institutions of the country, as well as the Government proclamations &c., disappointment has long seemed to attend everything in Hayti; nor can this be any matter of surprise, the soul and spirit of the nation never yet having been strung up, even to the principles and theories of its own adoption.

In seizing their liberties, the Haytians had indeed been men, but with regard to their right use, by the fair and free working of righteous laws, this required much more than merely the indignation which brought down slavery; bursts of fury did the one, but time and sound sense alone can do the other. Meantime, it may well be expected that many an error will be committed, and that many a mortifying failure will be realized; hence the failure of the greatly needed school of navigation, &c., &c..

The cultivation of the sciences, although frequently attempted, and a great variety of apparatus procured at an immense expense for that purpose, with the fullest conviction of the boundless resources which they would open in Hayti, yet has never been persevered in. It may be said that all this is unworthy, as indeed it is, but we have only to bear in mind that a sudden leap from childhood to manhood is impossible; with this simple fact before us, we have explained the whole case of Hayti as a nation, and notwithstanding she has not satisfied either herself or her friends, the fact remains, that her true element and dignity are found in her independence.

Want of progress, therefore, in the Haytian people, has not originated in want of capacity or intelligence, as may be seen in what has already been detailed, as to national documents, plans, theories, &c., &c., but rather in the absence of that moral culture, which, apart from creeds, has God himself for its element and object, and breathes that energy which alone can lead to the final accomplishment of great enterprises, whether national or individual.

Towards the latter end of August, 1846, President Riehé returned from his tour in the South, and was welcomed to the Capital with very great joy.

The details of this tour, some of which in reference to the suppression of the revolt, which was completely put down, would be painful in the extreme, must for the present be left to the future historian of Hayti. It should be noted, however, that whatever blood was shed in the putting down the wild and senseless Acaau in the South, delivered that part of the Island from a reign of terror, and established peace and quiet throughout the rest of the nation.

It should be mentioned, that these official tours through the country, by the Chief Magistrate, are generally both formal and formidable. On such occasions the President is generally accompanied by several thousand troops, and frequently by most of the chief officers of State, but perhaps the most singular fact connected with these official journeys, is the inadequacy of the pay of the private soldier for his support. How these armies subsist, is frequently a mystery, nor will the moral bearing of the case, during a public march, bear much inspection as to the properties on the road. The origin of this evil, doubtless, dates from the very birth of the nation, when every soldier lived as he could; why such an evil should have been suffered, in any degree, to continue, is another question. If there must be an army at all, a small and thoroughly efficient one, serving as a model of order to the nation, would unquestionably be more desirable than a large one, unpaid, unfed, undisciplined, and unclad.

The Government of Hayti, after this military march in the South, pursued its course in remodeling, reforming, and correcting; in fact, the general state of things at this time was hopeful. The Government was mild, and aimed at the progressive movement of the nation, as will be seen in the following passage found in an official circular, dated September 28, 1846, addressed to the Generals in the different Arrondisements:

"Enlighten all classes of the citizens; watch with attention the general movement; second and direct it towards the great object we wish to accomplish, which is the happiness of all.'

One of the measures carried out by this Government about this time, is specially worthy of attention. This was the reduction of the army pay, and also of all other employes, to one-half, for six months; nor is it less remarkable that this was submitted to without murmur, while it told most salutarily upon the finances of the nation.

It will be remembered that on the accession to power of General Riché, it was stated that the Constitution of 1816, drawn up under Petion, was, with certain modifications, to form the groundwork of the present Government; hence, on the 14th of November, 1846, the principal bodies of the State, comprising the Senators and the Secretaries of State, met for this important work, the result of which was ultimately a proclamation from the President, in which the following remarks will be found:

"Haytians! the pirnciples of amelioration have been established, and before long we shall doubtless reap the fruit thereof. I now again call upon you for help, in the accomplishment of this great work so happily commenced, and I am sure you will support me in endeavoring to give something like certainty to the future hopes of the country."

It is true, the Anglo-Saxon would rather see the full and free operation of institutions of another order, such as call out the expression of the people's will, without the fear of tumult; but Hayti was never formed into this shape of existence—she was never put upon this tack: her Republicanism has consisted principally in the absence of a Crown. She never would have taken birth as a nation but for the sword, and when thus started, she must soon have ceased to be, had she not lived sword in hand. Her case was unquestionably peculiar, hence her course has bëen so also; she therefore inevitably became military, and it is not surprising, however much to be regretted, that she remained so. In fact, it is rather surprising, that even the theory of free and civil institutions should have found admirers at all in such a country; nor will anything be more easy to understand, than that military rule and power are utterly incompatible with free and civil institutions, hence all the struggles of Hayti. Arms here have ever been struggling with reason, and even reason herself has taken up her own enemy in self-defence, and strange to say, has even become military, until "confusion worse confounded' has been the result.

But all mortal hopes are passing and uncertain. President Riché, from whose Government so much was expected, died on the 27th of February, 1847, after a comparatively short illness; his Government had begun to create great expectations, and to inspire confidence. He died at half-past seven on the morning of the date mentioned, and in less than two hours after, the Senators met for consultation as to a successor.

On the 1st of March, following the death of President Riché, General Faustin Soulouque was chosen President of the Republic of Hayti, by the Senate, and official information to that effect was sent to the chosen General, by a deputation from that body; a more unsought, or less expected honor, was perhaps never conferred upon any man.

The election of a President by universal suffrage, appears to be a thing greatly dreaded in Hayti; notwithstanding all the reigning love of Republicanism, the fear seems to be, the tumult of a people untrained to the habit of a free expression of opinion on great national questions, and in fact, there is truth in this. Yet, whether the tumult dreaded, would in this case have involved more bloodshed, confusion, and shame, than what really resulted from the present choice, made only by a few men, will be for the present and future generations to judge, or whether it might not have saved the nation a retrograde movement, which cost it immense loss and suffering, to have allowed the free voice of the nation in the selection of the Executive.

In presenting a man before the people for election, as President of the Republic, the national honor would render it impossible that he should be in any way incompetent, while the very struggle of the nation—well managed—would be educational in its effect. It is true, the elements of party feeling, in a nation which is made up of every shade and hue of complexion, may be more numerous and complicated than elsewhere, but there is no color among men which does not admire fair play; nor could, nor would, there be so much to fear from open and straight-forward work, in the choice of a Chief Magistrate, by a whole nation, as from the limited and timid judgment of a few in such a matter, even though they might be perfectly honest in their choice and decision.

From the sketches already given in these pages of the past history of this country, it will be seen, that from the beginning numberless causes had been at work, and powerfully contributed to sow largely the seeds of every kind and degree of discord, and to set fire to the evil passions of our nature.

To the man of really Christian views and feelings, it would doubtless be painfully edifying to trace out the root and origin of these fearful passions, which broke out in Hayti about this time, although to do this perfectly, would be beyond any mortal pen.

Party feeling on the unhappy question of color, was one prominent feature in the national convulsions of this time; jealousy of power rose high, between the two great divisions of the nation, and it will not be surprising that numerical power should, in this case, have been on the side of ignorance. These leading facts may, perhaps, partly help to the right understanding of all that followed.

It is by no means intended here, to enter into the details of these matters, from which such fearful convulsions resulted; suffice it to say for the present, that in all public quarrels, more or less error will generally be found on all sides, and that while mutual recognition of imprudence would be much in accordance with the general fallibleness of human nature, it would also lead to a manly conciliation of public feeling, as well as the ultimate consolidation of the national interests, while contention as to the side of right or wrong would be useless, not to say, in such a case, pernicious.

The details of the disastrous events of 1848, which marked the beginning of the power of General Soulouque, will doubtless one day be brought out, if not by those who mingled in these fearful scenes, at least by those who will have received the facts from eye witnesses, but this cannot be, until all mere passion upon the subject is extinguished. A shade might well be thrown over this dark period of Haytian history, but these lessons of the past point out those fearful rocks upon which nations sometimes dash and wreck, serving as warnings for an erring future.

Nevertheless, the event of the 16th of April of this year is too national in its character, and too important in its bearing, to remain utterly unnoticed. Party feeling of every kind, relating to class and politics, which had now long agitated the nation, on this memorable day broke forth; hence on the morning of this Sabbath day, the army, having met at the national Palace in the Capital, as usual, several of the foreign Consuls being also present, one of the military conflicting parties outside, now evidently wrought up to a climax of passion, fired a volley of ball cartridge, into the crowded assembly inside, killing some and wounding others. This somewhat mysterious event was followed, some few hours afterwards, by the meeting of other armed parties at the seaside, one of which consisted of Government troops, the other of citizens, partly armed; to the latter, orders were given to disperse, but not obeying promptly they were fired upon, and many left dead on the spot, such was the strife and bitterness of the moment.

Many fell on this memorable day; some were shot, as at the Palace, when danger was not dreamed of, others were fired upon by the military authorities, because they were in arms against the Government, while others were shot, untried, yet in the name of summary martial law. In fact, the present moment seemed to be chaos itself, let loose on a work of desolation, which ultimately spread through the whole nation.

The journal of the Wesleyan Missionary, then residing at Port au Prince, contains the following remarkable notes on this event:

"SUNDAY, April 16, 1848.—We were sitting at home, when suddenly the sound of a volley of musketry, evidently at the Palace, to which we were pretty near, struck us with terror. In a moment the whole city was in consternation, and for a long time there was no reply to the question, What was the matter?

"Dreading a general conflict, of which we had heard for a long time prophetically, I immediately resolved on placing my family on board some vessel in the harbor, which was soon done, and I left them, being necessitated to do so; but to return again to the ship, although in the harbor, that night, was impossible. A conflict at the sea-side, and precisely at the place of embarkation, had taken place. No one dared to stir, reports of pistols being heard every now and then. My family and myself were therefore separated during that dismal night, and in fact repose was perfectly out of the question; I however had taken refuge myself at the Swedish Consulate, which was near the sea. In the morning at day-light, we saw from the gallery where we were standing several brought down for summary military execution. Three of these unhappy men came under our special notice, neither of whom were pinioned; and arriving near the place of execution, which was close by us, the three ran; one escaping down the street, was pursued and shot; another running into the English Consulate, which was just opposite to where we were standing, was protected under the British flag; but the third running towards the house where I spent the night, was overtaken by his pursuing guards at the gate, where the sight of his death, which took place before our eyes, and which involved a horrid use of the sword and also some dozen balls which were sent through him, turned me sick.

"At last I ventured out, accompanied by a friend, and crossed the place of last evening's conflict, where some eighteen or twenty dead were still lying on the ground in their gore. Here, taking a boat, I at last reached my anxious family, which had spent the night in great uncertainty about me. I found them safe, but not without having been in danger. The contest at the sea-side, the previous evening, had very naturally attracted the attention of Mrs. Bird, who, without any idea of danger, looked on from the vessel where she was standing, until our old nurse, who had been more accustomed to the sound of flying balls, reminded her that shots were darting in all directions through the rigging, etc., and begged her to lay down on the deck, by which means she probably saved her life."

On this matter, as a whole, there is indeed much to be said. If it be easier to prevent national evils than to cure them, then we shall be driven back in this case also to the great question of Primary Christian Education. Again we say, and never shall we cease to say, that had such been afforded to the masses of Hayti, and earnestly carried out, from 1804 to the year now before us, there can be no doubt that the scenes of blood which so painfully distinguished the early part of President Soulouque's power would never have taken place ; nor can wars or revolutions or any other difficulty ever justify, or in the slightest degree excuse, the fact that this was never attempted with any serious and conscientious resolution to drive it through, so that not a child in the Republic should be left in ignorance. In fact, under such circumstances, the nation never would have been confided to a man whose advantages of education, Christian or otherwise, were utterly inadequate to the post he was called to occupy.

Doubtless, vital error has been persisted in on this great subject of universal primary education of the educated classes of Hayti. It has not been understood that this is the true source of universal development in every conceivable sense, that a laboring man at the plough, with a little knowledge, is worth more as such, to himself, his family, and his country, than if he were in total ignorance.

Happy will it be for Hayti, if her own errors, at last, should have the effect of opening her eyes to the fact, that genuine honesty, which is not afraid of universal light, through all her administrations is all she needs to have peace and security, but without which she may tear herself to pieces.

The spectacle of a nation rent and torn by intestine commotions and mutual recriminations, is indeed a sad one; but grief and sadness was now, for a short time, the unhappy portion of the Haytian people, and many a sorrowing heart at that time sought consolation and relief by seeking God ; some, doubtless, sought him sincerely in the national Church, while others devoutly sought the mercy of Heaven, both for themselves and their afflicted country, "au Temple Protestant." Hence, the latter place, at this time, began to be crowded, and the symptoms of a religious movement were unmistakable; in fact, it seemed highly probable that the Wesleyan Church at Port au Prince would soon need enlarging, a circumstance which could not be looked upon with indifference by those who saw no salvation out of the pale of the Church of Rome. In the estimation of such, this was one of the most alarming indications of the then state of things; in fact it was viewed by such as a fearful omen that Hayti was on the high road to ruin, and Protestantism was considered as incompatible with the safety and stability of the nation. Hence, from the Cathedral pulpit loud thunders were heard warning against the dangers of the day, to which many, in listening, were set upon inquiring whether this was really the spirit of Christ? Some too, by this means, were induced to go and see for themselves whether Luther really had a cloven foot, as it seemed to be reported he had; but finding that such was not the case, did not hesitate to walk openly with him.

The march of Christian truth, apart from Rome, by these frowns from high quarters, received a momentary check, but the blow was reserved for a future day. It is indeed true, that such blows and shocks are more injurious, ultimately, to those who inflict them than to those on whom they are inflicted; the smitten pile sinks deeper and becomes firmer beneath each blow; such, too, is the case with eternal truth. But the common sense of mankind has long seen the utter impolicy of religious persecution, in any form or shape. The Haytian character, however, is not intolerant in religious matters, as will be seen in the fact that the Wesleyan Missionary, then residing at Port au Prince, was allowed to preach in the public streets of that city, as in fact at that time he frequently did, — a liberty perhaps never allowed before to a Protestant Minister in the capital of a Roman Catholic country. In fact it is highly probable that Methodism, under Soulouque, never would have suffered violence of any kind had not the idea been set to work by those who pretended to superior knowledge, and taught unblushingly that he who would be unfaithful to his religion, as a Roman Catholic, might also and consequently prove unfaithful to his Government. Then danger was supposed by the ruling mind, and in some other cases it was probably feared, with even sincerity. It is true that the possibility of such fears at all would argue no small amount of ignorance; this, however, was not the fault of the ruling power of the day; in such a case the fault was with those who, knowingly, had chosen ignorance as their national head, rather than knowledge.

During the year 1849, another act of folly was committed by this already unhappy Government, which consisted in a fruitless effort, either to conquer or win over the Spanish part of the island, which had revolted under the Government of Riviere. Hence, on the 6th of March, President Soulouque left his capital with a considerable military force for the Spanish frontiers. Something like secrecy was attempted at first as to the real object of this great movement, but little therefore was known of the army until their return, except that on the 24th it was announced, at the sound of the drum, which is the usual way in Hayti of making Government proclamations, that a victory had been gained over the Spaniards; and on another occasion it was vaunted by a few partizans of the Government that the Haytian flag was now flying on the walls of Santo Domingo! All, however, was cleared up on the 6th of May following, when, between seven and eight o'clock in the morning, the President entered Port au Prince amidst a great roar of cannon and other military noise, which might with great propriety have been spared, for we soon learnt that the whole enterprise had been a most disastrous affair, the entire army having been nearly surrounded at what is called Dessalines' Pass, from whence the President himself and his men had to fly in great haste, after having suffered almost starvation for five or six days in this fearful mountain ravine, where the very sandals of the men became food, and some being reduced to such a state of weakness as to be scarcely able to bear the weight of their own arms.

Thus, alas! have the unhappy masses of mankind often suffered for the ambition of a few. Hence, light and knowledge diffused through and possessed by the entire people, constitute the true defence of their liberties.

Great and gigantic struggles were now going on in Hayti. Now and then the whole nation would seem to heave with convulsive throws, as though determined to throw off some fearful weight of oppression; but all was useless, and he who was discovered in his daring attempt to disturb the public peace by proposals in any form of revolt, was tried and shot.

It is however pleasing, in the midst of these painful scenes, to be able to recognize the silent meanderings of the river of life; hence, we pause to contemplate the unostentatious success of the Wesleyan Missionary, J. T. Hartwell, at Cape Haytien, who, in the midst of great difficulties as to the creation of funds, succeeded in completing the erection of a church and mission-house; the former of which was opened about this time. His fellow-laborer at Port au Prince was to have dedicated this house of God to its sacred purposes, but was prevented by indisposition.*

Thus, amidst the ruins of the fallen Cape, where but a short time previously all had appeared barren and discouraging, the seeds of Christian truth, by the instrumentality of the zealous and judicious Missionary on that station, had taken root, and some had began to love and serve their God in earnest.

The Wesleyan Mission, or rather Protestant Evangelical truth, at Cape Haytien, owes much to the persevering and intelligent zeal of the Rev. J. T. Hartwell. The utmost efforts of Soulouque's Government, on his arrival at power, were made against this Mission. The President wished to withdraw or annul the lease which had been given on these premises by the preceding Government; but the wise and resolute attitude of this worthy Missionary ultimately triumphed.

* A good school-house was subsequently added to those really eligible premises by the Rev. C. H. Bishop, whose useful labors will not be forgotten on this station.

But another phase of Haytian civilization was about to appear. It was thought that, considering the almost chaotic state of things, some great national diversion of thought from the sad scenes which had afflicted all might prove salutary. These at least were the specious reasonings of the day; but doubtless, pride and vanity were no small powers in changing the Republic of Hayti into an empire! This astonishing change took place on the 26th of August, 1849, when the President and his lady were temporarily crowned in the cathedral of Port au Prince, and the reign of the dynasty of Faustin the I. commenced.

The sceptre of despotism is indeed an iron one, as the sequel of this strange metamorphose will show. The great afflictions of the nation had nevertheless, as we have seen, turned some thoughts to God, who, in some cases, was sought through the medium of Protestantism, which in—now imperial eyes—was a crime, as will be seen from the following extract of the Wesleyan Missionary, at that time stationed at Port au Prince:

"SUNDAY, March 24th, 1850.

"To-day, the Government having ordered a general recruiting for the army, the whole city was in unusual movement.

"During the morning service, at which our esteemed native Missionary Heureaux had officiated, a body of armed police was observed to surround the church, and as it subsequently appeared, with orders to seize each young Haytian on going out. Some nine or ten were thus unceremoniously seized and conducted to 'La Place.' The young native minister just named, was met as he descended from the pulpit, by the policemen who had come into the church for that purpose, and led off as their prisoner.

"On arriving at 'La Place' myself, I was told by the Governor, that I had no voice in this matter; but I persisted in declaring that the young man Heureaux was a Minister of the Gospel, and that he was my colleague. The Governor of the city, evidently pleased that I had no more than that to say, simply replied 'Then take him away with you!" With regard to the others, as a foreigner I could do nothing, but was compelled to see them walked off, like so many criminals. The simple fact that they were treated as prisoners, when they ar-arived on board the men-of-war, to which they were sent—not as sailors—and told that they would have to learn what it was to change their religion, will show the nature of the case. Such was priestly power over weak imperial minds."

This was a heavy stroke; it is however but just to observe, that it was not at all the spirit of the Haytian people. European inquisitorial bigotry was behind the scenes.

The moment had now arrived when an effort of some sort should be made in favor of religious liberty. A memorial was therefore got up, on the general question, addressed to one of the Secretaries of State, and of which the following is a copy, as it subsequently appeared in the Wesleyan Missionary notices.

"PORT AU PRINCE, June 19, 1851.

"MY LORD:—Being persuaded that a full and free expression on the subject of religious liberty, cannot be offensive to a Government which has avowed itself to be the friend of toleration; I take the liberty as the friend of humanity, to address a few remarks to you on that subject.

"We only ask for the extension of virtue and Christian knowledge, the same liberty which is accorded to many things which are pernicious to society, such as the African dances, which can have no other effect than that of encouraging superstition and vice, and of diverting the attention of the masses from that industry which is essential to the prosperity of the nation. We beg that Ministers of the Gospel may have the same liberty as is awarded to the chiefs and queens of vicious dances. Oh! allow the light of celestial truth to shine upon the mass of the people in every corner of the empire.

"But it will, perhaps, be said that the religion of Christ exists already in Hayti, and has existed for a long time. I grant, indeed, that the symbols of Christianity, either in wood, or gold, or silver, or other material, have long been known in Hayti; but the Christian Religion, anciently, caused the idolatry of Greece and Rome to disappear, upon the same principle that light and darkness cannot blend; that is to say, that error and vice have always fled before the light and power of Christian truth; but what shall we say of that Christianity which leaves vice and error entire?

"My Lord, I have traveled through nearly the whole of the French part of Hayti, but alas! what have I seen? I have seen, it is true, a mild, docile, and very hospitable people, and I have never met with but the greatest respect, both from the authorities of the country and from the people generally; but in a moral point of view, with regard to Education and Civilization, general information and knowledge, I have not been able to help asking, if the Christian Religion really does exist in Hayti, where are its fruits? for the Gospel was never really preached any where without producing the happiest effects. When, therefore, I hear it said that the Christian Religion already exists in Hayti, I naturally ask, where are those institutions to which the religion of the Saviour never fails to give birth, wherever it is truly seated in the heart? Where are those establishments which ought to adorn the plains and mountains, where Christ is said to reign?—those institutions where the faculties and capacities of the rural population should be developed, and where the general habits should be formed and purified? Where is the noble institution of the Sabbath?* that day of rest, which is the gift of heaven to mankind, and so much needed by humanity at large to keep up the remembrance of our obligations to the great Creator, and to cultivate

* The public markets were, at this time, held in Hayti on the Sabbath day.

the religion of the heart. Yea, my Lord, if the Christian Religion really exists in Hayti, how shall we account for the absence of those things which it cannot but produce, wherever it exists? I might have entered much more into detail, and might have deplored many other evils, such as the great neglect of marriage, and the thousands of children disavowed by their fathers, and who, like the savages of Africa, are without anything to cover their nakedness; but I will stop here, and beg to be allowed to re-assure your Lordship that it is not proselytism that the Wesleyan Communion has in view in Hayti; no, this Communion offers her humble services to the friends of humanity of every nation, to help in arresting the progress of vice; to promote the general and universal regeneration of mankind, and lead them to glory and immortality by means of the religion of Jesus Christ, which it is desirable should be established in the remotest corners of every country.

"The order of nature and of God, both in the moral and the intellectual world, is progress and improvement; hence, thought and conscience are left free, and God has given to every man every kind of liberty, except that of doing evil. He has charged the Governments of the world with the care of liberty, the maintenance of order, and the chastisement of vice. Hence, my Lord, while we are thankful to the Haytian Government for that measure of religious liberty which is accorded to that portion of the human family which is committed to its care, we would at the same time ask that religious liberty, that gift of heaven, should be accorded as God himself would have it; yea, as He himself has given it, namely, fully, entirely, and without limit! His Majesty the Emperor of Hayti has already given it in a Constitution, which, in that respect, is worthy of both himself and the nation. We, however, beg that Religious Liberty in Hayti may be, not a dead letter, but a glorious reality.

"The friends of Hayti in Europe, and especially in England, will sincerely deplore to learn that religious toleration in Hayti, so fully and amply declared by the Constitution, is, in reality, limited to only certain towns in the empire.

"If, my Lord, my feelings and opinions were sectarian, I should scarcely have dared to speak so unreservedly on this momentous subject; but it is not as an Englishman, or as a Wesleyan, that I have spoken. As a friend of humanity, and especially so of Hayti, I am anxious that she should take her place among the enlightened nations of the earth; but I hesitate not to say, that this will never be the case while the great mass of the people, in the plains and in the mountains, are left in ignorance and deprived of the means of Education and Civilization. The friends of Hayti have long deplored that, instead of a hundred thousand children under instruction, scarcely ten thousand are enjoying that advantage—a truly lamentable fact, which opens widely the mouths of all the enemies of the African race, and fills their friends with grief.

"It is truly painful to me to find myself under the necessity of placing these remarks before the public of Europe; but, as it has been officially announced to me that religious toleration is now limited, it is necessary that the Philanthropists of England, and elsewhere, should know that their efforts to do good in this country can not now be extended to the whole population, in order that they may be saved the expense of such plans and enterprises as could not be carried out, and which we have lately had the misfortune to incur uselessly, from the confidence we had in the Constitution and institutions of the country.

"I cannot for a moment doubt, my Lord, but that your urbanity will forgive the liberty I have taken in writing to you frankly and freely on this great subject. My object has been to place before you more fully the motives and desires which influence our proceedings in Hayti.

"Believe me, my Lord, I more than ever desire the happiness and prosperity of Hayti."

It is, however, but just to say that the generality of the really intelligent and thinking part of the Haytian community were both ashamed of and indignant at this outrage on religious liberty, which called forth this public appeal to the Government. But the despotism of the day was supported by a powerful army, and a still greater power of ignorance in the blind masses of the nation. All, therefore, were obliged to suffer in silence. Nor will it be surprising, that with such views and feelings on the part of the Government, the prosperity of Protestantism should have received a check; the more so as about this time every Wesleyan church in the Republic, as well as others, were in a state of remarkable prosperity; for as it often happens in such cases, the course pursued by the Government drew both the attention and the sympathy of the whole nation more than ever to Protestantism.

About this time, the foundation-stone of a Wesleyan church was laid at Jérémie; but before the four walls were completed, public feeling, from various causes,* having been strongly expressed against Protestantism, the Imperial Government sent down orders that the entire work should be suspended, and in fact, altogether discontinued, without assigning the slightest reason for such a proceeding. After great efforts, however, in various quarters, in the form of appeals to the Government on the subject, the building, after some months' delay, was allowed to proceed,† and notwithstanding the most strenuous opposition of a purely popish nature, this neat little house of God was solemnly dedicated to its sacred purposes, on the 28th of August, 1851—the Thursday of that week having been preferred to the Sabbath, that being the great market day. The opening service commenced at 8 A. M. on the date mentioned,

* Official minds religiously swayed and duped by confessors, etc.

† The cause of religious liberty was, in this instance, as well as many others, greatly indebted to the wise and friendly interference of the British Consul, then residing at the capital.

and was conducted by the Rev. M. B. Bird, of Port au Prince; the evening service being assigned to the Rev. C. H. Bishop, who had but recently arrived from England, and who, as the Missionary pastor of the Station, had, through many difficulties requiring great prudence, brought all the toils and anxieties connected with the erection of this building, to a happy termination, thus affording the highest and most grateful satisfaction to those who deem the Word of God to be man's sole guide on earth, by the interesting events of this memorable day.

Great ceremonies had been appointed for that day at the Romish church of the parish, and as they were said to be extra, they were thought by many to have been simply in opposition to the proceedings of the Protestants on that day. But notwithstanding this, the Roman Catholics of the town crowded the new Protestant church, at the opening services for that day, showing thus a spirit of independence, very much in accordance with the Haytian character.

It would indeed be great ingratitude not to mention here, that the Wesleyan church at Jérémie was built by and at the expense of A. Folsom, Esq., a zealous American Methodist, who had long resided at Jérémie as a merchant. Happy is it for the cause of God and truth, such noble hearts are at least now and then to be found.

The Wesleyan church at Jérémie is a neat little building, seating about two hundred, and is well situated.

The Imperial Government seemed now to be consolidating; from the temporary crowning, however, to the final and permanent coronation, nearly three years intervened, during which time great efforts were made with the court of Rome to obtain an ecclesiastical dignitary, duly authorized for the solemnization of this great event, but without success, there being at this time no Concordat on the part of Hayti with Rome.

On the 28th of April, 1852, the pompous and imposing ceremony of a real coronation, of both the Emperor and the Empress, took place on the Champ de Mars, which is situated at the back of the National Palace at Port au Prince.

The position of the Champ de Mars is exceedingly beautiful; its elevation commands a fine view of the vast bay of Port au Prince, which is some hundred miles deep, and in the midst of which stands the spacious island of "La Gonave."

On the southern side of this immense bay, rises a splendid range of mountain scenery, which is verdant and lovely, where fertility would pour out wealth to any amount, at the command of well directed industry, and where the lower hills, towards the foot, are crowned with forts and dwellings.

The plains and mountains on the northern side of the bay of Port au Prince, are also grand, but much more distant from the capital, while the sight of the city, standing upon a gentle slope, which gradually rises from the sea shore, affords an imposing panoramique to the traveler approaching it in front by sea, all giving special charm and beauty to the little well watered plain, on which stands the capital of what at this time was the Haytian empire.

On this spot was erected for the day a tabernacle of immense dimensions, built of wood, as to the frame, and covered in with canvass. The interior was fitted up as a church, having a Romish altar, with its usual decorations of flowers, flaming tapers, and all that was considered as essential to the grandeur of the occasion. The national colors were tastefully arranged throughout the interior of this vast tent, which was capable of containing some seven or eight thousand persons. In fact, notwithstanding all the ridicule which attached to the whole case, it was an imposing spectacle. A nation, small as it was, was here represented, and it must be supposed that the motive, on the part of the well meaning, was national and individual security, even though it might be under the name of an empire.

As early as three o'clock, A. M., on the last mentioned date, the roll of drums was heard, calling the troops together, and reminding the inhabitants of the capital of the great event which was to distinguish that day. Soon after daylight, "le Champ de Mars" was filled, with all of brilliant and gay, both civil and military.

At an early hour, the roar of artillery, the shouts of vivas, the din of arms, with the confusion of bugles, trumpets, and various bands, at different points, announced the approach of the Imperial state carriage, which, for splendor, was worthy of the occasion, and was drawn by eight noble American greys.

On arriving at a side tent, at some three or four hundred feet distance from the main one, the Imperial family alighted, and from thence, after a rather long pause, all being well adjusted, his Majesty, duly robed and sceptered, accompanied by the Empress, marched with a brilliant procession of newly-created nobles in open air, until they reached the entrance of the great tent, and then continuing under its spacious canopy, they ultimately arrived in front of the great altar, now loaded with blazing tapers and gorgeous decorations of every kind; here seats were provided for all parties, according to their rank and honor.

The costumes on this occasion, of most of those who held offices of any kind, were designedly antique, rather imitating the court and time of Louis XIV. In fact, the splendor and riches displayed on this occasion, although it seemed to throw one back to another age, by the antique, not to say grotesque appearance of much that was seen, gave at the same time an elevated idea of the wealth and taste of the Haytian people. Nor would any European infantry have presented a neater or more imposing appearance than was seen in the Haytian soldiery on this occasion, while the attire of the simple citizens was that of gentility, and worthy of the day.

Numerous priests were in attendance; but there was neither sermon nor oration on the occasion; the chanting, however, and general music, was good, although wanting in good brass instruments. The Emperor crowned himself, and then the Empress.

At the end of this pompous ceremony, the roar of cannon broke forth again, which, with the sound of arms, and the confused music of widely scattered bands, all mingling together at the same time, overwhelmed everything; yet all passed off well, and the shades of night were welcome.

It might be admitted, that all this took place at a

time and under circumstances when some great national change was needed; but whether the change from a Republic to an Empire was the best that could have been hit upon is quite another question; whether there was not rather in all this a departure from sound principle and sound sense must be left to the future judgment of Hayti and the world.

A better form of Government than that over which General Boyer presided in Hayti, for nearly a quarter of a century, especially carried out in all its spirit and bearings, need not have been desired, except indeed that it did nothing in any positive sense for the masses.

Good, to be genuine in its effects, whether of a moral or purely political nature, must be positive and active, yea, and of sufficient power to dislodge evil. But the too negative character of the good under Boyer was not equal to the moment, nor will such good ever be equal to the necessities, either of Hayti or any other part of the human race; hence with regard to Hayti, we see that in 1851 country people were accused before the authorities of both a superstitious and cannibal use of human flesh. It is indeed to be feared, that there was more or less truth in this dreadful accusation; but even supposing the thing to have been in reality untrue, the bare possibility of such a report, in a country making any pretensions to Christianity, is most deplorable, and should lead every intelligent man in the nation to see and feel the necessity of an universal Christian education through the Republic, such as should become literally individual, without exception. Nor should Christianity be a mere national name, but a living power, diffused through the entire Haytian family.

But interest, ambition, and a thousand other considerations, again created the desire on the part of the Imperial Government to make another attempt upon the Dominican Republic, in the eastern part of the island, either to win it over to the Haytian empire, or subdue it by conquest to its sway. Mighty efforts were now made to collect an army of as great a numerical force as possible for this purpose; the whole military machinery of the nation was put in movement, and on the 10th of December, 1855, the city of Port au Prince was in a high state of excitement. The troops which had been summoned to the capital for this eastern march, came pouring in from the southern part of the island, and they, together with those already in town, began to move out, to be ultimately joined by northern regiments.

Thus the melancholy clang of arms again rung through the streets of Port au Prince, to the great affliction of many a quiet and industrious family, for it must be remembered, that a Haytian army is made up of men who, in consequence of the inadequate pay of the Government, principally support themselves, their lands, industry, and commerce, constituting the main hope and resource of their families. This simple fact will show at once the ruinous tendency of a Haytian military march, both as to officers and men.

Soon after midnight, on the day following the last date, viz., the 11th of December, the remaining regiments were in movement, and about four A. M. the Emperor himself, with his staff, moved out.

All were in high spirits, but the hilarity of the soldiery arose from the assurance which had been given, that war was not intended; the old vague tale, that the Haytian party among the Spaniards in the East, was now really strong, and again only awaiting the arrival of another Haytian force, to guarantee them in an open revolt from their own Government, was renewed, and with this assurance, which only an unthinking mass could believe, these deluded troops went out gaily.

The Spaniards, however, being of a vastly different mind, were prepared, and when the opposing parties met on the Spanish side of the frontier, the deceived Haytians, who had been told there was to be no war, found themselves fiercely attacked by the Spaniards, and the discovery of this deception by their own Government raised a storm of indignation which placed the Emperor himself in a most unhappy position. He now, having as much to fear from his own men as from the Spaniards, was compelled, with those who adhered to him, to retreat towards the northern frontiers of his own empire.

It should be observed here, that the feeling of the great mass of the Haytian people towards the Spaniards of their own island, is perfectly friendly, and that there was nothing in the case to excite war-like passions.

During the stay of the Haytian army at Ounaminthe, on the northern frontiers of the French part, one or two worse than useless attempts were again made on the Spaniards, by which the Emperor, becoming con vinced of his helplessness, again turned his course towards his capital, which he entered at midnight, most ingloriously, on the 14th of February, 1856, without the noise of cannon, music, or anything else, a silence which was singularly marked by an unusual degree of common sense.

This effort, however, had been intended to be a mighty one, as may be seen in the simple fact, that nearly thirty thôusand men had been drawn together from different parts of the island for this great enterprise; and there is every reason to believe, that it involved a considerable and useless loss of human life, and also of cattle, to say nothing of the uncalled-for injury, inflicted upon the internal and general interests of an already suffering country.

Nothing can be more deplorable than that men, entrusted with a nation's welfare, and having every material and resource to secure the general happiness and prosperity of a people, should, instead of faithfully fulfilling that high commission, plunge all into a sea of misery, either by a positively wrong course in everything, which must soon bring on the ruin both of the governing and the governed; or by one so negative in all of good, as to involve, although less speedily, yet not less certainly, ultimate consequences, equally unhappy and deplorable.

The energies of the nation for good were thus left to sleep, being without any wise direction, while all the natural resources were left locked up by sheer inaction, or rather by a false application of the national energies to ambitious purposes.

From a pamphlet on the mines and general resources of Hayti, published in 1844, the following extracts will give some idea of the immense resources of Hayti:

"From the year 1494 to 1504, gold mines in Hayti were worked with considerable profit.

"In 1694 an official report of Charlevoix speaks of gold as even abundant in the eastern part of Hayti; but disputes having arisen, the Spanish Court ordered that the mines should be filled up.

"Silver also is said by the same writer to have been found in abundance in the eastern part of the island.

"In 1503 quicksilver was found by Ovando, on the spot where he was building a convent. This mine is also said to have been closed, by order of the Spanish Government, in consequence of certain difficulties with the monks residing there.

"Iron also is known to be abundant, and is found in different parts, probably throughout the island.

"Copper is known to exist. Moreau de St. Méry, speaking of the copper mines in the mountains of Maymon, declares the yield to be abundant.

"In addition to the metals, sulphur and coal have been found in considerable quantities.*

Since the publication of the pamphlet, from which the above extracts are taken, petroleum has been discovered in the eastern part of Hayti, which it is ascertained is of the highest quality, while it is probable that it is not confined to one locality.

But besides these valuable resources, still more abundant wealth is found in the climate and soil of the country. Nature in Hayti is continually prolific; she yields incessantly, and is never checked by the chilling blast of winter, of which she knows nothing.

A certain quality of sweet potatoe comes to perfection in less than three months, all the year round.

In Hayti, as in the other West India Islands, many of the simple vegetable products will yield three

* W. G. Smith, M. D., long resident in Hayti.

times a year, while many others, such as the grape-vine, etc., will afford two crops the same year.

In fact, the Haytians are in the midst of abounding, yea, over-abounding wealth. That misery, from want of any kind, should exist in such a country, is intolerable; nor will the best friends of Hayti excuse her in such a case.

In addition to the abundant resources already mentioned, must be noted, woods of the most valuable kind, not only in immense quantity, but also in great variety, including mahogany, etc.*

On the subject of the great resources of Hati, the following extract from the preface of the pamphlet already referred to, is particularly worthy of attention, as coming from a well-cultivated mind, more or less allied to Africa:

"It is time that Hayti had recourse to her many natural resources, and thus to rid herself of her financial embarrassments, by availing herself of the advantages of her incomparably rich and fertile soil.

"In many parts of the world, the cultivator of the soil is necessarily the slave of an unfavorable and varying climate, while we have the advantage and enjoyment of one which is ever prolific.

"At the same time that our plains are ever under summer heat, our mountain heights afford perpetual spring, equal to that of Southern Europe.

"With very little labor on our part, our soil affords us even greater abundance; while, at the same time, our fertilizing streams abound, as we all know.

* For a long time it was considered to be doubtful whether the Island, standing in the immense bay of Port au Prince, called "La Gonave," was of much worth; this, however, is now no longer doubtful; mahogany is known to be plentiful there, as well as an important variety of other rich wood; nor are its resources yet fully known.

"These things, up to the present moment, (1844) have been forgotten; while at the same time, in a financial point of view, our foreign debt might, by such abundant means, soon be effaced.

"The European would, doubtless, accept our offers to bring out our productive resources to a yet far greater extent: woods of great variety yet remain to be brought forth, of which but few, even of the Haytians themselves, are aware of the value."

With regard to the mountain regions of Hayti, there is everything in them, as to nature, to charm. The climate, in some of the greatest elevations is, in winter, absolutely cold during the night, while the mornings and evenings are perfectly invigorating. Fertility frequently reaches the mountain tops; where, by the aid of a cool temperature, the productions of the northern latitudes might be realized.

The grand drawback in the great elevations would probably be the absence of springs; but, with suitable tanks, well built, the rains would be sufficiently abundant to supply every want at the same time. Mountain springs are not uncommon. In fact, the old French Masters of Hayti were not far from right when they declared St. Domingo to be the Paradise of Frenchmen!

It is, indeed, true that the population of Hayti, apart from the army, is small, and its capitalists are but few; the arts and sciences, and in fact all that really stirs up man to action, have been lost sight of by war and discord.

It is to be regretted that the boundless natural resources of Hayti have not had the effect of convincing the whole Haytian family of the error of limiting the education of their children merely to the correct use of the pen. A Government considering itself paternal, as has been the great idea of most of the Haytian Governments, and having the entire control of the national education, might well turn the thought of the people to this great question. The resources of the country, the unmistakable spirit of the age, as well as the general and true interests of the nation, now demand a competent knowledge of science; in fact, science now stands closely allied to commerce, manufactures, agriculture, and every other branch of industry; and is, therefore, the key which unlocks these resources of nature, over which God has made man an accountable steward; nor can any nation of the present age have these resources closed up through indifference, without being guilty of glaring ingratitude to the blest Creator, and most certainly exposing itself, either to the well-merited frown and contempt of mankind, or to the danger of being overwhelmed by the great ocean of civilization which is sure to rise around it.

Science is the book of God, and its great truths should be known to our children, as coming from God.* If mind could be made visible to mortal eye, the grandest sight on earth, relating to man, would be a mind expanded and adorned, with all the truth of God, scientifically and morally! Poor, therefore,

* The difficulty of introducing elementary science into the schools of a purely commercial and agricultural people, has long been felt in the Wesleyan Establishment at Port au Prince; but let the Government, as well as the various Boards of Education, take up the subject of science, as bearing upon all human interests, and especially as the key of the boundless natural wealth of Hayti, and all difficultywill cease.

if not even dangerous, is that education of either childhood or youth, where these elements are not found; nor, perhaps, is there a country in the world where the evil effects of a partial, or simply secular education, have been more fully demonstrated than in Hayti; yea, here is one of the secret springs of her unnumbered woes.

These remarks are not intended simply as reproachful to the Haytian nation; rather, the present reasoning is suggested by the astounding signs of the times, to which it is impossible to be blind. Electric telegraphs will soon encircle the globe. Steam is driving on the interests of the earth in every possible way, both as to traveling and manufactures; and, although we may hope that ultimately the commerce, science, and Religion of mankind will render war incompatible with the general interests of the human race, and even impossible—yet, at the same time, even at present, no nation or people can remain mere active spectators of this grand world-wide movement. Isolation in any sense, or for any people, would seem to be now impossible; there may have been, and even still may be cases in which temporary isolation may seem to be just; but if the human race is one family, such cases must be regarded rather as transient and preliminary than otherwise. Permanent isolation is utterly incompatible with that almost annihilation of distance which may be said even already to have resulted from the general improvements and march of the age.

The various tastes, capabilities, and intelligence of each branch of the human race, seem to make it strongly appear that man of every hue and tongue constitutes but one vast family, each member of which being destined to that which to others would probably be impossible; this may be seen also in the fact, that each division of the earth has productions, etc., peculiar to itself, thus leading us to the conclusion that the interests of men are all mutual, one and the same; and that, therefore, an universal brotherhood is not a dream; international hate is, therefore, deep ignorance, and must ultimately give place to the harmony of common sense and peace, that the prosperity of the world, in all senses, may go on.

The dawn of Christian civilization is rising over the whole earth; nor will it be possible for any one nation or people to stand still and see this great sight; this, in the nature of things, cannot be. All are, and must be, participators in this great drama. The ark, rising with the waters, saves the human race; woe, therefore, to the nation that does not rise, for the tide of progress is irresistible.

Hayti, like every other nation, must rise, or be overwhelmed. She cannot now shut out any element from herself, by which divine Providence is working for the general good of the human family. The days of exclusion, with all the reasons by which they were originally justified in Hayti, have passed away; and, whatever laws would now act as bolts to keep out anything which stands allied to human dignity and prosperity, must yield. The great nations of the age have treated with her on terms of the most perfect equality—not one honor or privilege is refused; nor can she repel her own friends in any sense, or for any reason close her doors; she cannot be exclusive, while the greater nations of the age have thrown themselves open both to her and to the world.*

Let it not, however, be supposed that Hayti, in any sense, has been standing still; her advance has, indeed, been slow, yet her commerce is sufficiently indicative of action and industry to afford the strongest assurance that, under sound civil institutions, the produce and general wealth of the country would very greatly increase.

On this subject it is but just to observe, that the difficulties of the Haytian Republic have been such as are rarely heard of; nor can we here stay to reason out whether these difficulties were evitable or inevitable; certain it is, that a military system of the very worst kind has weighed upon every arm of the nation; and yet, notwithstanding hindrances seldom experienced by any people, there has always been an evident eagerness to earn, which goes strongly to show that, with fair civilian institutions, there would be fair results.

In an American pamphlet, published in 1853, it will be seen that, at that time, the exports from Hayti were about 40,000,000 pounds of coffee, immense cargoes of logwood, mahogany and other woods, beside large quantities of cocoa, hemp, rum, cotton, honey, etc., etc.†

* One of the articles of the Haytian Constitution, when this work was commenced, excluded the white man as landed proprietor from the soil of Hayti.

† B. C. Clark, of Boston.

CHAPTER XI.

DOMESTIC FEATURES OF HAYTIAN CIVILIZATION.

The family is the nation.—Boys and Cigars.—Woman in Hayti.—The Freedmen of the States.—Efforts in their behalf.—Wooden cross not Christ.—French character from a tropical mould.—Haytian Costume.—Haytian table.—Haytian furniture.—A native Artist.—Music in Hayti.—Domestic service difficult.—Funerals, Baptisms, Marriages.—Funeral of a General.—Masonic Funerals.—Schools of merit encouraged.—Sitting at doors.—Public roads.—Must be free to be great.—Mothers absorbed in Commerce.—Divorce.

O! Save me
From the man, whose giant mind, but makes him
Clever to deceive; the hollow soul, where
All of hell lies fairly hid under a
Mask of light.

ONE of the grand lessons not yet practically learnt in Hayti is, that a nation is whatever its families are; the domestic circle well formed, so also will be the nation, hence it will naturally follow, that untrained families will form an untrained nation. This principle will at once give us the right to examine, even minutely, the interior and detailed life of a people—nor are we to hesitate before the fact, that this is one of the most important of questions, highly worthy of the attention of the faithful statesman, the Christian, and the philanthropist. We are however compelled to admit, that the formation of the domestic circle, never has been considered to form any part of the Governmental anxiety of the rulers of Hayti; to legislate upon this subject would indeed be difficult, but the power of a living and ever-working example in the great dignitaries of a nation, would be an effectual frown on vice in any form.

Yet the lamentation never ceases in Hayti, that the people are not prepared, etc., etc., nor can there be any doubt but that this long reigning idea has greatly contributed to make Hayti what it is. Politically as well as domestically, its effect ought indeed to have been stimulating, but it has rather been stagnating, not to say withering. Mere rudiments have been lost sight of in Hayti, hence, mathematics are not unfrequently studied, and to a great extent mastered, in a domestic chaos; the ensemble of a splendid structure is admired, but it is forgotten that the house should be built upon a rock, whether religiously, politically, or otherwise, and the minutest details of the building are at the same time to be fully entered into.

The domestic training of Hayti, by which is here meant the entire mass of the nation, is a fearful question; it would be unjust to say that there is absolutely none. But a few well trained families in a nation, constituting a mere fraction of the whole, could not form the character of a people.

Paternal control doubtless exists in Hayti, but the exercise of it requires a training and a style of sense which are but rarely found on these shores. In fact, the possibility of forming either the domestic circle or the character of youth, in a Christian sense, in a nation where concubinage and libertinage prevail, may be fairly questioned. A nation under the power and spell of such a state of things is most unhappy. Early yieldings to vice, in such a case, will be inevitable, as may be plainly seen in the fact that the boy and the cigar are too often met with in Hayti, while the same may be said to be the idol of the man, from which he can only part when it is wrenched from him by sleep: and generally the very criminal, as he marches to the place of execution, clings to this indulgence to the last.

It will not be surprising, if the unformed character, from want of domestic training, should neither know nor care much as to the value of time. This, to the foreigner in Hayti, is frequently an immense inconvenience, while it involves, beyond all calculation, national loss, not only of character, but of wealth.

Perhaps one of the greatest hindrances to the right formation of youth in Hayti hitherto has been the military impressment, which now, and for a long period, has frequently been done as soon as a lad has been capable of bearing arms; so that the alarming fact stands before us, that the greater part of the youth, forced into an undisciplined army, which is not needed for a foreign foe, and where one-half of life is wasted in indolence, gambling and vice. To expect the formation of a manly, virtuous, national character from such elements, were to expect figs from thistles.

But where the vast majority of a nation present more of a domestic chaos than otherwise, what can be, what must be, the position of woman?

It is only just to mention that there are many daughters in Hayti of well formed character and great accomplishments. Compared, however, with the masses of the nation, these are but exceptions; in fact, the general training and position of woman in Hayti is an exceedingly painful subject of consideration.

Commanding female influence, founded upon sound and useful education, strengthened and confirmed by Christian virtue, is wanting,—a fact which perhaps more than any other, has let loose vice upon the nation. On this subject much error has been committed. There has been a great eagerness for the education of boys, while the girls have been left in comparative neglect. Had the mothers of the Republic been cared for,—had the eagerness for education been rather in favor of the girls,—the industry, and entire moral element of the nation had now unquestionably been of a far higher tone, its revolutions fewer, and love of arms far less.

The formation of female character is doubtless vital to the best interests of a people. Here the enormity of concubinage again appears. The mother in this case feels that her dignity as such is lowered, and she is conscious that her daughter sinks with her, while, at the same time, society at large is injured.

> My mother and my sister wise and pure,
> My country and myself are safe and sure.

The domestic training which tells upon the character of a people, and in fact forms it, as in England and America, can only result from the long roll of generations. Nevertheless, the nation can only be what the family is, and the family, in domestic training, will depend upon the mother. A nation ever in the presence of female virtue, will and must show a moral attitude and power not otherwise to be acquired.

One of the grandest spectacles of the present, or perhaps any other age, as to its moral bearing, and singularly worthy the attention of Hayti, was that noble movement in the United States which followed the abolition of slavery, and which amounted almost to a rush of hundreds towards the South, whose object was to bring the freedmen under the influence of Christian instruction—an effort probably without parallel in the annals of history, and which soon acquired the glory of placing many thousands under those elevating influences of preliminary mental and moral culture which prepare men for free and independent life. The fact is sublime, of an army of honest and hearty pioneers, armed with pens and spelling books, etc., and, above all, with the Word of God, both in their hearts and in their hands, like true Missionaries, bent on tearing up ignorance and vice by the root, and planting the seeds of plain, sound knowledge, with the hope that not one freedman should remain in ignorance, but should be, as soon as possible, capable of understanding and fulfilling his duties, as a Christian, Republican citizen.

Such a spontaneous burst of Christian patriotic feeling gives the true idea of the means by which the world is to be converted to God. Armies must go forth, their arms mere truth, rather than here and there a Missionary, whose stand is indeed the nobler because he is solitary,—yet what is one among so many? But the main question suggested by this grand move is, Why has not Hayti done this long ago? Had it ever been truly upon the conscience, or really in the heart of the various Governments that have ruled Hayti since its independence, both the means and the power have ever existed to do so,—but nothing is more evident than that Christianity, without its life and power, is little worth. The form of Christianity has long been given to the Haytians, but a wooden cross is not Christ!

As in the domestic description of a people details become necessary, it may not be uninteresting to bring out some of the home customs and usages of this small but remarkable Republic.

Considering the peculiar history of Hayti—the circumstances which gave it birth—its ardent and ever-glowing climate, and the splendors of its luxuriant scenery, it is natural to expect that there should be many singularities in the general character of its civilization which would give it special identity and interest.

As might be expected, considering the fact of its having been a French colony, almost idolized by France, Hayti still bears all the impress of the French character, as to its present habits and manners. It must, however, be well noted, that all of French in Hayti has been formed in a tropical mould, and that consequently there are many traits in it which could not be seen in France itself.

Among the more intelligent classes of the Haytian Republic, the hereditary notions and general bias are French, especially as far as real civilization may have advanced. France, in nearly everything, is the Haytian model. This is simply natural, the French language being the only medium of intercourse and knowledge. The civilization and institutions of Europe and the United States are all viewed only by means of a French press, and consequently with French hues and tints. There are, indeed, exceptions; some having received their education in England, and others having effectually studied the English language, without leaving their country, have more or less acquainted themselves with both American and English institutions.

But the character, progress, and general civilization of Hayti, can only be rightly understood according to the point from which all is viewed. The great masses of the people are of African origin, while their advantages, as to even primary education, have been little or none; yet if the comparison as to civilization is to be with its own first moments of freedom, it will unquestionably be found that the advance has been great; but if Haytian progress, in this respect, is to be measured by an American or European standard, then it will be found wanting.

Hayti must be judged by those controlling circumstances which have formed and ruled her; hence her progress can only be fairly estimated by those who really know her.

The dress and costumes of the Haytians may, in a general way, be said to be such as prevail in France. It may be said, however, that the Haytian peasantry, like that of the West Indies, generally are smarter, more fashionable, and more gay, than that of Europe. This, perhaps, may be attributable, to a great extent, if not principally, to an ever gay and splendid climate; hence at their national festivities, or on great occasions, and at their public assemblies, the displays of dress among the Haytians are in brilliant accordance with their native clime. The men of all ranks display the tastes of Paris; while the ladies of all shades between black and white, still retain the custom of wearing, as the head dress, either the purely white or gaily colored Madras handkerchief, which is sometimes so gracefully arranged as frequently to amount to elegance, especially with the darker hues. Bonnets are used principally by Haytian ladies of good education, received either in Europe or at home, of which the number is increasing rapidly. The immense and costly shawl is by many still preferred; while among the wealthy and more advanced female youths, the Parisian attire is more rigidly adhered to; but snowy white is in the tropics justly admired and sought, both by men and women, if not as real and full dress, certainly as the best suited to perpetual heat.

Perhaps it ought not to be matter of surprise that in a climate almost invariably bright, love of ornament should amount to a weakness, on which immense sums are continually expended—an exhausting expenditure, which might doubtless be far better applied—the embellishments of the mind being of infinitely greater importance than mere external decorations. In fact, it must be confessed that not only important necessities are sacrificed at this empty shrine, but real gentility and good taste. This is mentioned more in the sense of fact than otherwise; for it cannot be denied that this is a human weakness, and is by no means confined to Hayti, prevailing as it does everywhere.

It is presumed that these details, while they will

not fail to interest, may at the same time serve to illustrate the point now in view, which is the degree of exterior civilization attained by the bulk of the Haytian people, as viewed from their original starting point, which it is conceived is the only fair means of forming a correct opinion on this question.

It might indeed be said that not much is gained by such a mode of judging, nor is it pretended that the progress of Hayti, in this or any other respect, is entirely satisfactory; much more might and ought unquestionably to have been done—nevertheless it is not to be forgotten that a people thus clad, and who even carry out their love of appearance to an extreme, must by their own industry have procured the means of feeding and supporting their tastes, and might serve to show how the revenue of this small Republic has not only covered its own national ordinary expenses, but has also met the annual claims of France, in reference to an indemnity already explained.

But the glowing picture of Hayti now before us, and to which yet more might be added, has nevertheless its shades; nor would it be honest or fair not to point them out as essential to the completion of a national picture. It must then be remembered that what has now been advanced has special reference to public appearances.

The displays of ornamental wealth are of course confined to great or remarkable occasions, when jewelry, from the highest quality to the very lowest tinsel that glitters, is in demand.

But the shades of the picture which we are now endeavoring to paint, are to be seen in private and domestic life; hence, having gained the cool retreat of home, after sweltering beneath a scorching sun, in the close and confined prison of some new and gay Parisian fashion, a relief is naturally sought, which forms a striking contrast between the interior and exterior of life. Let it not, however, be forgotten that an oppressive climate forms the picture now before us, and enters into all the details of domestic life.

But the ladies' imprisonment in the tight and snugly packed up attire of the latest fashions, inflicting even suffering in the fervid temperature of the tropics, forms yet other shades in this picture; ease being found at home in general looseness, which as a temporary relief is doubtless natural; this, however, is not peculiar to the Haytian. The European and North American, under the same circumstances, throw up their stiffened order, in the domestic retreat, and are compelled to submit to the power of heat. Nevertheless a general slovenliness is matter of regret, whatever the cause, and indeed intolerable.

Nothing can be more natural than the shades of the picture here drawn; yet at the same time, nothing can be more sure than that for want of good management, they constitute the source of all the domestic disorder which has ever been deplored in Hayti, and which to endeavor to conceal, would be simply out of place. Female education and training alone can correct these evils.

Upon the principle, therefore, that the nation is whatever the family is, we may say that whatever the city homes are, such will be the streets, etc.

That there are certain parts of the most civilized and polished cities of the world, far worse than some of the streets of Port au Prince, as well as other towns of the

Republic, is well known; but this does not alter the fact that the streets of this city are utterly unbecoming of that civilization which we have a right to expect in the municipal management and care of the Haytian capital.

It is singular that each householder has a right to build over what in England or the States would be called the pavement. It is not indeed enclosed or shut up from public use, but an upper floor, supported by posts, is brought over the pavement, which in some cases may be two feet above that of its immediate neighbor; so that what is understood as a pavement for foot passengers is perfectly out of the question—there being no municipal arrangements or interference in these matters; foot passengers, therefore, prefer to walk in the middle of the street, rather than have the annoyance of continually stepping up and down.

The shades of a picture are indeed necessary, but they must be nicely touched and correctly placed—otherwise all would be a failure.

We hope, however, that ultimately well organized systems of education, based upon the modest and virtuous precepts of the Christian religion, which shall be brought to bear ere long upon the female part of the population, will place Hayti at least on the way to her destined hopes. Meanwhile, before reaching her desired goal, it cannot be concealed that among the lower classes great looseness prevails, entering far too much into all the ramifications of private life; hence frequently, where means exist, the most costly articles are thrown aside from sheer wasteful inattention and want of economy, that useful agent in the management of limited and hard-earned means, which perhaps is even looked upon as rather a proof of avarice than otherwise; hence poverty here, as in Europe, is made wretched by the absence of thrift and care.

It must not, however, be forgotten that lights as well as shades have already been spoken of, as beautifying and completing this picture of national manners.

There is a certain class of the Haytian people which are specially neat, clean and orderly, both in their homes and everything else. In some cases, this has doubtless been transmitted from olden time, but not in every case in the same direct and positive manner.

It is worthy of notice that in traveling, even in isolated places in this Republic, where it might least be expected, the weary foreigner or other traveler will occasionally find a table spread with the utmost neatness, inviting his taste, with also silver forks and spoons, and a repast made sweet by its simplicity and cleanliness. It is not pretended that this is common, but that it should be so only here and there, among a people so cut off from general intercourse with foreigners, is remarkable and interesting.

The Haytian table is altogether French, with, however, such modifications as might be supposed to result from climate and various other circumstances, such as tropical productions, etc. On this subject the Haytians may be said to have followed the general and perhaps instinctive dictates of nature; for it must be admitted that the tropics do not admit of impunity in diet.

The Haytian table, therefore, may be considered as wholesome and safe—well adapted to the conservation of health in these warm latitudes; although the national habit of a heavy repast in the evening after sunset, which prevails, is very questionable, and doubtless is very frequently injurious.

A slight and informal repast forms what is termed a first breakfast; towards mid-day comes on "Le dejuener à la fourchette;" but the principal repast, dinner, is after business hours, which in Hayti is five P. M., and consequently runs late into the evening.

In furniture, it will not be surprising if the educated Haytians should display great taste, as indeed is the case; for wherever the means exist, nothing is considered too costly for embellishment and accommodation in a respectable dwelling.

Carpets of woolen texture, in a continually warm climate, it will be easily understood, are not desirable; but variously painted oil cloths are occasionally seen, or on the ground floor, marble will not unfrequently be seen, although its safety as to health, in a warm climate, is perhaps doubtful.

Bedsteads, armoirs, or clothes presses, and tables, are generally of the splendid Haytian mahogany, made frequently with great finish in the country, both by native and foreign workmen.

Paintings of family likenesses, and native scenery, executed by Haytian artists, frequently embellish the parlors and halls of respectable dwellings, some of which are good, others inferior.

In the national palace, as well as the Senate house and Cathedral church, may be seen many fair specimens of Haytian talent; and notwithstanding the failures of some, abundant evidence will be found of the existence of both capacity and taste for the fine arts, were they only under suitable direction; but wars and revolutions must cease, and peace must afford prosperity and leisure for the cultivation of those higher branches of civilization. In fact, resources of every kind exist both in Hayti as a country, and in the Haytians themselves, as an intelligent people, to sustain a high degree of happiness and wealth.

Music also has engaged much of the attention of the Haytians; but up to the end of Soulouque's power, it must be admitted that on this subject all was unsatisfactory, except that it was evident that both capacity and taste existed among the Haytians for the highest culture of this interesting branch of human progress. It is, however, singular, that vocal music should never have formed any part of the national characteristics of Hayti, notwithstanding the existence of a decided taste for good and elevated poetry, of which good specimens are not wanting among the Haytians.

The piano is an important item with all whose means such an instrument would become; many also both read and execute music with taste and style.

With regard to furniture, as a general rule it is expected that, from the highest to the lowest, the house must be furnished according to the means of the parties before the bridal day—a rule which in itself is doubtless good; it will, however, easily be seen that in the case of those with scanty means, a rule clashing with human pride would fail, and concubinage might be the result, especially in a country where marriage is not absolutely exacted, or rather where concubinage is not absolutely frowned down.

The question of domestic servitude is at the present time surrounded by every difficulty—nor can this be said to result from ignorance only; still, where mere ignorance is taught, equality, without its inevitable exceptions, it is likely to be misunderstood. A fact which simply shows that ignorance will understand even sound principles in a sense which will degrade itself, thus demonstrating the necessity of the education in common sense of the masses.

Many have attributed this domestic inconvenience to indolence; and in part, the idea is no doubt correct; but there are other causes—false notions of social independence, and that supremely false notion, of European origin, that labor is degrading, has proved a serious obstacle in this important department of Haytian life. Nor has there been any national effort to teach, by means of a really Christian education, that vice only dishonors. In fact, that style of education which shows, that vice alone is degrading, has ever been wanting in Hayti.

Funerals, baptisms, and marriages, form yet other remarkable features in Haytian civilization; all and each of which being attended with great display, whenever the means of the parties will admit of it.

In any other country, however important might be these landmarks of Christian civilization, they are viewed more as forming a part of the ordinary train of life than otherwise; but in Hayti these events stand prominently out. Certain it is, that in New York, Paris, or London, such crowds as follow ordinary funerals in Hayti would be impossible, in consequence of the absorbing occupations of the people. In Hayti, such occasions are demonstrations of affection and respect; and although it is not desirable that this should be diminished, yet it is quite certain that greater national activity would decidedly modify these usages, however laudable.

At the death of any one of respectability in Hayti, it is the custom to send round richly ornamented handbills, printed sometimes with gorgeous vignettes, announcing the family bereavement, the place from whence the funeral should leave, the hour, and whether the service will be at the Roman Catholic or Protestant church. At such time there will be a large attendance, whether the departed may have been Protestant or otherwise, while the general appearance will always be genteel and respectable. Hundreds will in such cases follow the corpse; and although even richly attired, yet without the slightest order, each one walking where and as he pleases. Should the funeral be that of a Haytian Protestant, the Roman Catholic relatives and friends of the deceased will not for a moment hesitate to crowd into the Protestant place of worship, observing at the same time the utmost decorum during the service.

The case of funerals is here noticed, as showing a religious phase of civilization, which is specially worthy the attention of the English and American Protestant. The solemn air which marks such occa sions among the above-named peoples is not seen here; that silence and awe which the presence of death ought to command, is here unknown; pleasant conversations and cigar-smoking go on, as the procession moves confusedly along; the bearers of the dead—if there be no hearse—will feel quite unrestrained as to loud speaking, or, with the ruder classes of the people, as to even laughter. These are indeed painful facts, and they are mentioned here purely to show that religious culture on these subjects has been neglected in Hayti.

> The awe of death strikes not on minds untrain'd
> For fellowship with God, by heav'n ordain'd.

It is specially worthy of notice, that notwithstanding Hayti is a Roman Catholic country, there has never been any distinction as to place of burial. Protestants and Catholics are buried in the same graveyard, so that the priest and the minister will often meet on the same ground.

Military honors are also rendered to the Protestant soldier, according to his rank, as in all other cases. In fact, it may be said that Roman Catholic Hayti is, in this matter, far in advance of some of the nations of Europe.

At the funerals of the uneducated classes, the lamentations and cries of the bereaved are generally loud, even to screaming, so that on some occasions it is perfectly deafening at the grave, but among the more educated grief is suppressed.

The honors which are paid at the death and funeral of a general, according to European and American ideas and usages, are extraordinary as to the manner in which all is done. At the announcement of the death of a distinguished officer, a company of artillerymen is despatched to the house of the deceased general with a small cannon. This company remains stationed before the house of the departed, where, to the great discomfort of the sick and nervous in the neighborhood, minute guns are fired, until the removal of the corpse for interment, while at the same time military music will go on in the house of the dead.

This seeming want of reverence for the dead is deeply painful to Protestants generally, and especially so to foreigners, on their arrival.

That death should command so little solemnity, seems to argue the absence of that deep Christian feeling which Protestants consider an essential part of the Christian religion, and which enters very largely into a really Christian style of civilization.

It is right to note here, that the funerals of Freemasons in Hayti are generally conducted with great decorum. On such occasions the Freemasons themselves walk in single file, one row or line on each side of the street, with the hearse between them; thus affording very frequently an imposing sight. Ladies, however, are left with the irregular crowd on these occasions.

Marriages are generally numerously attended in Hayti, and are mostly celebrated at the house of one of the parties, or perhaps at the residence of a friend, before a well-chosen and sometimes brilliant company.

In the Haytian Republic, marriage is recognized by the law as a purely civil contract. Hence, it is not considered to be valid unless performed by the civil magistrate—the religious part of this institution being apart from, and independent of, the civil law. A purely religious marriage would not be at all recognized by Haytian law.

The civil magistrate, therefore, having fulfilled the

duties and formalities of the law, with regard to the marriage act, the Roman Catholic calls in the priest, or the Protestant calls in the minister; or, if the parties should be one Roman Catholic and the other Protestant, as will occasionally happen, then the civil officer, priest, and minister, follow each other, thus making the ceremony of a triple character. A marriage may occasionally take place at the Roman Catholic church, or at the Protestant, but this is rare.

At such times another opportunity is afforded to the Protestant pastor of speaking faithfully on the general question of public morality, as essential to the general well-being of mankind, and showing that polygamy stands reproved before the fact that the Creator gave to Adam but one wife, and that a faithful and well-sustained monogamy secures the greatest amount of care and watchfulness over the rising generation. In fact, such occasions bring out the whole of this great question, as bearing upon the honor and the true interests of the human race.

Concubinage in Hayti is doubtless one of the many unhappy relics of those European vices practised under the withering shades of slavery, which the Haytian nation has never yet had the moral courage and power to despise, or rise above entirely.

The key to the explanation of this great evil, and its long continuance, is doubtless to be found in the fact, that there has not been that deep and enlightened religious conviction which leads to action, as to the imperative and absolute necessity of raising woman to her right status in society. As a theory this has never been doubted, although perhaps never seriously entered into. Hence, there has been no moving power in carrying it out; this would require Christ rather than Voltaire; hence, for many years female education was comparatively neglected in Hayti, and consequently true civilization has been checked in its progress.

That there has been great improvement in this country, on the subject now before us, must be admitted, and we may hope that the time is not far distant when female education in Hayti will be such as to lead both daughters and parents to look with contempt upon concubinage.*

Much yet remains to be accomplished; vice and ignorance are still powerful, and can only "now be subdued by a generation or two of laborious perseverance. It is doubtless beginning to be understood that the true interests of the nation are found in Christian domestic virtue; and sound example will ultimately overcome those ruinous evils which have so long acted as a moral blight upon the nation.

Let it not, however, be supposed that there are no virtuous marriages, or well-ordered families in Hayti, where good training and education are objects of the deepest solicitude. There are not wanting in this country families where no amount of sacrifice would be deemed too great to secure the educational interests of the children; of this the managers of the Boys' Wesleyan Boarding School at Port au Prince have had ample proof. In connection with this establishment, parents have been known to undergo

* "In fact, it must be admitted that, with regard to the upper and more educated classes of society, legitimate marriage is now the order of the day."—W. G. Smith, M. D.

great privations, with long-continued perseverance, in the interests of their children; while others, doubtless thinking to do better still, have sent their children to Europe, and are now beginning to send them to the United States of America, being ready to drain the very last of their resources to secure for their offspring the advantages of science and a good education. Much, doubtless, may be hoped to result from this spirit of sacrifice on the part of the Haytian parents of the better classes in the interests of their children, which, in the best sense, is emphatically the interest of the nation.

One of the distinguishing peculiarities of the Haytian character comes out in the fact, that schools of real merit are encouraged, whether they are conducted by Roman Catholics or Protestants; such at least has been the case hitherto. Nor is there much, even at the present, to be feared from the closer ties with Rome by means of the recently established Concordat.

It is not indeed meant that there is no religious bigotry in Hayti, as a Roman Catholic nation, but it is here simply meant, that as such, she has greatly advanced in religious liberty, and that probably no other nation of that creed has ever surpassed her in this great matter.

Baptisms form another feature in the national usages of Hayti. Sponsors readily stand for children, and they are really faithful and true to the solemn charges which they thus take upon themselves, at least as far as the general wants of the child may be concerned, in case of the death of the parents. In fact, special attentions are paid to such a child under any circumstance; and in the case of family poverty, it is frequently taken altogether under the care of those who stood for it in baptism.

It should be observed here, that the Romish Church receives all to baptism, legitimate or illegitimate. Whatever may be the motive for this indiscriminate reception into the Church, it must be admitted that many an unfortunate child thus finds useful friends in the sponsors which stand for it in baptism.

It must, however, be admitted, that baptism in Hayti, although a solemn sacramental rite of the Romish Church, has been most singularly and deplorably abused. Hence, mills, steam-engines, houses, etc., are said to be baptised before they are used. This is doubtless an inexcusable abuse of a practice which in its origin probably had simply in view to implore the blessing of God in the use of these things. It is, however, a lamentable fact, that this abuse has been pushed to a fearful excess of folly, having degenerated into riot, etc.

With regard to the baptism of children, it has not unfrequently been known in Hayti, that Roman Catholics have stood sponsors at Protestant baptisms, and that with a full understanding that the child should be taught the Protestant faith. Doubtless a Roman Catholic Concordat, should it be continued, may ultimately change this usage.*

Another singular habit among the prevailing customs of the country is that of individuals and families

* One of the Wesleyan Missionaries calling one day on a priest whose acquaintance he had formed, was specially welcomed by the observation that he, the priest, but the previous evening had had his new house baptised.

sitting at the door in the open street, especially if there be a piazza to protect them from the sun. To a foreigner, this, although not unpleasing, is remarkable. In the English West Indies, the more retired habits of English life have, in this respect prevailed, but in Hayti the practice here referred to is universal throughout the Republic. Climate has doubtless had much to do with this custom, although that openness which is peculiar to French habits, has perhaps originated it. The enjoyment and ease of this custom is considered to be increased by throwing the chair obliquely against a wall or post, the feet resting upon one of its bars. Frequently little groups are thus seen openly sitting at ease, enjoying friendly converse in the cool breeze. It is possible that this custom has done much to originate the habit among Haytians of saluting all they meet, known or unknown, the street parties being numerous, and the impoliteness of passing on without noticing them would be quite likely ultimately to wind up a politeness of this kind into a sort of tyranny.

Suitable education and Christian moral training forming the inner home, with good public circulating libraries, had perhaps prevented, or changed these habits, and filled many a lost hour in a far different manner. In fact, the want of reading habits and the love of sound reading, is an absolute misfortune to any people. The mind unstrung must necessarily engender habits of indolence and ennui.

Nor need it be any matter of surprise if liberty, that greatest, sweetest gift of heaven, as to this life, should have been abused in Hayti, or if the great truths of human equality should have been here misunderstood. If each Haytian, when he first broke his chains, should have felt as though every town, house, yea, the very atmosphere were all his own, it would be quite easy to forgive him.

> Chains suddenly thus burst, would fill the soul
> With bounding raptures, which bewilder all.

The general state of the interior of the country, as to public roads, etc., is another department of great importance in Haytian progress and general civilization.

With regard to the highways, the course and direction from one place to another is, indeed, plainly traced; but the state and quality of the road depends mostly upon nature; hence, if the soil be clayey the road will, in many places, be utterly impassable during the rainy season, in consequence of such depths of mud as will not unfrequently become the grave of unhappy asses, traveling on with their load to the market—this animal being very much in use among the country people of Hayti. In fact, these little hardy creatures are well adapted to the scanty means of the Haytian peasantry; hence, on market days, they are ridden or driven into all the large towns by hundreds. It is even an extraordinary sight to stand on some of the main roads of the suburbs of Port au Prince and watch the long train of donkeys, women and children, all loaded with various marketable produce; in fact, it is a sight indicating no small amount of energy and activity, and seems to remind the foreigner that it is rather a want of judgment in the direction of the national energies than real indolence, which is so seriously injurious to the country.

The reparation of the public roads is not absolutely neglected; but whether, in many cases, it would not be better for them to be left alone, rather than to have the attention which they sometimes get, is, indeed, a question. Military companies are sometimes sent out, by neighboring Generals, to repair the public roads; but this being a task imposed without interest, it will not be difficult to understand how it would be done. Piles are sometimes driven into the ground, from one side of the road to the other, by the sides of which are placed, horizontally, long logs of wood—a most unhappy arrangement for the traveler and his horse, the spaces between frequently endangering both, while the very mention of a vehicle on such highways would be entirely out of the question. It is difficult to suppose that such was the old French Colonial mode of repairing the public ways, the roads in France being generally very good; but, whatever might have been the origin of this style of road-making, it is simply inexcusable from the fact that stones are generally, if not always, to be found in the neighborhood, by which the great national boon of good roads might be easily secured; yet, up to the present moment, the clumsy and even dangerous old mode of reparation prevails, although probably it would cost even less to do better; for, the labor thus done in the name of patriotism or the State, is not, and cannot be a sound motive. A man may lay down his life in a battle for his country, while it could not be expected that he should drag out a whole life time in penury, with a family hanging upon him, in the name of patriotism, which does not compensate him for his labor.

Hence, the friend of progress longs for railways in Hayti. It is true, the great question in such a case would be, will it pay? But this question demands reflection. The hope of success would, perhaps, be in the fact, that railways create traveling and transport, and hence that they create their resources.

That railways in Hayti would, in many places pay, cannot be doubted. Neighborhoods might be named where the population might be supposed to be sufficient for an attempt.

The countless swords, etc., which have been purchased for Hayti during the last fifty years, to worse than no purpose, turned in this direction, as to their costs, had doubtless long ere this have settled this great question by the creation of incalculable wealth.

It will be easily understood that a people long shut up in themselves, as the Haytians necessarily were for their national safety, might, after many years, fall into a contracted, if not even a despicable class of ideas. This, it is to be deplored, has been the case, at least to some extent, as to the mass of the people; hence the great adherence to old customs. That such a people should seem to say, we do not wish to do better than our brave and noble forefathers, would not be very surprising, however deplorable.

With regard to the predominancy of old usages, we have only to remember that the plough, even yet, is scarcely known in Hayti, notwithstanding the splendid plains which invite its use;—up to the present day each one goes forth single-handed with his hoe.

A feeble attempt at a telegraph at Port au Prince, simply in the sense of an experiment, was recently made; but the operation soon ceased, there being no necessity for it in the city.

More or less, however, has been done in Hayti. Hence, sewing machines are not unknown in the Republic; steam engines also are in use, for the grinding of the sugar cane in the plains. Saw mills, by steam, have been introduced, although at the present time no longer in operation.

Perhaps one of the most singular facts connected with Hayti at the present moment is, the utter inefficiency of the military system, notwithstanding the nation has been more than exhausted in its support for more than half a century past. Compared with the wants and advancement of the age, the Haytian army is in every sense in arrears—being but little in advance of what it was in 1804. Nor are the details of military discipline very different from what they were in the beginning of the national career. A centinel with his chair and cigar is still expressive of the disciplinary tone of the Haytian army. The Haytians are, nevertheless, ready for both military and every other improvement. Every reproach, up to the present time, has been due to their leaders, who, in many cases, have been far removed, by good education, from ignorance, and might have introduced those improvements of the age, both in arms and military tactics, which would have made an army of 5,000 men equal to 20,000, and thus have promoted immensely the agricultural industry and interests of the country.

Steam has now began its career in Hayti; hence

coasting steamers are, at the present time, in use; and, to those who have known much of the past in this Republic, they are a vast improvement upon the old mode of traveling.

The following sketch of a coasting journey, in old style, is found in the journal of a Missionary already named:

"On the first of November, 1843, in the evening, we embarked on board the small coaster "St. Josephe," about seventeen tons, for Port au Prince, having spent a week or two, for a change of air, at Gonaïves, with our warm-hearted friends of Cornwall, in England. The only accommodation for myself, my wife, and child of four years, was the hold of the vessel; before which was placed, on the deck, the cooking stove; so that when the wind blew awkwardly for us, the smoke would be absolutely insupportable; while, at the same time, we dared not venture on deck for fear of being roasted between the cook's fire and the sun, there being no awning. Such then was traveling in Hayti; in fact, it was absolutely distressing. Towards the end of the journey two of the sailors quarreled; and, although it came to a fight, there really was not room enough on this tiny deck for the operation. They could only strike each other with one hand, being obliged to hold on to a rope with the other, otherwise both must have gone overboard for want of room. A more perfect release than to get away from this miserable little floating den, and safely to land at Port au Prince, could scarcely be imagined!"

Among the many strange customs prevailing in Hayti, and one which has descended from, no one knows who or where, is that of begging to be excused on separating from any one, either accidentally met or otherwise; hence, the little urchin, frequently with nothing but a shirt on, and that sometimes ragged, having executed his errand will, on leaving, invariably pray "Excusez," and, with a gentle bow, gracefully draw his naked foot along the ground as he retires!

Naked children, in the streets, is a sight to which foreigners have to become accustomed. This, no doubt, is to be attributed principally to climate, and is probably more or less prevalent throughout the tropics. It is, nevertheless, a habit to be condemned; nor is it for a moment to be supposed that it could, or would be tolerated among an educated people. This is, unquestionably, a great evil; and is one of the many roots of that general looseness which prevails through the entire country, as may be seen at the various streams where public washings are carried on at far too great a sacrifice of female delicacy.

The custom of using a handkerchief as a covering for the head is prevalent amongst the men of Hayti, and is no doubt connected with the question of health; nevertheless, the head thus covered with a handkerchief closely tied on, and a hat over all, especially in the case of a military officer, has much of the grotesque about it, whatever be the motive.

Carriages are but little used in Hayti, although they are by no means unknown in the capital. The horse and saddle are the chief means of traveling in this country; and it must be admitted, that the Haytians, both men and women, are generally good equestrians. It is, however, to be regretted, that the breed of horses is almost entirely neglected in Hayti; yet, as pacing and easy riding horses, there are perhaps none better.

It would be unjust to Hayti not to make the fact prominent, that as a people, the Haytians are renowned for their hospitality. It would be quite correct to say, that this is a national characteristic, and contributes much to the comfort of the weary traveler, who crosses the mountains and the plains of the interior, especially as taverns are rarely if ever known or met with in Hayti; but the cottager's dwelling is always thrown open to solicited hospitality, and every comfort is afforded which may be at command.

The nurses of Hayti are overwhelming in their attention, and the sick foreigner is greatly soothed by their unceasing care. In fact, this almost sleepless attention is peculiar to the entire West Indies. This may arise from an instinctive consciousness that sickness in the tropics is generally rapid in its course, and especially the fever of hot climates; but whatever be the cause, it is admitted that the care of the sick in the West Indies is much more assiduous than in colder climates.

Hayti and the Haytians present a splendid field for progress of every kind. With regard to the natural resources of the country, as we have seen, they are immense, whether we consider its woods, its minerals, its commerce, or aught else, which, together with its unbounded fertility, might produce unlimited wealth. For this, however, there must be peace and perfect security.

The geographical area, or superfices of Hayti, including adjacent islands, are superior to those of Ireland. A population of from eight to ten millions would leave yet room for great increase. In fact, the Haytian territories, filled by a population thoroughly industrious, and more or less educated, showing a nation which would command commercial and naval fleets, steam and otherwise, of her own construction, would present a convincing spectacle to mankind of progress; her revolutions would thus be superseded, and become impossible, for want of both time and disposition; while the slavery of arms, poverty, and ignorance, would cease. Hayti, under favorable circumstances, would be quite equal to this.

Men must be free to be great; their tongues and pens must be free, and every Government must listen to plain truth from an enlightened people, such as the Haytians ought to be.

Under such circumstances, thousands of the descendants of Africa, from all parts, would flock to the shores of Hayti, bringing with them either the wealth of gold, or that which is of yet greater worth, the wealth of strong arms, sound sense, and industry.

We have now, therefore, before us a general sketch of the social progress of Hayti during upwards of sixty years. It is not presumed that it is satisfactory, either on the part of the Haytians themselves, or of those of their foreign friends, who have been anxious spectators of their onward march.

Here we would again repeat, that Hayti must be fairly judged. Let her origin and infancy as a nation be honestly taken into account; let her progress be viewed in connection with the countless drawbacks which have clogged her course, in innumerable ways; swarming and powerful enemies hovered round and hung upon her, during the struggles of her birth; fearful elements also in her own bosom, soon convulsed her; while her masses—without any fault of hers—presented a mere chaos of ignorance. Even her victories and final success over the mighty power with which she had to contend, filled her with vanity and pride, which has never yet departed from her: let all these facts and withering elements be taken into account, and it will be seen that if Hayti has not progressed rapidly or satisfactorily, the reason is evident; while at the same time let it be candidly admitted, that she has fairly demonstrated her possession of all the elements of true civilization.

The most advanced countries of the age have required many centuries to reach their present status, and although they had not at their starting all the surroundings of science, etc., which Hayti has had, it must not be forgotten that she started from an immensely remote point in civilization, and under circumstances as unfavorable as could well be imagined. Nor is it to be expected that with the greatest advantages she, in little more than half a century, should accomplish what has been with others the work of ages; and yet many of them are still greatly in arrears as to really free institutions.

Another peculiar feature in the Haytian community, is the fact, that an immense amount of business is done by women.

This no doubt originated in the fact, that the military service has been such as to take the men away from their homes; hence, in the agricultural districts, the women and children principally reap the crops of coffee, which is the staple article of exportation, and which, during the year, requires but little care or attention. In fact, it will be easily seen, that in the absence of the men, the whole toil must devolve upon the women.

In the towns the women are engaged in general retail business; and it must be admitted that some of them show great tact in this branch of industry. Credit to an immense amount is sometimes given them by the great merchants, and wealth to a great amount is in many cases accumulated. Indeed it may be said, that the Haytian women are really commercial, a fact which has perhaps had more to do with the peculiar cast of Haytian civilization than we are apt to think.

Let it only be imagined that the mothers of a community are absorbed in commerce, and it will be easily understood that domestic training must suffer, if not entirely disappear. This may be industry, as indeed it is, and in itself perfectly laudable; but the system is unhappy.

A nation of families, formed upon this model, will and must be wanting in one of the main branches of really Christian civilization, and in fact, in nearly all that relates to the best formation of the domestic circle.

It is quite certain that a large family, fully and minutely cared for, by an entire and assiduous attention to all the endless wants of domestic life, would quite absorb every moment of a mother's care, and that care being almost universally wanting, the entire nation suffers, and the national style of civilization will, to a great extent, be shaped by this fact.

> The mothers of a nation give it form
> And shape.

What, under such circumstances of domestic privation, will be the position of the rising generation of girls? The fathers are absent; neither word, nor look, nor influence, can therefore be expected from that quarter. The mothers are indeed present, but the formation of their homes, in any truly domestic sense, cannot even be expected from them.

The diffusion of true, well founded moral principle, as superseding mere nominal or national creeds, which can never bind, will ultimately be the true and great corrective in all that relates to the vital interests and real elevation of Hayti.

The subject of divorce unquestionably stands closely connected with the great question of Christian civilization, and therefore demands here a passing thought.

Any law in a community tending in any sense to lower the dignity of marriage, or in any way to lessen the importance of that institution, is deeply to be deplored, as affecting most unhappily not only the general position of woman in society, but also as lowering the standard of genuine civilization, and thus opposing the elevating purposes of the great Lawgiver, with regard to the human family at large, both numerically and also with regard to physical and mental development.

Nevertheless, divorce is obtained in Hayti with comparative ease, marriage being simply a civil contract, and only existing at all in the eye of the law, when performed by the civil magistrate; neither the priest nor the minister are, in any legal sense, recognized. It is not in any sense performed in the name of God, who himself established it in the garden of Eden, but essentially in the name of human law, and with the understanding that that law is not immutable.

It is much to be regretted that the great principles of the marriage institution are but little, if ever, dwelt upon by the Romish clergy, when they are called upon to perform this solemn rite. If on such occasions the bearings of this great institution on general civilization had by the national clergy been habitually explained, during the course of more than half a century past, doubtless it had not been in vain, and probably the national morality had been of a higher tone. But the Roman Catholic clergy have generally contented themselves with the mere ceremonies of the church, which leave the heart untouched, and the mind unformed; hence the higher duties on the subject of marriage, and the development of its importance, have been left to the Protestant clergy, who, deeming mere ceremonies to be utterly useless, have generally aimed, on such occasions, at laying before the Haytian community the ruinous evils of libertinage, concubinage, and unscriptural divorce, at the same time showing the elevating power of marriage in all respects upon society.

That laxity on so vital a point should be without its unhappy effects on the general moral character of the nation, is not to be supposed. Negligence upon this point will inevitably tell upon the coming generation, and ultimately lead to vice and great unhappiness, the more so in a community where infidel principles have so much shaken the public mind and conscience as to the claims and authority of Christianity.

The diffusion of true religion, as superseding mere national and nominal creeds, demands therefore the most serious consideration of the Haytian people, as affording the only hope of the universal practice of sound principle on this great question.

CHAPTER XII.

Soulouque falls.—Geffrard the choice of the People.—Geffrard slips into Port au Prince.—Hayti Representative.—Exclusive Creed.—The masses as they ever were.-Cannibals executed.-Youths sent to Europe by the Government.—Steamers now familiar to Port au Prince.—The long Wharf.—Water works commenced.—Blowing up of the Arsenal.—Introduction of Gas.—The Foundry.—Improvements in Music.—Haytian Markets.—Prisons.—Penitentiary.—Religious Liberty.—Concordat.—Boyer blameable.—Protestant statistics.—Methodist Financial Committee.—New position of the United States.—Call upon the Churches.

The prison of a gloomy empire falls,
And day again upon the captives dawns,
Happy if now their brighter lot they know!

The fall of the Emperor Soulouque may be considered as a great national event in Hayti; notwithstanding nothing could be more natural or even inevitable, for the voice of Providence seemed to say: "So far shalt thou go, and no further!"

At one time there was more or less reason to think that the Empire was strong and firm; but despotism was unquestionably its soul, and it finally served as a lesson for those who are ever harping upon the necessity of an iron rule in Hayti. In the Empire, as a system of government, there was iron enough. Doubtless a firm hand is needed in Hayti, as well as elsewhere; but an iron one has never yet succeeded among these lovers of liberty and equality.

In fact, even in Hayti, the Empire, as a system of government, was behind the times; and the spirit of the educated classes, even those of them who were the friends of hard rule, as well as the sunken masses, which at one time half worshiped the Emperor and his hollow dignities, gradually grew cold, and ultimately opened their eyes, at least in some degree, to the fact that a Chief, without any education whatever, was a misfortune to a people; besides which, the great military marches, North, East, and South, so often repeated during this gloomy reign, became at last utterly insupportable to every class of the nation. A move, therefore, to shake off this fearful incubus, was ultimately the result; and General Geffrard became the choice of a Provisional Government, formed on the 22d of December, 1858, at Gonaives.

At the commencement of this movement, great fears were entertained of a struggle between the Imperial troops and the Republican army, now forming under General Geffrard, especially as it was quite understood that the Emperor would most certainly maintain a fierce conflict; nor can it be doubted that this was his intention, hence his great preparations for what appeared to be a great and fully intended blow; but however determined may have been this crowned chief, his subjects were now exhausted as to further patience both with Imperialism and its despotism; and this movement against the Empire, while it was well and efficiently directed, was so completely backed by the spirit of the nation, that success became certain.

The Republicans leaving Gonaives, and taking St.

Mark's, gradually approached the capital, under their newly-chosen President.

The Imperialists had sallied out once or twice to meet the advancing forces; but all their efforts being useless against the Republican arms, they returned, and shutting themselves up in the city, artillery and infantry were planted wherever they could command the roads by which the Republicans might enter the capital.

But all was now hopeless; the sceptre had evidently been wrenched from the grasp of an unfit hand; and during the night of the 15th of January, 1859, General Geffrard entered the city of Port au Prince, at an unguarded point, which he knew well where and how to find; and the formidable army for the support of the Empire literally and promptly vanished—not a man stood by the falling power.

Soulouque had imprisoned Mrs. Geffrard, with the hope of forcing her to give information of her husband, who he knew had fled or was concealed. As might easily be supposed, the monarch ignominiously failed in this base effort; and the conqueror, on entering the city, broke open the prison doors for his devoted wife and daughters, the latter having voluntarily followed their mother. The political prisoners also were liberated, and some of them soon proclaimed through the streets the heart-breaking tales of ten, twelve, or more years suffering.

There was great wisdom in choosing a dark night, for the great national metamorphoses from Imperialism to Republicanism; for while the shades of night made it easier for the victors, they also conveniently concealed the wholesale desertion from the Imperial army, which took place at such a rate that even before sunrise that morning, Imperialism had utterly disappeared, leaving Republicanism as complete as though such a thing as a crown had never been heard of in Hayti; except, indeed, that the unfortunate Emperor was now a prisoner in his own capital. He, however, was allowed to take refuge at the French Consulate, with his suite, etc., from whence he embarked on board the "Melbourne," an English transport, for Jamaica.

It is not intended here to enter into minute detail, with regard to the state of things in Hayti at this time, although it might be exceedingly interesting to do so; nevertheless a general outline of things is due to the many friends abroad who have long watched, and are still watching, the onward movements of this important though small Republic; we say important, because, however unworthy, Hayti is a representative nation, as to the African branch of the human race.

At the time of the arrival at power of General Geffrard, it will be admitted that Hayti had sunk to a low level, as to general progress and development; not indeed from any designedly evil course pursued by the former Imperial Government, although its corruptions were confessedly great, but simply because the ruling elements had been for some dozen years altogether in arrears of the age. Yet it is probable, not to say certain, that the best intentions existed, especially with some, but the knowledge necessary for leading the country on in the general improvements of the day was wanting, not indeed in certain classes of the country, but simply on the part of those who really had the reins of power, and who, by sheer force of terror, had silenced both tongues and pens; hence the failure as to real progress in Hayti was as natural as it was great.

General Geffrard therefore came into power amidst a chaos of things, and it will be admitted that the efforts, at the commencement of his Presidency, for an onward movement, were great and laudable, giving signs of real vitality, and affording great hopes for the future.

One of the first great measures of the new Government was in favor of education; and it must be acknowledged that the views taken of this great measure, and the scale of operations proposed, although not embracing the rural masses, was extensive, and much was unquestionably done. Both sexes shared in the solicitude of the Government, as to the establishment of public schools; and perhaps it may be safely said, that in a short time it was found that education had never before existed on such an extended scale in Hayti.

The nature and bearing of this effort for the rising generation, is another question. Whether the moral culture which was brought into action in this case, was of that elevating, ennobling, and unsectarian character, which would be desired and sought by many, in both America and Europe, is doubtful. The national clergy was expected to visit the various schools thus brought into existence; hence the idea of moral culture in Hayti, did not aim at more than the formation of a national, Romish and exclusive creed; and notwithstanding the now greatly enlarged sphere of education, it is doubtful whether in this

Haytian population of some 700,000 souls, more than 10,000 were ever at any time receiving the advantages of education, if indeed so many. Neither the great masses of the interior, or even of the towns, were yet reached; in fact, the day has not yet come for this Republic, when shame of ignorance as to a degraded mass, compels the ruling power to see that every child in the nation should be taught to read. Happy will it be for Hayti, when the liberty to be ignorant within herself shall cease!

Nevertheless it will be admitted that this Government struck the most powerful blow which had ever been given in this country, to one of its still-existing African superstitions.

It is not to be concealed that Vaudouism—a superstitious dance, of African origin—is still followed and practised by many of the long-neglected masses of Hayti, not only in the interior, but also in the capital of the Republic. This dance has a religious bearing, and involves the eating of human flesh, supposed to be sacrificed to the god Vaudoux.

A most unhappy case of this nature coming to the knowledge of the new Government, was brought into the Criminal Court, where it was proved that a child had been stolen, murdered, and eaten, not from want, but in the name of Vaudoux. The guilty parties—eight in all, among whom were several women—having been fairly tried, were brought out and publicly shot, as an act of security to society.

The justice of this dreadful example is of course not to be questioned; but it remains equally certain that neither Hayti nor any other country can be morally regenerated by such means. The opening of the eyes of the masses, by means of Christian primary education in early life, is the great hope in such cases;* and it is infinitely to be deplored that the full consciousness of the existence of this wide-spread evil in the Republic, has never been sufficient to rouse both the Government and every enlightened citizen, to such activity as would sweep away an iniquity so degrading to the whole nation, by those educational means so clearly pointed out by the common sense of mankind, and which God has so fully placed within the reach and power of every enlightened and well-disposed Government. If, therefore, ignorance is a nuisance in a Christian Republic, then let the education of every child in the nation be obligatory.

With the idea either that it would be impossible to educate the whole nation individually, or that it would be good policy for the masses to remain as they are, at least for the present, it has always been the aim of each Government to form a national nucleus of intelligence; and it must be admitted that great success has attended the education given with these limited views. It must, however, be remembered that the success here referred to is of a purely mental character; the moral element being entirely neglected, as to anything like formal culture; yet a sufficient number of intelligent men and women have been raised, to give the fullest assurance of what would have resulted from the individual education of the nation. The inevitable result, however, of

* It is a fact well known that this public act of justice was utterly without effect, except that it made the practice more secret; hence similar cases have occurred since. The god Vaudoux, in these dark minds, must yield to the true God.

such a course long pursued, would be the formation of a species of aristocracy, which in a Republic where the most ignorant have from the beginning been taught an absolute equality, would operate most injuriously, in innumerable ways—as, in fact, it has done.

At the restoration of the Republic, a resolution well worthy of notice was adopted, which was that of sending a number of intelligent youths to France, for the purpose of acquiring a knowledge of different branches of industry. The idea was doubtless good, but the results of such laudable measures have hitherto been frustrated by the military system, which has so long drawn into its ruinous vortex the entire youth of the nation.

It is true that with regard to national education, in the full and entire sense of the expression, Hayti has failed. Nevertheless she has so far succeeded as to demonstrate her entire capacity to represent, with her younger sister Republic, Liberia, the African branches of the human family.

It is worthy of notice, with regard to the last-named Republic, that at its capital, Monrovia, there now exists an university, on an entirely efficient scale, with the power of distributing literary honors, and having as its just and natural source the education of the masses.

Had the national mind of Hayti leaned this way, her superior pecuniary resources had made the same great national glory easy of acquisition, long since.

The hopes of Hayti were perhaps never more raised than they were by the great movements of the 22d December, 1858, as may be easily imagined, when it is remembered that they so hopefully dispersed the long night of despotism, under the name of an Imperial Monarchy.

Doubtless the desire for progress of every kind, so ardently manifested at that time, both by the Government and people, was perfectly honest and sincere. Much was proposed, and much was set on foot, but the true rigor of sound moral principle was wanting.

Among a vast variety of undertakings, attention was soon turned to a small steam navy, and also to the establishment of a line of coasting steamers, the latter being done by the organization of a native Steam Navigation Company, to be encouraged by a yearly grant from the Government, to whose call they should be held in case of necessity.

The present improvement is the more acceptable to the public, from the fact that it is on a fair commercial principle, depending thus on its own merits and worth for success, and it is hoped that ultimately it will be fully developed, extending its operations to the entire Island, including both the French and Spanish parts.

There may be, therefore, now seen in the harbor of Port au Prince, three naval steamers in the service of the Government, and five coasting steamers belonging to the private Haytian Steam Navigation Company, already referred to; nor can it be denied that this is a great advance upon the past.

To those who are accustomed to see forests of masts, commercial and naval, these notes may indeed appear trivial; but by those who know anything of the infancies of new countries, the few steamers already upon the Haytian waters, and under the Haytian flag, will be greatly appreciated, as affording much hope for the future; and in fact, with regard to the coasting steamers, it is greatly to be hoped that when military duties shall either have ceased altogether, or shall have been reduced within reasonable limits, they will become commensurate in numbers, etc., with the great resources which nature everywhere offers in Hayti—affording at the same time, as they will, greater facilities for more constant and extensive intercourse with the various seaports of this great Island.

Also with foreign countries, intercourse by steamers now began to assume an interesting and promising importance; the Haytian Government at the same time showing every disposition to encourage this increased intercourse with the world by yearly grants, which in certain cases were made, thus bringing America, England, and France into closer and more extensive commercial connection with this little Republic.

The fact of several commercial steamers carrying on a successful business with this Republic, may be considered as proof of the resources of Hayti, which are now beginning to be practically known. One result of this increased intercourse at Port au Prince may be seen by immense enlargements for commercial accommodations at the custom house of that capital, and also the remarkable addition of a wharf, advancing into the sea some 600 feet, with tram-ways, etc., for facilitating the transport of goods from the shipping to the custom house.

Progress and improvement as to ocean communication is now therefore a fact; but with regard to interior communications, not only is there a total absence of steam, as to public railways, but the ordinary highways, as we have already noted, are precisely as they have been from the beginning, except that they have generally deteriorated in all respects.

It is true that with regard to public railways for general traveling, it is very greatly doubted, and perhaps by competent judges, whether the population of the Republic is sufficiently dense to warrant any attempt of this kind, on any large scale; in fact, any attempt on a large scale would perhaps be impossible, without foreign capital.

One great fact, which might afford some reason to believe that railways in this country might answer better than is generally thought, is that an immense amount of produce is utterly lost in the interior, simply for want of means of transport. In the present state of the public roads, heavy timbers of great value are lost; immense mud holes, dug by heavy rains, embarrass on no small scale the very interests of the country; whether the amount of property lost by such impossibilities of traveling, would not greatly help, in the way of compensation, is at least worthy of consideration. In fact, railways bringing to the various seaports of the Republic the great timbers of the interior, where public saw-mills might be established, would create great industry in the country, and at the same time greatly increase the supply of its own wants, as well also as its exports.

Under the restored Republic, it was in contemplation to establish water works for the capital, on such a scale as should meet the wants and necessities of the whole city, not only as to ordinary supplies for the population, but as the best protection against those fearful conflagrations which must long be inevitable among an uneducated, untrained, and consequently careless mass, where almost a whole population may be said to be ever on the move, with lighted cigars, whether at the carpenter's bench, among bales of cotton, or otherwise.

It is right to notice that this great enterprise was not simply proposed, but really commenced, by the Geffrard Government. Immense sums were applied to this purpose, and the whole work begun, by the importation of a large amount of piping and general apparatus. The great reservoir was dug, and greatly advanced as to the mason work.

This may be considered as a great and laudable undertaking, and when fully carried out and completed, will doubtless be an immense stride in general progress. For the present, however, it is greatly to be deplored that circumstances have checked the progress of this admirable and greatly-needed undertaking. National troubles intervened, and all was suspended; hence the great fire of 1866 had full range, a fourth of the city being entirely consumed.

Another sad proof of national carelessness occurred about 4 A. M. of the 12th of September, 1866, when the arsenal blew up. This event was indeed one of the most fearful nature. Upwards of 30,000 lbs. of powder exploded, which covered the entire city with every description of shot, some of the heavy ones damaging the houses, and all more or less threatening human life. At the hour mentioned, the whole town was alarmed; but what at first seemed to be the shock of an earthquake, was soon explained by whizzing balls, etc.; bolts were started a mile distant by this dreadful shock; some lives were lost, but not many; an immense amount of property was destroyed. It was said by those who remembered the similar explosion which occurred nearly forty years previous to this one, that the latter was more terrific than the former. In the present case, many houses in the neighborhood of the arsenal were literally shattered to pieces; and in fact, through a great part of the city, many houses were seriously injured. That so few lives should have been lost, in so fearful a catastrophe, is surprising.

During 1861, an attempt was made on a small scale to introduce gas-light into the city of Port au Prince, of which the following are a few historical notes:—

In 1859, the Wesleyan Missionary, long residing in the above named capital, visited the United States of America, on his way to England, his native country, with his family, after nearly twenty years' residence in Hayti. In both the States and Europe he pleaded the cause of female education in the country of his long residence, with the intention, on his return, of establishing a public seminary for this purpose, on such a footing as should have been an honor both to Hayti and the great cause which it was intended to represent. But notwithstanding the purpose and proposition were both universally applauded, the effort was a failure, the details of which would bring out a sorry tale, of many professing and wealthy Christians, who in the same breath both applauded and rejected all direct appeal to them. A small sum, however, was collected; but the whole amount being less than £100, and therefore altogether inadequate to the expenses of the undertaking in view, was lent for the purchase of a small gas apparatus at New York, which turned out to be a perfect success, and continued in use at Port au Prince for upwards of two years. It was indeed limited to the Wesleyan Missionary establishment, which consisted of church, two dwellings, school, etc. As might be expected, this great novelty in Hayti attracted public attention, and these small works were visited, examined, and admired by the President of Hayti, accompanied by his Ministers.

The Wesleyan establishment, in this case, was simply intended as a starting point for the ultimate introduction of gas to the whole city of Port au Prince; but this also proved a failure. A slight accident occurring, the neighbors sent a protest to the Missionary, against the making of gas so near to them, with orders to demolish everything in twenty-four hours! This was supported by the authorities, who requested that all should be suspended for the present, and thus ended the first attempt to establish gas in Hayti!

This was at least a well-meant attempt by a friend of Hayti, to introduce into the Haytian Republic one of the most admired improvements of the age. Whether this laudable enterprise should have been allowed utterly to sink by the enlightened authorities who had so much admired it, and who so long had witnessed its successful working, or whether public spirit was not wanting in this case, would need but little reflection to decide. It might indeed be said that other things were more wanted in this Republic;

but for fifty years past this has been said of every proposed improvement in Hayti, and nothing has been done. Unquestionably it were better to begin something, than never to begin anything, simply because many other things are wanting.

Much, however, as the failure of the introduction of gas-light into Hayti is to be deplored, the failure as to the founding of a good Protestant Seminary for female education is yet far more painful, and in fact humiliating, especially to the Missionary who had this thing at heart, and who was left unsupported, notwithstanding the most laborious efforts on his part, by a Christian public.*

It is but due to the restored Republic of Hayti, to notice the fact of the establishment of a Foundry at Port au Prince. The mere erection of iron buildings on a respectable scale, although of but little importance in either Europe or America, may be considered in Hayti as an event; the attempt itself is praiseworthy, although the remark might be applied here also that other things yet more urgent were needed.

The steam force at the establishment in question, may be less than one hundred horse power, but the general machinery, or rather the general distribution and application of the power, is well planned and efficient, and if only well worked and sustained, under good direction, might unquestionably be of

* The remaining funds for this great purpose are still available; and it is greatly to be hoped that heart enough will yet be found, if not among the men, at least among the ladies of all the churches of America and England, to enable this Mission to take up the great question of female education in Hayti, upon a scale which shall acknowledge, what Hayti has never yet fully done, the true dignity of woman!

incalculable advantage to a country so entirely agricultural as Hayti, where implements of all sorts are continually needing repair; where now also ocean steamers are in constant need of such repairs as are practicable only by means of such establishments.

Unhappy events, of a revolutionary nature, paralyzed this as well as other great national undertakings. Nevertheless the buildings of this establishment, which are mostly of iron construction, are worthy of a national idea of this sort; and although the whole enterprise languished long through political strife, it may ultimately become efficient. Its management was at first under French engineers, who although perfectly competent, were singularly unfortunate in all respects, both as to their arrangements with the Government, and also as to their health; for it must not be forgotten that the tropics are trying in no ordinary degree to European workmen.

Among the distinguishing peculiarities of the restoration of the Republic, should be noticed the subject of national or military music.

Up to the end of the Empire, it must be admitted that public music in Hayti was altogether in arrears, notwithstanding the decided taste and ear of the Haytian people for this useful and charming science. This inspiring power evidently tells upon the very gait and march of the troops; while as a science, it forms a salutary mental exercise for a numerous class of persons, going far to show that whatever is done, either in a military or any other sense, should be completely done, even though it should be on a limited scale, military or otherwise.

Competent men, both civil and military, were sent

for from France, and the result is very apparent; nor can it be doubted that with a right and efficient direction, the Haytians would equal any people in the world, in this exquisite charm of life.

With regard to military organization and general discipline, it might be well to note here that a corps called "Tirailleurs,"* was formed, and having been well disciplined by foreigners, their appearance, with their new music at their head, was perhaps the most martial that has ever been seen in Hayti. The mass of the army, however, was much as it had ever been, that is to say wanting in real military discipline; in fact, it must be admitted that Hayti, in the very thing which she has most and so long adored, viz., all that relates to the sword, is very far, not to say shamefully behind all the military and naval tactics of the age.

In municipal arrangement, much still remains to be hoped for. It must be admitted that the streets of Port au Prince, in all respects, demand improvement; but above all, the markets present a scene the most thoroughly African that can well be conceived—dangerous as to epidemics, etc., from the vast accumulations of every kind of refuse.

The butchers' stalls, although not really neglected, are nevertheless uninviting; while vegetables, fruits, etc., are arranged on the ground, the venders being frequently screened from the sun in some ludicrous manner in the shape of a crazy shed, or otherwise.

It is therefore greatly to be hoped, that the powers and the financial resources of the municipal body will be enlarged, and that iron markets, upon the prin-

* Riflemen.

ciple of "les Halles de Paris," such as was contemplated by the worthy Mayor of Port au Prince in 1863, will be fully carried out, with the brilliant accompaniment of gas, as was already intended. It is indeed infinitely to be deplored, that the new Republic, which had broken down a despotic Empire, should not have had a sufficient amount of perseverance to carry out such plans as, in such a case, would have done honor to Hayti, and also to its African character.

We cannot here allow to pass unnoticed, the great question of reformatory and prison establishments.

It is to be regretted that in this important branch of modern Christian civilization, there is not only much that is wanting, but much to be undone.

The unfortunate beings incarcerated for moral delinquency of any kind, seem to be much more under an avenging than corrective power. There seems to be no reforming influence or design within these wretched walls; nor does it seem to have been considered by the Government, that the time, mind, and muscles of these unfortunates, might be employed in such a manner as to be of great moral benefit to themselves, and at the same time of great public utility.

A thief caught in the city under the Empire of Soulouque, would frequently be beaten with sticks by policemen, as they drove him to the prison through the public streets, and in fact greatly ill-treated; a most unhappy spectacle in all its bearings, both as to the prisoners themselves, and as to society at large.

It has ever been the usage in Hayti that criminals should work in the public streets, under the surveillance of military police, with heavy chains upon their legs. It is indeed inconceivable, that sights so thoroughly lowering to the public mind, should be possible under any enlightened government. Such however is the case; and it is to be deplored that higher views have not prevailed on this important subject.

The prisons themselves, although tolerably clean, and generally well-supplied with water, are poor in discipline and without moral culture. Crime, although indeed prevalent, is certainly not so much so as might have been expected from the ignorant state of the masses; but the thought of prison-life being turned to any advantage, either to the prisoner himself, in a moral corrective sense, or to the public, as to general utility, seems not for a moment to be entered into. Life, time, resources, and all that is hopeful as to reformation, seem to be utterly flung away, as to prison-life in Hayti.

An attempt at the penitentiary system was indeed once made in Hayti, and even great expense and preparations were made in erecting suitable buildings, etc. A military officer of intelligence was sent to Jamaica, during the Empire, to study the system carried out in that island, and on his return a full and well-drawn up report was presented to the Government. All was admired and applauded, but beyond this little was done, except an entirely inefficient attempt to carry it out.

The buildings for the Reformatory, which bear the name of "Maison Centrale," still remain, with their forges, and all needful arrangements for blacksmiths, whitesmiths, etc., etc.; all which are now used, either for Government or public service, as may be, but as an establishment having for its purpose the working out of moral reformation, it is simply a failure. Nor is this in the slightest degree surprising to any who know Hayti, where indeed intellectual culture on a good scale, although not general, is well carried out, but where moral culture either for prisons, penitentiaries, or general education is but little known.

We now turn our attention to one great subject, in connection with the general progress of Hayti; one, too, vitally bound up with true civilization, and dear to all. The subject of religious liberty.

Hayti, following in the train of mankind generally, has not always been faultless on this subject. She too, has persecuted creeds, which she deemed not her own — thus following in the wake of nations greater and old than herself; she has, it is true, done this genteely by paying all expenses, and respectfully requesting the first Missionary advocates of the Bible who reached her shores, to withdraw; although even this stood connected with some mobbings, peltings, imprisonments, etc., etc. Not, it is true of the Missionaries themselves, but of the natives who had adhered to them, and had thus dared to think for themselves in religious matters. Soulouque also dishonored both himself and his country, in the same sense, at least to some extent, notwithstanding the Missionaries themselves were not sent away.

But the restoration of the Republic placed religious liberty upon its right footing; and it should also be admitted, and suitably noticed, that every Government in Hayti, since 1843, except the late

Empire, has been, upon the whole, liberal upon the religious question.

Grave considerations and reasons are indeed assigned for the establishment of an Ecclesiastical Concordat with the Roman Pontiff. We will not however here, farther enter into these reasons than to notice approvingly, that a purer clergy than the one which served Hayti previous to the establishment of the present more legitimate hierarchy was indeed needed in the Republic; but time alone will develope whether the advantages sought by means of a closer alliance with Rome could not have been more fully realized and carried out by other means.

We are not here speaking in any sectarian, or even religious sense. The simple question now before us is, whether the ecclesiastical system of Rome is not in arrears of the advanced views of the educated part of Hayti? Whether, in fact, such an ecclesiastical compact is not incompatible with the spirit of the age; not so much from any religious conviction, as from the innate desire existing in all men to be in all respects free, being responsible to God alone, in all that relates to the conscience? *

* The following notes on the Concordat between the Court of Rome and the Haytian Government have been furnished by a friend for this work.

Apart from the funds for the general support of Roman Catholic worship in the Republic, as well as the heavy expenses of clerical seminaries, the Roman Catholic hierarchy appointed by the Concordat are allowed to draw on the public treasury in the following order:

The Archbishop	20,000	francs	per an.
The two Bishops, 1,200 frs. each	24,000	"	"
The Grand Vicar of Port au Prince	4,000	"	"
To four other Grand Vicars	12,000	"	"
To each of the forty Clergymen, 1,200 fs.	48,000	"	"
	108,000	"	"

That the reigning spirit of Hayti is such a love of liberty, and too, in such a sense as Rome was never yet disposed either to give or tolerate, is quite certain. How these plain facts may harmonize, is a question for the future to develope. That there was much wisdom in the course so long pursued by Hayti on this subject, in the past, is very probable; notwithstanding the general character of the Romish clergy previous to the Concordat formed by the Geffrard Government.

Religious liberty, however, under the reinstated Republic, may be considered to have been complete. Whether so much could be said of any other Roman Catholic country in the world, is doubtful. Notwithstanding the advanced ideas of France on this subject, it is not meant by this that Protestantism might not meet with difficulties of a local kind in Hayti, from perhaps a bigotted village priest or magistrate; but there is reason to believe that in such a case, both the Government and people generally would be on the side of right. This, however, as we have seen, was not always the case in Hayti. Boyer evidently dreaded entire religious liberty, as something for which Hayti was not prepared, notwithstanding she had been quite prepared for this, both under Petion and Christophe; both of whom had introduced Protestantism to their people—yea, and protected it. Nor was it ever, under them, in the slightest degree, molested by the people; rather its presence among them was greatly respected. Nor was there ever the slightest clashing heard of between the two communions; there was the utmost religious liberty both in the Kingdom of Christophe and in the Republic of Petion—each was resolved that both Romanism and Protestantism should stand together before the people, and that all should, in the freest manner, choose for themselves. These remarkable men, evidently, had but one thing in view, which was, to give the fullest religious liberty to all, not simply in a general sense, but individually, and to maintain it in perfect peace. The Romish clergy of those days, saw many of their own flock using their own judgments in religious matters without an opposing word. This was done in peace; there was indeed no Concordat in those times.

The plea, therefore, of the Boyer Government, that the people were not prepared for the toleration of Protestantism, as we have already seen, was unfounded. The truth is, that Boyer himself was not prepared for this, and that Christophe and Petion were; while, at the same time, both the latter were resolved on the maintenance of peace, and the entire liberty between the two creeds, certainly, Boyer had no such resolve at all.

Protestantism has now been before the people of Hayti half a century, and it is not to be supposed that its influence is very limited. It has worked, like silent leaven, throughout the length and breadth of the nation; hence the power and extent of Evangelical truth in Hayti is not to be judged by the number and size of the various little churches of the Protestant communion, now scattered over the Republic, nor even by the number of members attached to those churches.

The "Gouvernement Provisoire" of 1843, doubtless, took an immense stride on the great subject of religious liberty; and, it may be said, that all was maintained in this respect, until the unhappy days of General Soulouque; who, nevertheless, under better advisers, had doubtless done better, for his own good will can never be doubted, but his mind was unopened by education.

It is, however, gratifying to find that the Christians of the United States of America are now beginning more seriously to turn their attention to Hayti; and it is equally to be hoped that the annihilation of slavery in the model Republic of the age, will lead these Christian sons of freedom, of every denomination, to turn their attention fully to their many neighbors, who are rent and torn by internal revolutions, and who so deeply need the soothing power of genuine Christianity. It is also gratifying to feel assured that, no other sword than that of truth and righteousness, will be used in this great work of sweeping out indolence, ambition, and ignorance!

Upon this principle, we here with pleasure record the arrival in Hayti of the Rev. J. T. Holly, of the Episcopal Church of America. This worthy servant of God landed in Hayti on the 26th of May, 1861, at the head of a Mission Colony of one hundred and eleven persons, from New Haven, Connecticut, of the United States of America; their object being two-fold—to form such a home for themselves in this land of ill-understood freedom, as should exert such a Christian Missionary power on the community and country, which they had adopted with such truly Missionary feeling.

The place of residence, which was assigned by the President of Hayti to this little pioneer Christian army, was an estate belonging to the government called Drouillard, about three miles outside the city of Port au Prince. Nor were they wanting in energy and enterprise—in this respect they were fully American. But it is hard for men of northern latitudes to understand the power of a tropical sun, and the care and prudence which the preservation of their lives demands under its prostrating influence. The care thus needed, during the first year, is too often thought to be mere indolence and timidity; hence many of sterling worth in this Colony fell victims to a persevering, indefatigable, but ill-directed industry; and, at the end of nineteen months after their arrival, the ranks of this noble Missionary band were so thinned by sickness and death, that a different course altogether was deemed desirable, and adopted. The pastor became a resident in the city of Port au Prince; where, it is earnestly to be hoped that one so worthy, will be long sustained by the Episcopal Church of America, which has already put forth such laudable energy in behalf of Hayti.* Great discouragements, unquestionably, crowd on all Missionary labor in the Haytian Republic; but the resulting increase from the preaching of the Gospel to every creature, is of God. All reasoning is silenced when once duty becomes plain; as, beyond all doubt, is the case with Hayti.

That Mission work would be more efficient by sending forth large Christian companies for the evan-

* Since the above date of 1861, the American Episcopal Mission of Port au Prince has received the entire frame-work, in wood, of a small church, parsonage house, and school, which now stand as embellishments to the Capital of the Republic of Hayti.

gelization of the world, rather than solitary Missionaries, might be easily understood; but such enterprises in the tropics, without the greatest prudence, would inevitably involve great loss of life. Farm labor, under a vertical sun, to a northern constitution, imperatively requires a gradual introduction,—the cooler hours of the twenty-four must first be employed, and the fierce heat of the torrid zone must be faced by degrees.

The arrival of the last named pastor completes the following statistics, which will afford a general view of the amount of New Testament truth which has been brought to bear upon Hayti, by various denominations, since the arrival of the first Wesleyan Missionaries in 1816.

PUBLIC PLACES OF WORSHIP IN HAYTI, APART FROM AND INDEPENDENT OF THE NATIONAL ECCLESIASTICAL ESTABLISHMENT OF THE COUNTRY.

Denominations.	*Number of places of Worship in each place.*	*Computed number of attendants at each place during the year.*
English Wesleyan Methodists.		
Port au Prince	1	600
Fond Cheval	1	40
Jérémie	1	100
Gonaïves	1	100
Cape Haytien	1	200
Gros Morne du Nord	1	40
L'Anse á Veau	1	40
Cormunin	1	40
IN THE SPANISH PART.		
Puerto Plata	1	50
Samana	1	100

African Methodists."

Colored Americans.		
Port au Prince	1	150
Arcahaie	1	50
Jérémie	1	50
Santo Domingo	1	50
Baptist—English.		
Jacmel	1	300
St. Raphael	1	50
Baptists—Americans.		
Port au Prince	1	100
St. Mark's	1	50
Episcopalians—American, etc.		
Port au Prince	1	200
Cabaret Quatre	1	30
Colored American Immigrants dispersed through the Republic without Pastors		400

EDUCATIONAL STATISTICS.

Probable number of Children sent from different Protestant Schools since the commencement of Evangelical Missions in Hayti.

From the Port au Prince Wesleyan Day School	1000
From the Cape Haytien	500
From the Gonaïves	500
From the Jérémie	400
From the Jacmel English Baptists	200
From the Port au Prince American Baptists, etc.	100

Those who know anything of the nature and intense antagonism between the Church of Rome and those whom she deems heretics, will look rather with wonder, than otherwise, on the extent of success which has attended Protestant labors in Hayti; especially when it is remembered that the numbers here given, both as to the public ministry, and also with reference to education, are nearly all of Roman Catholic origin.

Nor should the fact be overlooked, that the work of education at the different stations named, is carried on by pecuniary resources created in Hayti, by means of payments in the schools, and also by subscriptions collected wherever they might be found; at an immense cost of Missionary toil, known only to those who have been, and still are, thus personally engaged. Some idea, however, will be formed on the subject of general expenditure, relating to the various Mission properties in land, buildings, etc., now held by the various stations—purchased principally by funds raised in Hayti—and of which the following statistics will aid in arriving at a fair knowledge:

Cost of land and buildings among the English Wesleyan Methodists, and other Denominations, in the Republic of Hayti.

PORT AU PRINCE.

English Wesleyan Methodists.

Land and Church, (gold)	$15 000
Parsonage, School-house, etc., etc	12 000
Various dwellings on the same property	1 000
JEREMIE.	
Lands and Church	5 000
Parsonage, etc	3 000
CAPE HAYTIEN.	
Land and Church—a lease from Government.	5 000
Parsonage, School, etc	3 000
CAYES.	
Land and Church	5 000
FOND CHEVAL.	
A small Chapel, etc	100
CABERET QUATRE.	
A small Chapel, etc	100

JACMEL.

Baptists—English.	
Church, Land, Parsonage, etc................	12 000
Native Baptists—St. Raphael....................	1 000
African Methodists.	
Port au Prince Church, etc.................	2 000
Arcahaie Church, etc.......................	100
Jérémie Church, etc........................	500
Episcopalian—American.	
Port au Prince—Land, Church, Parsonage, etc.	3 000

In addition to the entire support of Education by Hayti itself, amounting to certainly not less than the sum of $2,000 per annum, in gold, more or less has also always been raised in Hayti towards the support of the public Ministry.

The Wesleyan Missionary Committee of London, in all probability, has expended on Hayti, as a Mission field, upwards of $200,000 in gold!—a great sum, considering the toil of raising it, but small, considering the work to be done.

The statistics here given, financially and otherwise, will doubtless throw some light on the extent and general results of Missionary labors of various kinds in Hayti; and the figures given will supersede the necessity of further enlargement for the present.

How the idea of abandoning such a Mission should ever, for any conceivable reason, have got any where into existence, is utterly inexplicable; yet, that such an idea has been broached in certain quarters of the Church, is quite certain.

Much, indeed, might be said as to discouragements in this Mission, especially with regard to the

English Wesleyan Methodists, who were the pioneers of Protestant Missions in this Island; and here we would begin with the fact, that the two first Missionaries were compelled to withdraw from this field of labor, as the result of persecution; after which, for many years, Protestantism was barely tolerated in Hayti, while every step and development of the Mission was exceedingly slow. The country also has been the victim of political convulsions; and, although comparatively great things have been done, it has been in the midst of great difficulties. Most of the European Missionaries, for reasons apparently sufficient to themselves, have gradually withdrawn from the field; while most of the native Missionaries have ceased to be connected with the English body, also for reasons sufficient in their own estimation, although remaining friendly.

The tenure of land in Hayti by foreigners is, doubtless, more or less discouraging to the operation of foreign societies—the holding of landed property being impossible to foreigners, except through the medium of native trustees.

Still, the aim of all Missions is independence. It is not to be supposed that either Colonies or Christian Missions were founded with any other idea than that of ultimate independence.*

Upon this principle, and with this special purpose

* Discouragement, therefore, on any such grounds or for any such reasons, on the part of those Churches from which Missionaries are sent, would be simply an error; the sole aim of all Christian Missions being to place in the hands of all nations the great power of Christianity; to teach them how to apply it, and to leave them to do so when the fair moment for so doing shall arrive.

in view, a financial Committee was formed at Port au Prince, in 1865, with the hope of creating funds throughout the Republic, for the general support of the Wesleyan Mission in Hayti. This was intended as a starting point for ultimate self-support; hence the first measure proposed and adopted by this native Committee was an offer to the Parent Committee of London of three hundred pounds sterling, on condition that five Missionaries should be sent to Hayti. This offer was made simply in the sense of help, but it was declined in England on the ground that to comply with, or accept it, would entail expenses which the home Committee was not prepared to undertake; nor is it altogether surprising, if confidence in Hayti should have failed in this case, considering all the difficulties already referred to in this Mission, and especially when the fact is added, that the hope of a native Ministry in Hayti seems, for the present, to be faint.

Nevertheless, the formation of a financial committee in Hayti, with a view to ultimate self-support, may be considered as an epoch in the Wesleyan Mission of this country; that it was worthy of the patronage and support of the parent Committee was admitted; that all refusal to act in the case should have had the most chilling and discouraging effect on all future effort, will be easily understood.

The case now before us, is the more to be deplored from the fact and certainty, that had the Missionaries thus requested been sent, funds to a much greater amount than the sum pledged, would have been raised.

Hayti is doubtless considered as not having fulfilled her national mission as to Africa and the African. This, painful as the fact is, must be admitted to a great extent; hence she has been looked upon as unworthy. This also is true; but if this is to be the ground-work of abandonment as to Hayti, the principle would lead to far more than would be desired. If only such parts of the earth as have deserved redemption are to be visited, where shall we go?

Whatever view may be taken on this subject, it is a fair question whether, if this Mission had been kept up, and the same increase of Missionaries as was accorded during the first thirty years of its existence continued, Hayti might as a nation have been put on a different track, and whether the impulse thus given, might not have led to another order of things.

It must not be lost sight of that the work of Christian Missions in Hayti is still essentially of a pioneering character. The Wesleyan Missionary Society of London have ever encouraged their Missionaries in this sense. Nor has the time yet come, when the great preliminaries of this noble work might cease. The pioneers are still needed, and will be, until the various churches already raised, and yet many others, shall be able to maintain and act for themselves. To allow them to disappear for any other reason than what the great Head of the church would recognize as impossibility, would be a crime.*

* A country deeply needing Christian Missions, and being unreservedly open to them, is unquestionably a call to the churches. That the case of Hayti is such a call cannot be denied. Whether those, who in obedience to the great call in question, have put their hands to the plough, have ever after a right to cease all further obedience to that same call, which as far as relates to necessity and an open door, ceases not, is a grave question.

It is now evident that divine Providence is bringing about a splendid concurrence of circumstances in behalf of the human family at large, and therefore more or less in behalf of Hayti.

During the past, limits and fetters of various kinds, both in and out of Hayti, have operated in an exclusive sense, not only as to Christian Missions, but also in many other respects. Conflicting views and feelings have long been working; but the time is coming for better things; the breaking down of old barriers has commenced; slavery has now been sufficiently shaken to assure us that ultimately the world shall be free in every sense.

For many years the attitude and position of the United States with regard to Hayti and the African question generally, was painful and unhappy. Now all in this direction is changed. In fact, the gloomy days of the past, in all these matters, are over; yet, during those times of darkness and discouragement, the messengers of the churches were sent from the Wesleyans of England. Long and through every difficulty have they labored; nor has it been in vain, as will be seen by the preceding pages. For many years, this field of labor seemed to be confined to its first pioneers; but the day is now evidently come, when hindrances on every hand are dispersed by an Almighty power. This interesting field of labor is now thrown open to all. It is hoped, and confidently expected, that the American churches will now think of Hayti. Let all the churches, whether of America or Europe, hear what the Spirit saith unto them in this matter, whether as to Christian education or the preaching of the everlasting Gospel.

The triumphs of justice in the United States by means of the late civil war, may doubtless be understood as a signal on the part of divine Providence of righteous purposes towards mankind.

A great nation, where the Word of God is in the ascendant, no longer under the iniquitous spell of slavery in any sense, either with regard to its internal politics or its general and extensive relations with mankind, is now unboundedly free to act in the diffusion of Christianity, by saying to the nations on the great subject of justice and freedom to all men—follow us. And it is to be expected that her armless armies will join other ranks, under the same Emmanuel, to raise the world, and aid in placing the human family on the highway to universal peace, knowledge, commerce and science. In this sense, Hayti may hope for her share in the general good; the more so, since the proof is fully before the world that she is prepared for all that the general church of Christ, from any and every quarter, is prepared to do for her. Nor is anything else needed for Hayti; her capacity to act and do for herself is sufficiently evident. The moral element alone is her failure. Here all indeed is weak and unhealthy. Let the Christian churches, therefore, of the world bring her health and strength, and she will rise to her proper level.

CHAPTER XIII.

The Immigration.—Its failure.—Assassination of the President's daughter.—Intended public meeting on the death of Lincoln.—The Tirailleurs.—Quarrel between the English and Salnave.—Geffrard's last Message.—Great proposals for reform.—The night of the 22d of February, 1867.—Geffrard embarks for Jamaica.—New Government.

Nations clos'd up, like stagnant waters, to
Corruption haste; let then the living stream
Come in.

Nothing indeed can be more deplorable than the great instability of Hayti. Truly nothing can be said in justification of this; and yet it is an undeniable fact, that there is much to be said of the development of some of the resources of the country, even in connection with this painful fact.

Military duties and revolutions, weighing as they have done upon the entire population, and ruinous as they have been, have not obliterated the proofs of real stamina in the Haytian nation.

Let it be remembered, that notwithstanding all that is to be deplored in this case, and although the national interests have been so crippled by great political shocks of every kind, all has nevertheless gone on, though poorly. The exports of coffee have increased, and an important cotton business of some 10,000,000 pounds per annum has been even created in the midst of the greatest political troubles. Education, although on a limited scale, has been kept up; the various interests of life have gone on; and notwithstanding a heavy national debt to France, which forms a continual drain upon the public treasury, wealth and even fortunes have been and still are accumulated, while the revolutions themselves have frequently brought before the world men of talent.

The proofs, therefore, are clear of the existence of immense resources in Hayti, both morally and physically, needing only fair circumstances to bring them out.

It will be seen from the preceding chapters, that during the first years of the Geffrard Government, all was hopeful, notwithstanding errors of judgment or otherwise, as to the general principles of Republicanism or political freedom; for it must be admitted, that Hayti has never yet understood fully the principles of free government in a really practical and working sense.

It should be noted here, that in the early part of the restored Republic, an intense desire was manifested for an augmentation of population by means of immigration on a large scale. Numerous agents were therefore employed by the Haytian Government to hold public meetings amongst the colored people of the United States, and lecture on the general subject of Hayti. By this means thousands heard of Hayti—its climate, fertility, boundless resources, and advantages of every kind were brought before the public by means of the press, and in every other way possible. In fact, by many, these descriptions of Hayti and its various resources were thought to be merely luring exaggerations. It is, however, a fact, that the climate and soil of Hayti do unquestionably afford extraordinary resources. But it must be remembered, that however extraordinary the resources of any country may be, the greatest prudence should be exercised when entire families are thus drawn from their homes.

Immigrants put in possession of even a rich wilderness, are at once in the position of pioneers; their task, in the midst of the greatest resources, will become hard, and many in such a case will die under their burden. Nor would the cry of cruelty, injustice and deception be very surprising in such a case.

That there was want of judgment on all sides in this great and laudable scheme must be admitted. Nevertheless, vast sums were expended by the Haytian Government in this case; and it must be owned, that many influential men in the Republic of Hayti had this thing really at heart.

Hundreds of families arrived in Hayti at a time. All hopes were great; but the difficulties of forming new homes, of adopting new habits, and of forgetting the enjoyments flowing from the high civilization which they had left behind, were distressingly great, and many sunk, unable to bear their load. The tropics worked fatally on these northern constitutions, although African in their origin; a thousand fears were very naturally the result. Hundreds returned, and the report of their disappointments, sufferings and loss, both of friends and property, soon ended further proceedings.

The effort was, nevertheless, well meant, and had it only succeeded, as it unquestionably would, had it been on all sides rightly directed, it would doubtless have been of incalculable advantage in all respects, not only to Hayti itself, but to those who came, and also to the great principle of independence, which to all Haytians is and ought to be dear! Nor ought this failure to terminate all future idea of this sort. Let the same object be still kept in view, and even more than ever in view; but instead of embarrassing numbers arriving suddenly, no suitable preparations being made for them, let the whole aim and plan be worked slowly, rather in the sense of a perpetual movement than otherwise. Let suitable positions for a few families be previously fixed upon, where water and fertility shall render success certain, and where, on their arrival, they shall be sent without delay. Nor let there be further augmentation, until the prosperity of those already at work is fully established and assured. Such a course pursued for twenty years, or on the principle of a perpetual increase, would ultimately become a vast success, and the reputation of the country would be permanently established.

For those possessing more or less wealth, Hayti might ultimately prove to be a safe bank, paying great interest on capital, well applied to a soil of boundless fertility. This field, also, in a literary sense, is worthy of attention, as to the bar, medicine, or the senate.

In fact, the aim and ultimate object of this great effort for immigration was praiseworthy. It evidently meant that Hayti needed this. It was doubtless thought that a more healthy moral element was desirable, than which nothing could be more true. But in addition to this fact, it is found that the population of Hayti is too small for the due cultivation of its wide territory, and from paucity of population, will result weakness and stagnation. Nor is it to be concealed that stagnation is a leaven for evil. Let then a healthier moral and intellectual stream come in; but let it come in safely to all parties.

The military system long prevailing in Hayti and the language are doubtless obstacles; but the former must ultimately and before long lose its power. Nor let it be forgotten, that in this attempt, under the government of Geffrard, this question was fairly and satisfactorily considered. In fact, a military despotism must become impossible. Let those, therefore, who feel aright on this matter, come to help this nation forward in the triumphs of peace and industry.

With regard to language, full and fair commerce will show the way in this matter; while it should not be overlooked, that the English language has already made great way in Hayti.

The great principle both instinctively and designedly recognized by the last strenuous effort for immigration, as well as in the same attempt of 1823, was, that no branch of the human race can become isolated. Man cannot exist alone in any sense; he was not formed for this, nor can it in the nature of things be. Hence it has been an unlimited blessing that from the time of Julius Cæsar, all Europe, so to speak, has poured itself into Great Britain, and the glory of the United States at the present time is, that they are now open to the whole human family. Nor has either of these great nations lost one iota of their identity by the overwhelming tide of immigration, which has long been flowing in upon them.

Hayti, therefore, has everything to gain by judicious, unceasing and well managed immigration. Let her only maintain her dignity by the enlightened, universal moral culture of her children.

But whatever there might have been of good in the Geffrard Government, the elements of discord, from whatever cause, could not be concealed. Swarms of enemies doubtless resulted from banishment, political executions, trampling on public opinion, extravagance in public salaries, supporting great vanity, and a thousand other things, showing decided want of moral ballast.

It was not, however, to be expected, that a great privileged class, such as was created under the Empire, and which had taken decided root, would be suddenly swept away without creating bitterness. Hence on the 3d of September, 1859, one of the most diabolical events that was ever recorded, dishonored the annals of Hayti. A certain party, resulting from the wreck of the fallen Empire, formed the fiendish plan of assassinating the President. History informs us that the Government had heard of this; but they unwisely allowed the plan to mature, probably hoping the more easily to seize the really guilty. Darkness was chosen for this deed. Hence in the evening of the last named date, it was planned that the married daughter of the President, Madame Blanfort, should be shot, with a view to bring out the father, who was to have fallen in the excitement, which would naturally result from their diabolical proceedings.

This innocent victim was shot by murderers who had aimed at her, through one of the windows of the room where she was sitting, engaged in reading at à table. The ball of the assassin went through her head, and life was soon extinct. But the friends of Geffrard understood the elements about them. Hence by their entreaties to prevent him from exposing himself, this base project failed.

The history of this unhappy case, together with the trial and execution, forms a volume of deep and unhappy interest, which is well known in Hayti.

It is therefore evident, that even from the beginning of the restored Republic, the elements were conflicting. Nevertheless, much was done as to national progress, as has been shown in the foregoing chapter.

But the true, sound principles of government have ever been wanting in Hayti. Hence the best intentions have failed by wrong measures. The great political sin of Hayti has ever been in not allowing her own recognized principles of Republicanism to have free action. The chief magistrate, Emperor, King, or President, has hitherto been the master and not the servant of his country. Hence he has executed his own will rather than that of the people. Arms, therefore, have been resorted to in all cases, rather than give up a power which in the end could only be sustained by brute force. Hence the military power under Geffrard sought perfection as a system; its music, discipline and uniform were all such as had never been seen before in Hayti.

Nevertheless, up to 1862, a House of Representatives, during the restored Republic, had been at work, in which there were men who could and did express themselves with decided ability. The result was, that the Government was in some cases seriously called to account. This was indeed a new order of things in Hayti; such, too, as was not readily appreciated by the ruling power. Hence, in the early part of 1862, this Parliament was dissolved, the President at that time having the power to do so. Nor would it be difficult, perhaps, to explain why the same Representatives were not returned by the people. It is however certain, that a different House was constituted, which probably would not have been the case, but for undue governmental influence; while at the same time, it is equally certain that the dissolution of this Parliament was the starting-point of much unhappiness.

Lowering clouds now commenced. The men who had legitimately spoken in behalf of their country, had been silenced and dismissed. The leaven of discontent had thus been deposited in the nation, and its power was soon seen. Murmurs here and there were increasingly heard, and the ruling power, feeling the symptoms of a revolutionary plague, concluded that the sword was the best protector. The order of the day, therefore, soon became military impressment. The country was thought to be in danger, although not from any foreign enemy, and therefore must be protected; or, to speak plainly, the Haytians were threatened by the Haytians, and arms therefore were necessary. Such, alas, has ever been the course of Hayti, and her victories have too often been over her own prostrate self.

A new military corps had been formed under the Geffrard Government, and was named "Les Tirailleurs."* This corps, consisting of some two or three

* Riflemen.

thousand men, was specially trained, as to discipline and music, by men from Europe. Their appearance was perhaps the most military, and as such the most imposing ever before seen in Hayti. They were petted and in every way idolized by their Presidential chief, and in fact, under the shadow of their arms, he deemed himself invulnerable.

In the early part of 1865, the revolutionary feeling of the anti-Geffrard party came to a climax, by the formation of a Provisional Government at Cape Haytien; and on the 13th of this same month and year, Port au Prince was in a state of great excitement.

A public meeting on the assassination of President Lincoln was to have taken place at the Wesleyan church on the last named date, at which a Secretary of State was to have presided; but the public excitement was such, that it was impossible for it to take place.

Hayti was therefore again in the throes of another revolution, the root of which was two-fold: First, the stand of Longfusse, who had been joined by Commandant Salnave, the former having been tried and shot, the latter escaping; secondly, the dissolution of the House of Representatives, which had evidently been a cause of great irritation. These two circumstances had rather been main-springs among a thousand others, which had long been at work, until the final result was that the nation was in conflict.

In the early part of Geffrard's power, the public press had clearly expressed the wishes of the nation, that punishment of death for political offences should cease. This, however, was not heeded; and it is deplorable, that under an enlightened Government, which dared the wishes of the better part of the community, so many victims should have fallen as a mere matter of policy. It would be painful as well as humiliating to reckon the number that fell under a Government of so much light and intelligence for political offences. But, "What a man soweth that shall he also reap."

The military power of the "Gouvernement Provisoire" at Cape Haytien was in a fort at that place, named "Bel Aire," commanding the main, and almost the only entrance to Cape Haytien. This fort was under the command of Commandant Salnave, who, under the Provisional Government, was soon named General.

Forces and troops were now got together by President Geffrard. An army of from six to eight thousand men was sent to the north, and attacks, skirmishes, and fights became frequent between the parties, in which many at different times were killed. But Salnave, with a handful of men, held the fort, "Bel Aire," and the comparatively great army of Geffrard long quailed before this handful of resolute men. Ultimately, Geffrard himself marched with an additional force; but all was useless, until a difficulty occurred between the English and the Salnave party. The former considering their flag to have been insulted, pursued the offenders, but in the pursuit became inextricably fixed and grounded in the harbor of the Cape, and was fired upon from the land. A bombardment by the British forces was the final result; the consequence of which was, that Salnave was dislodged, and with many others was taken on board an American man-of-war, then in the harbor. The way being now cleared, Geffrard and his army entered; but his taking possession, by means of foreign guns, was displeasing to all parties. Nor was anything made solid by this means.

At last a pause ensued, and Geffrard returned to the capital. Had he at this time remodeled the Constitution, established at once a four years' presidency, descending ultimately himself to simple citizenship, reduced his army to reasonable limits, and his own salary from $40,000 to $20,000 per annum; had he then pushed economy through the entire Republic and seriously set about the education of the masses, the name of Geffrard had been immortalized in Hayti. But he chose another course, and consequently changed his position with posterity.

The leaven of discontent was now working through the entire nation, and the Government felt that it must surround and sustain itself by arms or fall. The result was, that the Republic became one great military camp.

During all these movements, great truths would now and then be spoken in the Senate; nevertheless the Government was no longer called to account for its proceedings.

The public journals, some of which had spoken plain truths, now of themselves, voluntarily, ceased to exist. They had spoken truth in vain, and therefore they had now ceased to speak at all; thus they seemed to leave the national bark to drift as it might upon a troubled sea, which by right means it would not have been impossible to calm.

The marches and counter-marches, together with

the arming of a whole nation, purchase of large ships, etc., would naturally have drained even a rich national treasury. All public works and enterprises ceased — all was poverty; the public credit was shaken, loans became impossible, while the whole nation became disgusted and exhausted with fatigue.

To add to the public troubles, two great fires had occurred at the capital, and Port au Prince had been reduced to the greatest distress, thousands of families having lost all they had, and being left without shelter.

It will be evident from these statements, that political, commercial, and financial complications of a most ruinous nature, would be the inevitable result. How intelligent men, directing the interests of the country, could contemplate a threatening ruin, which it was in their power to avoid, without at once saving themselves and their country, is difficult to understand. Yet far more astonishing was the case of the President, who knew the will of the nation as well as he knew his own, and whose dignity, safety, and duty concentrated in being its executive; but an infatuation seemed to have seized all that were in power, and confusion seemed to seek its climax.

It will easily be understood, that the whole Salnave party, having been compelled to withdraw to foreign shores, it would coalesce with Geffrard's enemies already banished, and an army of no small force would by this means be united against his Government beyond the limits of the Republic. Nor did they fail in this manner to exert their influence and power. Many, too, whom they had left behind, as they well knew, sympathized with them, in addition to the many who had fled from Hayti during Geffrard's Presidency. In fact, the large exiled party of Soulouque, at the fall of the Empire in 1859, were now in sympathy, and unitedly contributed immensely to the general embarrassment; in truth, the elements now at work, both in and out of the country, were powerful and threatening; nevertheless it was felt by many that, with all the errors of the Geffrard Government, the country had in some respects advanced, and there were not wanting those who would have rejoiced to see that Government rising above its abuses rather than see all interests at the mercy of a sword-revolution; but the pride of one party and the bitterness of the other were both rising above all control, and it seemed inevitable that wreck should come on.

The national machinery, however, worked on. The subject of a periodical Presidency was broached by the President himself, but his proposition was surrounded by such a network of conditions, and above all, that the President going out of office should be allowed a handsome pension, with military honors, etc., that it failed and sunk the President himself yet lower in the estimation of the people.

The seventh article of the Constitution, by which Geffrard professed to rule, forbad the white man to hold landed property in Hayti. This subject was also brought forward for consideration by the President; modifications were proposed, which perhaps might have succeeded, but the agitations of the country increased, and the subject of peace and war between the citizens of Hayti absorbed every other.

The following message of President Geffrard to the House of Representatives and Senators, will enable us to form an idea of the general state of things during the latter part of his Presidency.

"*Gentlemen of the House of Representatives:*

"You are perfectly aware of the events which took place in the course of last month at Gonaïves, Hinche, Ouanaminthe, etc.

"These new outbreaks were indeed easily put down and order re-established, but they have had the effect of renewing alarm and increasing the uneasiness of the public mind.

"These events are not solitary or far apart from each other; they are evidently the continued efforts of one and the same unceasing conspiration.

"In the beginning of these unhappy movements, I had indulged the hope of being able to calm the violent feelings and passions in which they originated by a course of policy at once moderate and generous, but in this I have been disappointed; my moderation has been interpreted as weakness, and my generosity as timidity.

"Still, as to all attacks upon myself personally, I have continued to follow the conciliatory course.

"Yet the persistency of these factious men in carrying out their designs, and the ruin upon ruin which they continue to heap, have brought on circumstances which threaten the peace of society and the future hopes of the country.

"In such an agitated state of things, I should be wanting in duty if I did not suppress the finer and more generous feelings of my nature. Henceforth these guilty men shall receive what they seek; my hand shall no longer in mercy stay the sword of justice against them.

"Amidst such unceasing agitation and daring attacks upon the public peace, you, gentlemen, must have noticed a fact, which to me affords singular pleasure, for, while it is the strength of our Government, it must at the same time fill its enemies with despair. I refer to the entire calm which so evidently reigns throughout the whole of the peasantry of the country, who are still pursuing their ordinary course of industry in every commune of the Republic. With an admirable good sense they have resisted the tempting and ensnaring promises which corrupted men have offered. In fact, in all the agricultural districts these base intrigues have failed, and this explains the fact, that these agitations have been confined simply to the places where they have broken out.

"These troubles, agitations, and alarms, I repeat it, are the work of one and the same conspiration, carried on and sustained by a handful of unhappy men, most of whom have lost standing in society, either by judiciary condemnation or misfortunes which have been the result of their own imprudences, but all urged on by blindness, pride, covetousness, and hate.

"This party has evidently two centres of action, the first of which is among us, its purpose being to diffuse their own political views and tofoment in surrectionary movements, and also to gather round them the discontented and dissatisfied of all kinds.

"The other centre is on foreign shores, formed of men who, in their own country, were divided in politics, and hated each other, but now being animated by the same one purpose of fabricating calumnies and falsehoods, and of furnishing ammunitions, arms, and money to the disaffected at home, with a view to accomplish their design.

"What is the object of this faction? We know that it is to displace the present Government, with the hope of gratifying their own selfishness.

"Hence, what are its plans? In a correspondence which has been intercepted, one of the leaders expresses himself in the following manner:

"'The Revolution is inevitable; it will be bloody, bitter, and deeply distressing, because of the various shades of hatred made uniform by one fact, viz., that no citizen will be armed in favor of the tyrant, etc. Power will come out of even the inert.'

"This is their platform. We seek here in vain for names well-known for true patriotism, tried and proved by long service, or distinguished by personal virtue and merit.

"Behind the ramparts of the city of Cape Haytien, the cry was, 'Salnave!' On the arrival of the brave General Berthelemy, he was himself proclaimed to be the man of their choice. Before the city of Gonaïves, General Guerrier at once became their man; and each day will doubtless produce another.

"Only calumny, insult, and falsehood are heard of; but nothing really definite—not one new thought, nor even the form of a system that would inspire the assurance that the future would be any better than the present; in fact, the odious excesses of all kinds to which these men are given up, are such as were never heard of at any former period of our history.

"Assassination, incendiarism, pillage of both private and public property—no crime is too great for them—and to crown all, they seek to place the guilt of all their aims upon the Government.

"In vain do they pretend that it is one man only they attack. No one will or can be deceived by so low a subterfuge. The fact is, that it is upon society at large that they are making war.

"My aim shall be to protect society, by the fair use of every means which the Constitution may place at my disposal; and the ardor and constancy of my defence shall be in proportion to the intensity of the opposition with which I may have to contend.

"In the noble task which is imposed upon me by the circumstances which surround us, I shall reckon, gentlemen, upon your loyal support.

"Dark shades indeed appear in the general state of things; but after all, they are only to be found here and there. The position of affairs in the Republic at large, on the whole, inspires confidence—a fact which demonstrates that we are disturbed by a faction simply, the masses being quiet.

"For more than a year past, this faction has declared a revolution to be on the eve of taking place, and that this was visible at every point of the political horizon; but when revolutions are thus imminent, the nation rises at once, and no longer waits.

"Here, then, we have an audacious minority aiming at a

revolution; and, unable to create the needful enthusiasm, they seek to lead on by desperation.

"While these men are conspiring and laboring to ruin the country, the people—the true and faithful people—are enriching themselves by industry. Our home markets are full, and our exports were never greater, not even in the most prosperous times.

"On the 30th of last June, the produce of half the year only amounted to:

Coffee	40,000,000 lbs.
Cotton	2,000,000 "
Woods	50,000,000 "
Cocoa	2,500,000 "

"All other exports being in the same proportion. Let the public quotations be noted, and it will be found that all has been as remunerative as at any past date.

"Importations perhaps have not kept up in the same proportion, in consequence of our deteriorated currency, the cause of which will easily be found in our revolutions, and public conflagrations, all which disasters have been aggravated and increased by the financial difficulties of other countries, as well as the war in Europe which is just beginning.

"It is hoped that the fact and truth of things now before the world, will have the effect of establishing public confidence, and giving general assurance.

"I was anxious, gentlemen, to show you the solid ground on which we stand, before your separation for your various homes; persuaded as I am that you will do your best, in your different spheres, to tranquillize the public mind, and to discourage every tendency to disorder, which is so thoroughly ruinous to all interests.

"In the statements which I have now laid before you, I have also had in view to give that assurance to foreign nations which our commerce needs, and to create that confidence in us abroad, of which we conceive ourselves to be worthy.

"Gentlemen, in taking leave of you, I have the honor of saluting you with great sincerity.

(Signed) "GEFFRARD."

Few speeches, from either thrones or Presidential chairs, have been more plain and straightforward than the one now before us. There is no effort here to conceal or gloss over the difficulties or real state of things as they were at that time.

Hayti, according to the official statements now before us, was suffering at that moment from great internal convulsions, which were now viewed with alarm by the Government itself; nor need the fact be evaded that this state of things had too long shaken all interests.

The Message now before us shows that the long and continuous attempts at change, which were now beginning to shake the whole frame-work of society, had steadily and specially kept in view one man; the legitimate enquiry, therefore, simply is, whether the working of the Haytian Government had indeed been under the direction of one mind, or whether all had been done in conformity with the free, the fair, and honest working of laws and institutions, to which the Executive of all constitutional Governments is responsible, and without which anarchy and confusion must result—which no plea of the unfitness of the masses could justify. Geffrard's starting point should have been universal moral culture, beginning with his own Government. This would have saved both him and his country.

Hayti has even yet to learn the great advantage of allowing every division of power and authority full play, and rendering every functionary responsible for the right working of his department—thus relieving the chief magistrate of an immense weight of responsibility.

There is indeed something admirable in the fact that the masses of the people were generally calm amidst all the tumults which at this time agitated the Republic. So much could not certainly have been said of the late Empire. Here the masses rose, as well as the higher classes—a sad proof that the galling yoke was felt by all; hence, as we have seen, not one man stood by the falling monarch. The masses were indeed in this case unconscious of oppression, but they had ever been left stagnant in ignorance and vice, although possessing the soundest elements of every kind.

It may be seen from the Presidential message now before us, that there is ever much to be feared from enemies, which have either been banished or have banished themselves, to escape political execution. A man exiled will in all probability be desperate; and in a country liable to revolutions, the numbers compelled to fly would probably in the end form a strong force upon a foreign shore, and even become dangerous.

France, as a numerous people, might indeed be strong enough to resist almost any amount of armed exiles which she might have; but the case of a weak and small Government, having a large number of outside enemies in the position of exiles, is very different; while the intense eagerness to return, and the bitterness of banished men, who conceive that they are innocent of crime, will be easily understood.

Commercial and industrial activity went on, notwithstanding the paralyzing circumstances of the country, during so long a period. The male population, however, being nearly all under arms, much would inevitably depend upon the women of the land; nevertheless this would show how highly desirable to such a people must be a permanent peace. Could but a healthy national tone be brought about, there would probably be few nations of the same proportions that would surpass Hayti in general wealth.

On the subject of importations, as referred to in the Message now under consideration, we have only to remember that with regard to manufactures of any kind, nothing is done in Hayti. Hence, soap, lard, butter, rice, etc., are all imported, simply because the energies of the country are entirely expended under an unhappy military system, which, while it turns everything out of course, as to general produce and industry, at the same time corrupts, demoralizes, and in fact ruins the entire youth of the nation. Foreign markets, therefore, are resorted to on a scale that would never have been needed, if arms had not been the great occupation of the nation. In fact, the creation of a class of mechanics is a thing almost unthought of; such has been the extent of this national military camp; hence a formal apprenticeship to a trade is a thing almost forgotten under present circumstances, although at one time something of the sort existed in the Republic.

The true friends of Hayti, both native and foreign, are compelled to admit that the statements now made are profoundly to be deplored; for it is impossible not to feel that mankind were not born simply to bear arms.

Upon the whole, therefore, the official document of

President Geffrard, already considered, shows a most unhappy state of things. The entire structure of society is there shown to be shaken; all minds are agitated; all hopes are dim; the very money of the country has long become an article of merchandize, and is ever varying in value, thus showing a complication of things from which it will require no small amount of talent and good faith to extricate the nation. Nevertheless, all the materials for the formation of a right state of things are at hand.

The people need only a fair and open road, with the light of pure Christianity shining upon it, and unrestricted liberty to go on—that liberty which is unfettered by arms, and which needs only a Christian conscience, in the right sense of the word, to render it perfectly safe.

An enlightened, honest, and faithful house of Representatives, teaching and compelling the Government to do its duty, would prove both a main-spring and safety-valve to the nation; that such a House could be found in Hayti is very certain. The struggles of all nations are towards this point, while it is the realized glory of both England and the United States; nor would this fail to make Hayti worthy of herself.

But the surges of an inevitable revolution were coming on; rumors and agitations increased; commerce was nearly prostrate; only men in arms and military uniforms were to be seen.

Proposals of reform were now abundant, all of which were accepted by the Government, which was now opening its eyes to what ought to have been seen long before. All, however, was now some two years too late.

The political tempest was rising. Troops were hurriedly sent hither and thither. Men were uselessly harassed and fatigued, until decided discontent and disgust became manifest, ending at last in a most extraordinary explosion of passion, of which the following are the leading facts:

It will be remembered that a military corps of riflemen had been formed, called "Tirailleurs;" they had been the great hope and power of this now reeling Government. Barracks, on a comparatively large scale, had been built for them, in which they were to be lodged, fed, and disciplined, as this is understood and done in Europe; but the Haytian "Tirailleurs" were not prepared for such military rigidity, however brilliant; their pay, too, became irregular and uncertain; their food, also, which was prepared for them, was a great source of discontent. Each one, previous to the new arrangement, had prepared his own food in his own way. The new style was to them loathsome. These, with many other sources of dissatisfaction, had prepared them to imbibe the general feeling of discontent which was now animating the whole nation.

The result of all was a fearful plot, which might have swept off both the President and his family. Hence, during the night of the 22d of February, 1867, the whole city of Port au Prince was roused by the sound of volleys of musketry, which seemed to take place in the neighborhood of the palace. The fact, however, was soon known that the Tirailleurs were pouring out their fury in this manner by firing upon the palace.

Nothing could be more dreadful than this frightful

rattle of fire arms. It was hoped for a moment that blank cartridge only would be used in such a case; but the ominous whizzing of balls through the air, while they convinced all to the contrary, gave at the same time universal warning of danger. The thought of who might fall at the national palace, was harrowing; and this was greatly augmented by the report of a cannon which had been planted before the palace by the insurgent party, and which was replied to by the Government; in fact, amidst these flashes and reports of fire arms, with the exciting sound of balls flying through the air, all was alarm. Some innocent ones fell in the streets, and those who remained in their dwellings instinctively avoided all openings, from the dread of flying balls.

About 2 A. M. of the 23d, the scene was most exciting. The firing on the palace then began to cease, but the entire city was in an uproar, and the cry of "Vive Salnave!" seemed to be the watchword. In fact, the whole population appeared to be wrought up to madness. The Tirailleurs were seen by the bright moonlight of the early morning, stalking in all directions, armed and in small companies, without order; no one whatever seeming to be at the head of this mysterious and extraordinary movement. All were giving orders, but nothing definite could be perceived in anything that was done, only that the name of Salnave seemed to be the magic soul of this amazing movement.

Day-light came on, and with it the ascendency of the Government authority, which now pursued whoever might be found as having been engaged in this nocturnal movement. Some few were found in one of the forts at the northern entrance of the capital, among whom were some of high respectability. Thirteen in all were shot by their pursuers, and thus ended this unhappy affair.

The power of the Government was now evidently broken. The military corps on which all the hopes of the Executive had leaned, were the first to send the national ship adrift in the midst of the tempest. The gods which had been adored, had now been mysteriously seized with fury; and this was the winding up of an utterly wrong course pursued too long, by even intelligent men, who had been very confident in their system of management, and their knowledge of their people.

On the morning of the following 13th of March, it was found that during the previous night, President Geffrard, with his entire family, etc., had gone on board the "Destin," a French man-of-war, then in the harbor of the capital, and was then clear of the territory of the Republic, on his way to Jamaica.

It would be premature to say much at present of the Government which followed the withdrawal of President Geffrard. It might, however, be mentioned that a Provisional Government was formed, of upwards of twenty members; that this was superseded by an "Assemblée Constituante," elected by the people; that a new Constitution was drawn up; that the Presidency for life was abandoned for one of four years; reforms on a large scale were established, both as to the army and otherwise; the press was declared to be entirely free.

But reconstruction and consolidation, in such a

case, can only be the work of time. Doubtless the past will at last become the great teacher of Hayti. Commerce and contact with foreign nations will and must ultimately sweep away many hindrances to prosperity; while the loud calls for universal education, will rouse the nation to its duty. Christian Missions will doubtless increase, with also an immigration which will bring in the Christian element, and ultimately raise this nation to that high level of Christian civilization, of which it is well known to be entirely capable.

CHAPTER XIV.

THE CAUSE AND CURE OF HAYTIAN REVOLUTIONS.

Conspiracies, which seek the deep hid cave,
To blow the Revolutionary flame,
Are oft the offshoots of the Rulers' frowns,
On the loud thoughts of a free people's will.

In the estimation of many, Hayti stands answerable before the world for her many revolutions, nor is it presumed that she is not.

On this subject Hayti, for many reasons, has long considered herself exceptional. She is, however, before the world, and it is to be expected that many will judge her who are in better circumstances to do so than she is herself; for the simple reason, that those who are looking on upon a struggle are frequently better judges of its course than those who are actually engaged in it, and are therefore ofttimes blinded by passion.

If, however, Hayti is censurable in this matter, she can only be so in the same sense that England, France, America, or any other nation might be; for it is undeniable that this has been the foolish course of all nations in all ages of the world.

Fearful convulsions of humanity constitute, principally, the texts of human history; nor can it be denied that the finest nations of the age have arrived to what and where they now are through fierce and bloody struggles. It might, indeed, be said that as to Hayti, all this was avoidable; but however true this may be, it cannot be more so than of every other branch of the human race, either of the present or past ages; hence we are all driven to the conclusion that we have to do with facts simply as they are,—that the world, through all its generations, might have been better, cannot be doubted.

Whether Haytian revolutions, therefore, or any others, were unavoidable or not, is not so much the question at present as whether they are, in any sense, to be accounted for, or whether they are really the mere whims and freaks of an immature people. Such an inquiry, while it is only just to Hayti, might be useful to its future generations; for it must be admitted that the great cardinal points of right and wrong have been continually lost sight of, and hence the ever-recurring necessity of pointing out the rocks with which they have so often come into contact, and on which they sometimes have nearly wrecked; thus, at the same time, demonstrating the only sound principles upon which any Government can, with safety and real advantage, direct the interests of a free and intelligent people.

It will help us greatly in this investigation to call to mind, and to fix it well in our thoughts as a fundamental principle, that in every branch of human interest, whether politics, religion, or science, there are certain cardinal principles which cannot be departed from or violated with impunity: hence the inevitable law of lightning, being destructive wherever it strikes with power, we seek safely to direct its course.

We are not pretending to anything new here—

hence we note that principles, as cardinal as the sun, present themselves for every system of right Government, and from which any departure will involve such fearful consequences as no amount of military power would be able to control. Public opinion is not controled by arms—thought is not to be silenced by brute force—human interests and opinions, in a national or any other sense, can only be safely guided by the great principles of right. Plain as all this is, Hayti has yet to learn that all interests of every kind, private or public, must yield to this; in fact, this itself must become every man's interest, and whatever Government she may have, which cannot submit to this, must fall.

It will, however, easily be understood that more proximate causes of a local character, bearing with great pressure on each individual, will produce their more prompt and immediate effects; hence, the domestic wrongs of slavery, when once agitated, promptly worked out their results,—the violent death of Dessalines also, as well as the feuds between Christophe and Petion, may be reckoned among those domestic national strifes which are so often met with in history, although in reality unjustifiable and even censurable.

The task, however, which we now propose for ourselves is, to explain the causes and the cure of the Revolutions of Hayti.

In this inquiry, the simple principle of cause and effect will form the ground-work of our reasoning—avoiding all that is abstruse—plain matter-of-fact being all that is here needed.

The causes of the national evils in question lie deep

hid, and but too frequently are utterly lost sight of. It will, however, be imperatively necessary to bring them out into open day, in order that we may see our way clear in our present inquiry; nor are they at all difficult to recognize, notwithstanding they are not found upon the surface of things.

True liberty is, unquestionably, found in the Anglo-Saxon branches of the human race; hence our attention will frequently be drawn in that direction. It does, indeed, amount to a truism to say that plain right constitutes the pivot on which every honest Government turns; and yet it is an extraordinary fact, that some of the greatest vaunters of national liberty in Europe, were never yet free! and have shown themselves to be even incapable of liberty in its fullest and best sense; hence, plain as truth and right are, they are the very principles which must be unceasingly preached and perpetually held up to the view, not only of the statesman and merchant, but of every class and condition of men, such is the wilful blindness and depravity of man, especially when private interests clash. Yet, no plea as to national habit or education, can be accepted for the simple violation of right, either on the part of peoples or Governments; nor will any consideration, under such circumstances, shield either the governing or the governed from anguish.

It has not fallen to the lot of Hayti to have an Anglo-Saxon origin or training, as to the important municipal details which seem to be peculiar to that part of the human family; and yet there is not a people more prompt to recognize and distinguish between the great cardinal principles of right and wrong on any political subject. Hence the unceasing plea in Hayti itself, as well as elsewhere, that the people are not prepared for that which is simply right, is, and has long been a starting point, from which much error has even already resulted. In fact, it has ever shut up the nation within limits too small for its just moral instincts; and the result has been, what all have seen, increasing efforts in the form of revolutions, to break them; thus showing its instinctive vitality, and demonstrating that its tendency is to stretch beyond its narrow bounds; thus, too, showing that the true wisdom of the Statesman lies in rightly guiding and developing the national impulse. Nor is it to be concealed that when the pent-up crisis comes on, if the more powerful weapon of reason is not resorted to, it will be laid aside, and the sword will be madly seized.

The thought that the Haytians are not prepared for plain and honest dealing, is simply one among innumerable other errors; and, if it were even true, it should rather be the most powerful reason why they should begin a better course. But this is one of the thoughts of former times—one by which slavery itself was upheld, and therefore is altogether unbefitting the present day.

It must, however, be remembered that by the people in this Republic, is to be understood the educated classes; nor need there be any hesitation in such a case; for, notwithstanding, the most uncivilized understand, feel, and are indignant at injustice, it can not be supposed that the details, or true principles of Republicanism, are even remotely understood by a mass of people, which a false and unjust policy has allowed to be shut up in complete ignorance for more than half a century—an error which, it must be admitted, brings down a great weight of censure upon any Government making the slightest pretensions to Republicanism, in a Christian sense.

The descendants of Toussaint l'Ouverture have specially to remember that the wide range of all cardinal principles is filled up with minute details of every kind, inviting close attention, and forming a fit subject for study and research. There may, indeed, and will be differences of opinion as to the application and working of principles in certain details, arising out of difference of climate, habits, etc., etc., but with regard to the cardinal principles themselves, which constitute the great frame-work of the general Government, it will be very evident that they can not be sacrificed without bringing on unnumbered woes. Whatever fails, the main points, serving as pillars to sustain the whole fabric, must stand ; freedom must exist—this, indeed, has been felt in Hayti. The error has been in the details. Of a free press and free speech, a certain range is, indeed, needful ; nevertheless that range, limited by sound sense, must be considered as affording fair and honest freedom.

The use of the great cardinal luminary can be modified in any way we may see or feel to be necessary, but its presence and power could not be dispensed with ; and, however we may deem it necessary to manage its rays, it must fairly shine.

A free and educated people will become restless if the sun of all their hopes—which ought to be their own executive government—becomes obscured by error, and the chill will be instantly felt, which precedes the ultimate fever of those passions, before which all reason flies.

It may be considered as to Hayti, as well as every other country, that the two great necessities which may be called cardinal as to an independent people, are, Freedom and Knowledge, in the most Christian sense, as attaching to all parts of the population, high and low, and wherever these elements may be wanting, it should not be on the part of the people, experience having long taught in Hayti, that an ignorant mass will become both a snare and a fetter to any free government, engendering despotism, fraud, and vanity. In fact, it has been well said by a great orator of our day * that "true liberty does not come from governments, but from the people." Let, then, the entire people be raised by Christian education to the true level of their own interests.

Under a Republican form of government, and especially with a small nation, knowledge must be universal, or the clashings, where all are political equals, will become insupportable, if not fatal. In Hayti a fearful vortex has sometimes formed itself between the two extremes of ignorance and knowledge, and history has shown us the result.

The knowledge which combines the moral elements and which alone can sustain the national soul, must be from God. In Hayti, the starting-point of moral principle has been what men call honor, rather than God and his Word. Experience has long taught us in Hayti as well as elsewhere, that it is necessary to lay the greatest stress on this point; intelligence being more dangerous than otherwise without sound,

* H. W. Beecher.

well-founded moral principle. There must be a well-recognized "higher law;" knowledge in this sense may safely be universally diffused. A free and constitutional government requires this:—each man, in a right sense, then becomes sovereign; and being well able to command his own interests, enriches both himself and his country. And yet, strange to say, in Hayti it is admitted, with perfect *sang froid*, that her masses are in the deepest ignorance. How such a fact can be viewed and admitted by any Christian enlightened government or enlightened part of a community without the deepest solicitude, is inexplicable and strongly indicates that some one main thing is wanting. Nor can it be any matter of surprise that under such circumstances a withering element should be felt throughout the nation; its energies under such circumstances cannot acquire tone, strength, or development; in this sense the wheels of the national interests in Hayti have ever been clogged. Hence the status of the Republic has ever been low, even to humiliation, while material for revolutions has consequently been inevitable, abundant, and ever increasing.

The want therefore of moral culture, and universal education diffused through the entire population, has been Hayti's great and constant misfortune.

Doubtless, a measure of these advantages has ever existed in the Republic; and it is undeniable that there are characters of real worth in Hayti, but all is partial and limited; while wide-spread ignorance among the great majority of the people has undeniably been a fearful source of woe. The religion of the heart has been wanting, and pride and avarice have possessed education and power—thus creating in ignorance both suspicion and envy. The education which Christ sent his disciples to give to every creature has been imperfectly given in Hayti, and men, instead of turning their swords into ploughshares, and thus bringing out the national wealth, have turned them upon each other, thus paralyzing every interest and shaking every hope.

Certain it is, that had the people of Hayti been from the beginning Republicans, in the true and full sense of the term, with her masses enjoying but a moderate degree of light and knowledge, as to Republican citizenship and individual sovereignty, they had unquestionably been vastly different in all respects to what they now are; while they had by this means shunned many a revolutionary conflict, and saved some hundreds if not thousands of banished exiles; sound moral principle had formed the domestic circle, thus increasing and consolidating the general interests and respectability of the nation, and giving it its right stand among the most prosperous nations of the world. So true is it, that manly piety and public virtue promote the interests of the human family. But Hayti has ever remained not only in ignorance as to her masses, but a prey to the vilest and most degrading superstitions. The range of national knowledge has ever been limited to the few, who from the commencement of the national career, have invariably left to the ruling powers the task of enlightening the great bulk of the people as to general education. The education received by the few, whether acquired in Hayti or elsewhere, has not been of such a nature, either religiously or politically, as to inspire sympathy or uneasiness for the sunken masses, or lead them out among the rural population to diffuse the light they had, or in any sense to better their moral condition. With truth may it be said, that of such an education there exists but very little idea in Hayti; notwithstanding this, to an immense extent, is the style of education in the great neighboring Republic of the United States, where the aim and tendency is the education of every individual in the nation, especially in a moral sense, by means of Sunday-schools, and by even the moral structure of society; nor is this simply the work of the clergy.

The education of the few in Hayti, has been productive of a high sense of superiority, engendering a vast amount of pride, while at the same time the institutions of the country have taught the most ignorant an absolute and entire equality, thus placing both classes in a false position with each other. Nor does this fact fail to produce the most unhappy effects, leading, as it does, the most ignorant and incapable to aspire to honors and duties of which they are utterly incapable. Nor will it be difficult to understand, that with the idea of equality—in the absence of education—instilled into the mind by the very institutions of the country, failure in reaching office and emolument would ultimately engender a revolutionary spirit. Hence, the ignorance of the masses, with their well-understood claims to equality, renders the utmost caution necessary on the part of the Government in appointing to posts of office and honor.

In fact, in such reflections we are reminded at

every turn that Christian moral culture is the one thing needful for mankind. Literary education, never yet formed the conscience of any nation ; for this there must be a well-adapted training, by the inculcation of such moral truths as unfold the eternal destinies of man ; nor can it be questioned that horror of sword-revolutions would result from really Christian moral culture.

The necessity of moral education is now acknowledged; it is felt that the mere development of the intelligence cannot meet the wants of general, and especially commercial life, where all is paralyzed without sound moral principle and good faith. In fact, its want is ruin to all interests.

Hope of internal national reform, even after the most deadly revolutionary conflicts, is and must be lost while the general elements remain the same. It seems not to be sufficiently understood and felt in Hayti, that her disease is moral, and cannot be cured by the sword. Mere changes of men, although to some degree useful, will not reach the case. Nothing real or complete can be accomplished while the general elements and principles remain the same. Never was language more correctly applied to a nation, "Ye must be born again."

We come then to the conclusion, that the first great cause of revolutions in Hayti has been of a negative kind ; the right elements of society have been absent, and the results need occasion no surprise. There has been a moral void, which has been filled up with a chaos of evil, from which innumerable woes have sprung forth ; reasonings without end have followed—some have wished one thing, and others have declared another—politicians have brought out their theories, and aged men have given their experience, but each one has thought that Hayti was not yet prepared for the theory of the other.

Those, however, who have studied the systems of liberty which are considered to be the honor and glory of the present age, do not hesitate to declare that the principles of free government have never yet been understood in Hayti. The worn-out pretexts that Hayti is not yet prepared for freedom in such a style or sense has long thrown liberty into the shade as something rather to be feared than otherwise—in fact, as something impossible for Hayti. Nor does it seem ever to have been understood that the unceasing risings and heavings of the nation plainly indicate the deep need of the thing refused.

The leading idea of a true Republic is, that the people govern; in Hayti the leading idea, up to the present time, has been that the executive governs. Under really Republican institutions, the people discuss political questions, both privately and publicly, as being their own special interest and concern, relating quite as much to them, and even more, than to the executive; but in Hayti, for more than sixty years, it has been supposed that conversations on political questions or open discussions, would be dangerous, and therefore are not to be tolerated. Better days doubtless will come, but such has been the past.

The natural and inevitable consequence of such views has been, that public opinion has been frowned down. It is indeed possible to forbid, and even hinder its public expression, but its formation and silent working are beyond the power of man to control; thought will and must be free. To compel its secrecy by endless ramifications of espoinage, or any other means, is simply adding fuel to fire, which in the end will explode in some revolutionary form, and those who thought themselves the most secure, will be the first to writhe under the effects of their snaky proceedings.

A press, dumb by command of the ruling power, speech forbidden, and the very thoughts threatened with a sort of woe to all who dare to think aloud on political questions, are simply the component parts of a political volcano which must in the end break forth with great violence. Nor does it seem ever yet to have occurred to the Government of Hayti, that in these matters they have hitherto been pursuing an impossible course, or that by prohibiting speech, and almost thought, they have made themselves the authors of the revolutions by which they have been so repeatedly overthrown.

To an Anglo-Saxon, it would seem something almost superfluous to say, that the free and honest working of the Representative system is of paramount importance, or that if this be in any way interrupted great evils must inevitably result. It is true, that in great Britain the sovereign holds the power to dissolve Parliament, but the re-election of members is left free to the unrestrained choice of the people; in fact, the object of the dissolution of the English Parliament, on the part of the sovereign, is to re-consult the mind of the nation. Hence the freely chosen representative body becomes the tongue of the people, the nation's safety-valve, through which all revolutionary elements escape. Happy are the people where the national mind is free, and whose institutions allow free vent to those passions which among human beings are inevitable.

It is probable that the starting-point of all Petion's difficulties, apart from the great error of establishing a life Presidency, was the breaking up of the Representative Senators, which doubtless he could not have done had he not held the sword. This, too, was the rock on which Boyer struck; nor is it a little remarkable, that after so much experience Geffrard also should have followed in the same train.* In each case dissatisfaction seized the whole nation; this great constitutional wheel checked in its movements, all in each case went wrong, and the climax of of the evil was revolution, yea, and in each case having the Government for its source.

One of the secrets of the bad working of good institutions in Hayti has been the undeniable fact that Government influence has too much interfered in the general elections, an evil the more inexcusable from the fact that able men in this Republic are not wanting, of all shades, who are perfectly capable of entering fully into all the wants and necessities of their country. Hence, the Executive has executed its own will rather than that of the people, and despotism, which has ultimately seen no hope but in the sword, has been the result.

With a free and fairly working House of Representatives all else will become of secondary importance, justice fully and ever-reigning will satisfy; yea,

* It is true that the Constitution of the Geffrard Government gave the Executive the power to dismiss the Representatives. This step, however, was ultimately fatal to him.

such a government becomes the idol of the people, revolutions are shunned, and the road to progress is left wide open and kept clear for advancement of every kind.

The conclusions, therefore, from our present reasonings become inevitable, that a government interfering in any way with the free elections of the people, with a view to dictate or in any way control, becomes at once revolutionary. In fact, it is a conspiracy against the people, which, as Hayti has long seen by sad experience, leads on to most fearful evils. The principle involved here then is fundamental, any violalation of it is inexcusable, while its ruinous effects will be inevitable.

In Hayti, the people have ever been taught, that they are free and independent, in fact sovereign, and yet their Governments have seemed to believe that the people are unprepared for what they have ever been taught to expect: in such cases the force of arms will fail; nor will there be the slightest right to complain of restlessness, ingratitude, or revolutionary tendencies on the part of the people. Their sure and certain aim will be the overthrow of the Government, which is unfaithful to its own institutions, and all effort to stifle thought or hush the public voice, has so far been found to be useless. Cardinal principles departed from by the Executive will have prepared the way for its own fall; it would require willful blindness not to see that this is the spirit and tendency of the age; arms in civil government are becoming useless, and must disappear. Hence, armies meet in Hayti, but oftentimes a sense of right compels them to fraternize.

Want of higher moral tone in Hayti, and the absence of that Republican boldness which dares to speak out, is infinitely to be deplored. A man here will whisper, and at last draw the sword; nor will he perhaps hesitate as to his own life, while, as a consequence, he will expose many, but he will not beforehand abjure the sword and speak out unarmed, notwithstanding his greatest protection would then be, that he was not a conspirator, and that he simply meant right, but openly.

Those who know Hayti best, have ever been of opinion that the Haytians are a mild and easily governed people; perhaps this will not even be disputed. What then shall be said of the great political strifes of Hayti? The answer is simple and easy: If the people are such, let the Government itself be straightforward in its course, and the people will not derange it; but otherwise, let no one expect peace, not even from a people otherwise peaceably disposed.

Another cause of anxiety and agitation in Hayti, has come from her many banished ones on foreign shores. Political offenders have generally been exiled, or knowing that their lives, as such, have been at stake, they have fled, until at last a great opposing power has been formed outside, which never ceases to exert its utmost energies against the Government which may have driven them away.

In a small nation, it will be easily understood that opposing influences from the exterior would be more sensibly felt than in the case of a larger nation: each banished one will have his sphere of influence in his native land, where, by means of unceasing correspondence, he will perpetually work, until some great gap in the existing Government is made by some false step, perhaps brought on by exiled hate. Some forty or fifty of influence thus exiled and forced from their native shores, would be sufficient to keep a small nation in constant agitation, especially if the sympathies of the great political parties of the nation are with them, as will invariably be the result of any false political measure which may have been adopted by the Government.

In reference to Haytian exiles, it should be noted that in most cases they are supported by their friends and families in their native land; a circumstance and fact which will keep alive, on all sides, the keenest sense of dissatisfaction, and render the general elements of things and circumstances yet more conflicting and dangerous. In fact, the banished ones will never cease to hover about their native shores and eagerly watch the favorable opportunity when some one in sympathy with them shall raise the standard of revolt, and they themselves shall be able to come in again upon some dreadful revolutionary wave by which they may help to overthrow the power which drove them hence; and another start is made, perhaps to end in precisely the same manner,—a danger which will ever threaten while the revolutionary aim is rather a change of men than of principle. Nothing indeed can be more deplorable; the more so, from the fact that the remedy for such evils is so simple and ever at hand, which is simply to follow out the general common sense of mankind.

But the main cause of the revolutions of Hayti has

unquestionably been, that system of slavery which is called the military system. A soldier in Hayti, as in every other country, does not belong to himself, he is a slave, in however honorable a sense. In Hayti, however, it must be admitted that want of discipline, education, etc., etc., makes it, for the private soldier, even degrading. Hence, a nation in such a sense, altogether military, cannot be either free or noble. If those who adore the sword are to perish by it, what shall we say of Hayti? Truly her safety is in justice and reason.

It is probable, indeed, that some of the measures of Petion, although good in themselves, would never have been carried had he not been conscious of his military power. Nevertheless, it must be admitted that this was a most unhappy starting-point, especially when it is remembered, that as first President, every measure of his would serve as a precedent to posterity. His purposes and intentions were doubtless good, but even a good measure carried out by wrong means in a civil government, will lead both the present and future generations wrong.

It is indeed true, that up to the present time, it has been deemed impossible to manage public affairs in this Republic without arms to back up the civil power; but however true this may be, its perpetuity is impossible; reason must, and ultimately will, triumph over brute force.

Had the Pilgrim Fathers began their national career with the sword, America had by this time been a fearful scourge to herself and to the whole earth. So powerful a nation, perpetually armed, and with an army in the same proportion to her general population as in Hayti, the entire of the new world had ere this been desolated. The world may indeed bless God for the moral character of the founders of the United States of America!

The case of Hayti has indeed been different; but it is nevertheless evident that the course she has pursued has brought on revolution upon revolution, until she scarcely knows how to exist at all; and in fact, in the absence of those national safety-valves which the free working of free institutions affords, she will be compelled to turn her arms at intervals upon her own citizens, and in the name of law, hurry them out of existence.

It is not, however, difficult to understand that a nation composed of three such divisions as exist in Hayti, should have suffered from despotism, in some form or other, for so many years; in fact it seems to have become a settled conviction with many Haytians that Hayti, mild as her people are, must be ruled by an iron hand. This, however, has no doubt been the source of all that has afflicted the country. A people who have fully learned that they are free, will not fail to break any iron hand to shivers.

The following seem to be the three great divisions already referred to, as making up the general state of things in the Haytian Republic:—

1. The masses in deep ignorance.
2. A general military bias, with a great army.
3. An educated class, composing the minority.

Supposing the more enlightened minority to be well disposed to govern on the principles of Republicanism, their principles and motives would ever be in danger of being misunderstood by the uneducated masses, which have been left to themselves in a manner which posterity will never justify; nor would the army itself be very much disposed to listen to the idea of being simply the servant of the nation, and thus yield the entire power to the civil magistrate.

Protestations against the military system have been frequent in Hayti, but thus far they have fallen to the ground, and every attempt to put down arms has only increased them; in fact, to govern without them has long been thought to be impossible in Hayti;* notwithstanding it is perfectly evident that under their pernicious shadow the civil institutions lose their power; innumerable corruptions rush in, until all becomes insupportable, and the sword is again wielded to destroy the wretched progeny of evil which it has created—which, failing to do, as is generally the case, the whole Republic becomes a military camp; general officers are increased, until the vitals of the country are eaten out, and freedom dies amidst the cry of "Vive la Liberty!" Hence the noblest intentions have failed; banishments have resulted, and unhappy victims have been judged and cut down as political offenders.

Executions for political offences have no doubt powerfully contributed, among many other causes, to the frequent revolutions of Hayti, having unquestionably increased the evil they were intended to

* Impossible, for two reasons: 1st, The uneducated have been from their infancy so accustomed to see authority of every kind in military uniform, that they would scarcely have any conception of it in a plain dress. 2d, Each revolutionary party, on succeeding, having compensated its abettors by conferring military honors, they have become permanent, by an obstinate refusal to give them up, and bear them as honorary,

cure. In fact the imposition of silence upon a people by such means, on all political questions, robs a nation of its true dignity; espionage becomes necessary to a Government under such circumstances, and will impress upon a people a most unhappy character.

The freer the nation, the more open will generally be even the individual character.

There is a withering power in the use of arms, in the internal government of a country; before them, reason is dumb, while neither the Government nor the people are safe.

The remedy, therefore, for the evils of Hayti, is not to be found in arms; and the Government which cannot stand without them, is in a most unhappy case, for it exists necessarily, in such a case, upon a fearful volcano. Arms cannot convert wrong into right, nor can they give permanency to any false system; right must ultimately triumph; arms before it are mere straws; they doubtless have their place, but there is no freedom under their rule.

If, then, the sword belongs to the people, and not to any one man, let them say how it should be used; let the Executive consult them through their institutions, to which he has sworn fidelity.

The institutions of Hayti, faithfully worked, would supersede revolution, while they would secure every reasonable amount of freedom to the citizen. This too is what is sought and desired. In fact the struggles of the Haytian people have had for their object and end the free, fair, and full working of their own institutions, notwithstanding much evil has mingled with all their revolutionary movements.

It is, however, declared, both by foreigners and

natives, that the Haytians, as a people, are far behind their institutions. Such a fact of any people must be deplorable, because it seems to suppose the necessity of a despotism of some kind and degree, and seems to explain the sense in which an iron hand has long been thought to be necessary in the management of Hayti.

Let the Government of Hayti, with the President at its head, be composed of men who are at their posts with honest motives, resolved to lay aside, whenever it is necessary, their own private interests and views, having solely in view to serve their country; submitting themselves to an independent Senate, and an honestly and freely elected House of Representatives, which would truly represent the intelligence of the nation; free from all military influence, keeping the army in its right place, purely as the servant of the nation—and it would soon be seen whether the Haytians are prepared or whether they are not for honest, fair and straightforward work, on all sides. In fact there is absurdity in supposing that any people, even though ignorant, should not be prepared for transparent honesty, which has ever been adored by mankind, whether wise or ignorant.

That there is unpreparedness in Hayti, is evident; but let the common sense of mankind judge in this matter, and let the Haytians themselves be in earnest in their own best interests.

The cardinal principles by which a country should be governed are evident as the sun, and the range within them is vast. Details of every Republican variety will here be found, perfectly capable of being adapted and modified to both the people and the climate; but the great cardinal points can never be departed from, without fearful consequences, nor will there nor can there be any peace in Hayti, until the fundamental principles of right Government are practically carried out, and faithfully adhered to, both by the Government and people.

Whatever, therefore, may be wanting in Hayti, there needs no reasoning to prove that the people are perfectly prepared to receive the happiness and prosperity which right everywhere reigning would confer upon them, leaving them at the same time at liberty to enrich their country, by enriching themselves; that any people would be better prepared for such a state of things, than to be ever groaning under a galling military yoke, needs no reasoning.

If, then, it is certain that a Government in Hayti, sound in its general principles and administration, would secure the peace of the country, then it becomes a question whether the people are right or wrong in demanding it, and whether they would be men in the full sense of the word, if they did not. That this has been the general sense of Haytian revolutions, cannot be doubted; the fact, however, that they have ever failed in securing the object in view, ought now to teach the Haytians themselves that there are means for correcting abuses far more powerful than the sword; and if the national existence is not to cease, this must be studied, understood, and practised in Hayti.

There can indeed be no doubt but that senseless ambition has played its part in all the past, nor is it to be supposed that this will be easily annihilated; but wide-spread Christian education, and the fair working of the national institutions, would greatly circumscribe the limits of pernicious and empty pretension; and if this be the fact, then is the conclusion inevitable that both the cause and the cure of Haytian revolutions are evident.

It must, however, be admitted that the fact of revolutions is a proof of the existence of error somewhere. Certain it is that the Executive of Hayti has not generally considered himself the servant of his country, in a Republican sense; rather the chief magistrate has considered himself as ruler and master, forgetting at the same time that he who will have all, and do all, must be responsible for all.

Our reasonings, therefore, bring us to one great conclusion, which is simply that whichever party in a nation is not in harmony with the cardinal principles of a fully recognized and universally received Constitution, is revolutionary, whether it be the Government or the people.

In the case of the great French Revolution, it is evident that the people were revolutionary, they being resolved to change the existing system of things, by which they had been governed for ages. Whether the people were right or wrong in this case is not the question before us at this moment; but it may be fairly questioned whether this has been generally the sense of the Haytian revolutions—they, in nearly all cases, having had their source in the national complaint that neither the Constitution nor the institutions of the country had been adhered to, and fairly carried out, for the true advancement of the people.

The fair lay, therefore, of the question now before

us, is whether the people of Hayti, or the Governments which have presided over them, have been revolutionary?

It is impossible to suppose that the fair working and honest administration of popular laws and institutions, should be productive of revolutions; hence it will at once appear that the Haytian revolutions have not been the result of the mere whims and freaks of the people, yet it cannot be denied that they have been frequent;* we therefore are driven to the conclusion that sound moral principle has been wanting where it was most needed.

Our final conclusion is, that the cure for revolutions is preventive; this will be found in knowledge and freedom, in the sense already explained. Christianity firmly and deeply planted in the heart of every child in the Republic, by means of primary education, with woman raised to her just elevation in society, is the only salvation of Hayti.

* It may be worthy of notice that the revolutions of Hayti have been fewer than those of either its immediate neighbor, Dominica, or those of Mexico and the Republics of South America, as will be seen from the following statement:

From the fall of Dessalines, which occurred in 1806, all was comparative peace until the revolution of 1843, showing an interval of upwards of thirty years. From the fall of Riviere, which was simply a continuation of the revolution of 1843, until 1844, all was comparatively easy until the fall of Soulouque, 1859, with the exception of the case of President Pierot in 1846, which could scarcely be called a revolution, showing a period of fifteen years. The Government of Geffrard continued from 1859 to 1867.

It is true the national spirit must be characterized as restless; but the neighboring Republic of Dominica, as well as that of Mexico and those of South America, have been not only unceasingly restless, but their revolutions have been more yearly than otherwise; nor are we to forget that the national convulsions of both America and Europe have been sufficiently frequent and fearful! These are awful facts, condemning all alike.

CHAPTER XV.

AFRICAN CHARACTER AS DEVELOPED IN HAYTI.

From deepest shades of ever lowering fiends,
To brightest seraphs' ever glowing tints,
The proof of oneness through our race is seen,
Of every hue.

It may, perhaps, be demanded whether the scenes through which we have passed in the "Historical Notes and Sketches of Hayti," now before us, and which have led us through so much of blood, ambition, and revenge are, in any sense, favorable to the African character?

The question is a fair one—it demands attention; and, although many have come to fearful conclusions in these matters, the friends of truth and humanity, who are no respecters of persons, and are disposed to look upon the great family of man as being "of one blood," have only to let the history of the world speak for itself on this great question.

It is, indeed, a strange and singular fact, that to many of fair and honest views, this question has always appeared to be one of great, and even dreaded embarrassment;—this may arise from a tendency to view it in an isolated sense, whereas the plain truth is, that we have only to deal with this branch of human history as we would with any other—and the answer to the great question, so fairly proposed, will be found in the simple fact, that it is by one and the same road that men of all nations and colors, in all ages, have arrived at whatever has been deemed great or grand.

That there is, and ever has been, a more excellent way to true greatness than the one that has generally been chosen by nations and individuals, is very certain. This, however, is not the matter now before us. But the broad and unmistakable fact is evident that the White branches of the human race, although numerically in the minority in the great family of man, have waded through the crimson sea of war in its basest and fiercest sense, and through woes which no mere mortal could detail, to arrive at what has generally been understood, even by some of the greatest of our race, as dignity and grandeur.

Yea, dark and sanguinary has been the White Man's career, throughout the whole course of time.

Unless, therefore, the Black Man is a superior being to his lighter brother, he will not be better—worse, he cannot be. And, if all men are of one blood, as inspiration has long taught us is the case, then we may expect everywhere, and in all, the same dark labyrinth of intrigue, and the same blood-stained course.

Incapacity to govern, it is still said, and even proclaimed by some of the highest authorities of the earth,* is evident in the Black races; nor need any fear or hesitate to admit this fact, which will be found to be far more general than has been thought it has, and still does apply to all mankind in their first attempt to govern, and has ever continued to do so,

* President Johnson's "Message."

until thought, experience, and education have brought about a better state of things; hence the most crushing despotisms have been carried out with the minutest and most persevering tenacity by the wisest of all the past; and, even at the present moment, it is undeniable that Europe has still immensely to learn and to do in this great work of real freedom and true government.

The ages which it has taken the White Man to learn what he now knows, and to arrive at what he now is,—and he has still much to do and to undo as to the true principles of free Government,—afford a sufficiently humiliating proof of universal want of capacity, in some sense and at some period, especially in the sense in which it has generally been applied to Hayti, for really right national Government; nor is it possible to fix on any one branch of the human family which has not passed through a most imperfect and trying infancy on this subject. Hence, in the long study of ages on this great question, what errors have not been committed by immatured Governments! and what anguish have they not inflicted in the name of law and right!

The vast family of man, like the large family of a single pair, show the most opposite differences of character, capacity, and style; a fact which amazingly displays Creative wisdom, which has made so vast a variety in living intelligence compatible with equality in its most essential and noblest sense, and in fact opens to us a volume of beneficial results to mankind.

It must, therefore, be expected that the course of the Black Man will be the same as that of all the rest of mankind of every hue, as in fact it has been. Indeed, one of the greatest demonstrations of the homogeneity of the human family is found in the fact that the vices of all are the same, as to general depravity; while, at the same time, the fact is now acknowledged that the same great moral cure for man which is found in Christ, and his truth, faithfully applied, and unreservedly received, is found to be adapted alike to all, and is every where the power of God unto salvation.

It might be demanded, why has not Hayti followed the examples of free Governments, which form the glory of the age, and which she has so long had before her? This, doubtless, was her duty. But of what nation, out of England and the United States of America, might not this be said in a greater or lesser degree? And, even of the two last named countries, who would say that they are perfect?

Up to the present time, therefore, it is evident that the same moral level has not been attained by all men, nor have all the intelligent of the earth surmounted their weaknesses and prejudices. The great fact that vice and virtue are relative to God alone, and not to man or circumstances, has yet to be more fully studied. There is still a tendency to applaud in Cromwell what would be condemned in Toussaint l'Ouverture, and to allow that to be grand in Napoleon the I. which would be looked upon as barbarous in Dessalines. There is, indeed—as has already been said—a more excellent way to all that is great and good; but both the Black and White Man have equally shown perversion from truth and justice—they have each followed their own way; and intrigues, dark and foul, have marked the course of both.

The day has evidently come when all distinctions of color must cease, in every aristocratic sense, and when all must be lost in the simple truth, that man is every where the same. Hence, if the scenes through which we have now passed in following out, although in a limited manner, the history of the Haytian Republic, have been scenes of humiliation and woe, as they unquestionably have been, we have simply to remember that this is Man, whether in Europe or Africa. Light, moral and intellectual, must now make its way through the earth, until the true level and sense of universal equality shall be found, understood and maintained, with dignity to each and safety to all.

It might, indeed, be thought that what has been said of the White Man, as to the wars and sanguinary means by which he has arrived at the entire lordship of the earth, applies equally to the savage, who has done but little else than shed blood; yet, that it is to be observed, that the White Man has advanced in civilization with his wars, while the savage, with all his blood shed, has remained as he was. There is, indeed, truth in this; but if we are to decide here on which side lies the greatest amount of guilt and crime, whether on the side of those who knew better, or on the side of those who knew no better—it will, doubtless, become an awkward case for many of the most polished and refined among men.

The truth, therefore, is, that more or less of the fiend attaches to all men, civilized and savage;—

hence all men, wise and ignorant, need alike that power of God which alone can confound the reign of sin; a power, compared with which, all human creeds are mere weakness, whether national or otherwise. Men morally, whether they live in forests or cities, are poor, blind and miserable; nor can any thing be more evident than that man by wisdom never yet knew God. The healing of the nations is with God, whose need is every where felt, and who has nowhere left himself without a witness.

The fair question, therefore, before us is, whether there has ever been any true tendency in Hayti towards progress? Whether there has ever been any proof of the presence of a developing element in the nation? And whether it has shown any due claims to any degree of dignity? Should it appear that the root and power of real progress do exist among this people, the amount or degree of general advancement and national development will become of secondary importance—the tree really possessing life and vital power will rise and expand, however slowly.

These thoughts will, very naturally, lead us back for a moment to the commencement of the national career.

Here, then, justice demands that the elements, morally and intellectually, which made up the general state of things when Hayti first declared her Independence, should be fairly considered.

The scene which such a retrospect view brings before us, is not very easy of description. We here see a great mass of human beings which had, for some few years, tasted the sweets of liberty, now threatened with the renewal of the woes and pangs of slavery. They were, indeed, ill prepared for free institutions;—they were, nevertheless, prepared for all that was fair between man and man; and they were more than prepared to resist the renewal of their former chains. Surely, the full details of such a state of things would require something beyond human power; and yet this was Hayti's starting-point as a nation. A greater chaos could scarcely be imagined. Such were the materials with which the founders of this Republic had to build up the nation.

Nevertheless when the Whites, with all their brilliant aristocracy, and their most studied refinements of ease and luxury, withdrew from Hayti, did the Black Man really return to savage life, as his former oppressors often had declared he would?

To say that the progress expected has not been realized, is simply to say what no one denies; nations do not grow up to maturity suddenly; nor is this the order of nature in any thing.

Certainly it cannot be said of Toussaint l'Ouverture, and many others of his day, that they in any sense retrograded; in fact, it might be said of this distinguished Black Chief, that he had a horror of retrogradation; and it cannot be denied that his companions in arms were, many of them, remarkable and highly useful men in their day. History, indeed, shows that in those days which tried men's souls, Hayti possessed men of extraordinary character, tact, and courage.

That the case of Hayti on the question in hand, is one of great singularity, will, perhaps, be admitted; and, perhaps, posterity may discover that, upon the whole, she has rather deserved applause than censure, in so far raising a national edifice of the most unpropitious materials which could have been found.

If, therefore, a correct judgment is to be formed in this matter, it must be by a due consideration of the elements which made up the general state of things, at the national starting-point.

Had the Haytians, when once left to themselves by their former White rulers, abandoned the institutions of their predecessors, it would doubtless have been in perfect harmony with much that had been predicted of them by those who thought themselves their only saviors. This, however, was not the case; they not only sustained all that they thought good of the former order of things, but they did for themselves what no one else could do for them—they remodeled the political and social theories of men, whom they deemed greater than themselves; and, having abolished all that was aristocratic, they adapted all to simple Republicanism.

Attempts, it is true, at Monarchy have been made, but they have proved abortive and have failed.

Slavery and despotism fell; the ancient order of things ceased; the ground was cleared, and the gigantic task of re-casting and re-modeling the entire order of things remained to be accomplished.

The men who had long been deemed incapable, and, according to many, were to have sunk into oblivion or something worse, undertook the great work of re-construction; how they succeeded, we leave the page of history to detail. Certain it is, that Republicanism took the place of the lowest and most degrading form of despotism, and the laws and institutions were adapted to the general system of national liberty.

Nor were the founders of this newly-formed Republic inadequate to the great task of a fair distribution of lands, which had now become the property of the Republic—a measure of no small magnitude; which, as may be seen by history, was so managed and directed as to create at once a Commonwealth, give identity to the nation, and render it solid.

Truly there were no elements of savage life, or tendency in that direction, in the re-forming of the whole system of jurisprudence, and its adaptation to the new nationality. This, indeed, may not have been done according to the Anglo-Saxon idea of things, but it required no ordinary men to follow out the amazing complications of French law.

That all this, and much more, with all fiscal arrangements creating the pecuniary resources needful for their support, should have been well and fully carried out, is the best proof needed that the foundations of this national edifice were well laid, by a race of men who were deemed incapable; yea, even by their own fathers deemed incapable, so far as to be by them denied even the rights of men!

It must here, however, be remembered that the presence of high French families, both in the army and in the civil ranks of life, had undoubtedly produced educational effects on many of the Blacks, while the sons of the wealthy White Colonists had been allowed the advantages of a Parisian education.

It has been said that the Haytians found every thing prepared for them; it has, however, also been said that Africans, left to themselves, go back again to savagism. The last statement is simply unworthy of notice. In the presence of Haytian history, with regard to the former, let the inquiry be started, Who were the originators of civilization? or have there ever been any at all? has not civilization rather descended from father to son? has not the ordinary course been, that each succeeding generation has gone a step beyond its predecessors? Was it then necessary to a fair test in this case, that Hayti should have been cut off from the common order of God and nature? Those who reason thus, would then exact from Hayti the proof that she was something more than human.

What has any nation, in this sense, that she has not received, however much she may have improved the gift of heaven?

It is, indeed, true that pride and jealousy arrayed the Haytians against each other soon after their Independence, and that national fratricide, in the form of civil war, convulsed every thing. Deplorable, however, as this was, it is a remarkable fact, and one specially worthy of notice, that the two great parties into which Hayti at this time was unhappily divided, were each animated by a true spirit of progress—hence each one aimed at sustaining the cardinal principles of true and constitutional Government. Indeed, the emulation between the northern Kingdom and the western Republic is too great a fact in Haytian history to need further comment here; and, whatever there may have been to deplore on either side, and especially on the side of Christophe, certainly in neither case can it be said that there was any tendency to savage life; in fact, Petion's great motto was, that "education raised man to his proper dignity"! And, although it must be confessed that Hayti has not fully acquitted herself in carrying the principle of this great motto to its full extent, or in fact in any other respect as to general progress and civilization, yet the truth has ever been before the world, that both Commerce and Education have unceasingly gone on, however slowly, or however imperfectly; nor can it be said that their results are not, to a great degree, manifest.

Supposing, therefore, that the Haytians merit every censure as to civil wars, revolutions, and general want of progress, that has been passed upon them both by their friends and their foes, they, after all, have only walked over the old beaten track of all mankind in all past ages, from the days of Adam down to our own times. True, indeed, this is wrong, whether in an individual or nation, and cannot in any sense be justified; but if he only, in this case, who is innocent, is to cast the first stone, not a tongue would dare move against Hayti: we must, however, say of her that she is not blind to her own faults.

It is then evident that the Black Man of Hayti is no more affected as to his dignity as a man, by the course he has pursued in a national sense, than is the White Man, who has so often been, and in so many cases still is in precisely the same case, only that the amount of guilt is greater in the latter than in the former, from the simple fact of far higher pretensions.

The fact, therefore, remains undeniable, that the elements of true civilization have ever been preserved in Hayti. They may have been misused, misapplied, and misunderstood, and error may have produced a thousand evils, but the aim and intention of the ruling parties have undoubtedly, upon the whole, been good.

The frame-work of the national system has been in general in harmony with the age. Hence the representative system has always in some sense existed, and men of capacity have not unfrequently come forth. The press has been unceasingly at work, not indeed always freely, but its use has ever been highly appreciated. The style of social life, notwithstanding innumerable discouragements arising from such a vast amount of ignorance in the nation, which at times would seem to chill everything, and fill the Republic with mutual distrust and suspicion, has not gone down.

Marriage has unquestionably gained ground, and its national effect will be seen in the fact, that in families at all respectable, female morality and honor are well sustained.

Wealth has greatly accumulated, a fact which affords the fullest assurance that whenever fair national circumstances of permanent peace shall bless the Republic, the love of gain will soon change the whole face of things, and raise many to great possessions.

Education, also, although it has not reached the masses, principally because they have not availed themselves of their own free national schools, which are everywhere open to them, and have been established at their own national expense for their children, is nevertheless widely extending amongst both sexes; while the idea is often broached that it should be universally obligatory, a measure which ought doubtless to have begun with the nation.

Whether the European education which thousands of the youth of Hayti have received since the commencement of the Republic, has upon the whole been preferable to a good home education, as to the country generally, might perhaps be considered an open question. The fact, however, that many of the Haytian youth have returned to their country with much European vice as well as literature, will not surprise. Superior knowledge in such cases might, however, be expected, which, together with a well-sustained education received by many at home, will show a united power of intelligence, which, if well directed by sound moral principle, would tell upon the country. These facts assume the highest importance, when it is remembered that the Haytian Republic has ever consisted of two distinct classes—the one comparatively well educated, the other not at all. Hence the great bulk of the people, in their deep ignorance, are and must be far below their true level as Republicans; an unhappy fact, which has already produced its ill effects; such circumstances so often bringing into office utterly incapable men, who have been raised to a high post from prudential motives, relating to color or otherwise; while on the other hand, the ignorant masses have too often been the victims of designing men, who had more knowledge than conscience.

If Hayti, therefore, has not acquitted herself as a nation, let her at least be fairly dealt with. Doubtless blame and censure must attach somewhere; but a fair and candid examination of this subject, which would show difficulties peculiar to her case and general circumstances, would place her in a clearer light before her friends.

That infidelity in all forms and degrees has greatly prevailed amongst the better informed of this Republic, is a painful and undeniable truth. In fact, the tide of vice rises and flows from the first Europeans, who seized these shores, the first wave of which is seen in the murderous annihilation of the aboriginal tribes, the theft of Africans, the introduction of concubinage and even libertinage, with the merciless and degrading despotism of slavery. These were the seeds first sown upon these shores by European hands. Nor let it be supposed that they have not abundantly produced their unhappy effects, especially upon the formation of the original politics of independent Hayti. Doubtless it was here that the lesson was learnt of power in the hands of the few, thus giving birth to an aristocracy, which, with Europe at that time, believed that the masses did not need education—that they would be even dangerous with it, and were therefore better without it.

The Haytians of that day might indeed have looked to the recently-formed American Republic of the United States. But there slavery then existed without even a ray of hope that it would ever cease ; and the fame, yea very existence of Hayti, was hated by all the slave-ridden powers of the age. Even her neighbors, English, French, Spanish, etc., all felt that a free Black Republic in the midst of them was a shock to all their slavish hopes. Hence all Haytians were spurned from their shores, or if thrown there by wreck, the free Haytian was perhaps thrown into prison, for the crime of being free, and the fear of the dangerous contact of freedom with slavery.

Circumstances, therefore, highly honorable to Hayti, but which threw a deep, dark shade over all the communities around her, who thought themselves vastly her superiors, doomed this Republic to long isolation. The Haytians themselves also at the same time, feeling that the safety of their liberties demanded this, in their turn proclaimed that no white man should be a landed proprietor amongst them!

Hayti, indeed, resolved to be free as to slavery; but the moral chains of ignorance and vice, even to this day, hang upon her. Hence progress in its full and true sense, with her, has been impossible. To infer, however, from this, that nothing has been done, would be unjust and untrue.

It is now, therefore, for an honest judgment to be formed whether the Historical Notes and Sketches of Hayti, contained in the preceding pages, have thrown any satisfactory light on African independence in this Republic.

That it might and ought to have been better with Hayti in all respects, is true; but this is true of every nation under heaven.

At the same time, the construction of a free Republic, with institutions in harmony with the spirit of the age, from such materials as we have seen and examined, beyond doubt has in it extraordinary merit; and it will be for posterity to decide as to the degree of censure for innumerable errors, neglects, and persistent corruptions, or of applause for so much done under such unparalleled difficulties, which should be awarded to Hayti. That she has exposed herself to censure cannot be doubted, either by herself or her friends.

Whether, however, considering all the circumstances of the case, Hayti has not done what no other people or nation ever did before, is worthy of enquiry.

England, America and France have now fully acquitted themselves on the African question. The black communities, under their rule, are and will be fairly dealt with. Nevertheless, the principle here maintained remains unaltered and untouched, viz., that independence is the true and most effectual means of development for any people, and that it is to be preferred whenever it becomes necessary for any sound and sufficient reason.

That the United States of America could ever have been what they now are by any other means than that of independence, is certain. Nor need this fact at all lessen the value and importance of sound colonial government as the cradle of independence, as doubtless it was always intended to be.

That Hayti could never have had the same hopes and prospects as a colony, or the development which she has already realized, cannot be a matter of doubt. Her revolutions have indeed been injurious to her; but however frequent they may have been, they can only be viewed as political diseases, and if despite of them prosperity has been realized, the proof is clear that a fair order of things would have fully demonstrated the advantages and superiority of independence.

It is to be remembered that the colonial wealth of St. Domingue was foreign, belonging mostly to

French citizens, while it was also the product of unfair means; and if it were even proved that the wealth of the colony was greater than that of the free and independent Republic of Hayti, it would still remain a fact, that the Haytian Republic of 1868, compared with that of 1804, evidently and undeniably shows an immense stride in general progress. Nor can Hayti be otherwise judged, as to whatever progress she has made, than by comparison with herself, through her different epochs.

It must, however, be borne in mind, that in addition to the creation of all her own pecuniary resources, and the support of all her institutions, as to financial demands, Hayti for many years has met the enormous annual claims of France for landed property, due the former French colonists, the sum total of which will be, when completed, 60,000,000 of francs.

It is specially worthy of notice, that while every colony still surrounding Hayti is more or less dependent upon its parent Government, their armies, navies, functionaries, and sometimes clergy, being partially sustained from home, and also receiving every help and sympathy in the various public calamities of earthquakes, hurricanes, and fires, Hayti has fully maintained the most perfect independence in all similar cases. Whether, however, on this account or not, no friendly hand has ever, in such calamities, been stretched towards her, this is indeed no honor to the Christianity of her neighbors. But she has always understood her position; nor has she ever needed foreign help or desired it, except by the fair means of commerce.

It is unquestionably to the honor of Hayti, that in this sense, her independence has ever been complete. Most emphatically is it true, that she owes no man anything, and when her foreign debt to France shall have been effaced, her already sufficient resources will become far more ample than ever.

But after all, the fair view of the national wealth as resulting from independence, is only to be seen in the distribution of all the national resources and individual possessions. In this view of the case, it will at once appear that the individual and family wants of a half a million of free citizens, would be incomparably greater than in the same number of slaves, including even a few thousands of their masters, their wants being doled out of the avarice of their yet more degraded owners, while neither their homes, lands, wives, children, or even themselves, were their own. But freedom and independence, made all their own; and the transition from poverty to comparative wealth becomes evident. The aggregate wealth, therefore, of the free half million, compared with the same number of bondmen, without anything they could call their own, needs no comment. The present aggregate, therefore, of national wealth, viewed in this sense, would unquestionably surpass the highest colonial realizations.

Nor should it be forgotten, in addition to this, that the colonial exportations were the life of the country, drained not for itself, but to be exported for the support of chateaus upon foreign shores.

Let also the fact be kept in view, that since the independence, immense fortunes have been realized in Hayti, both by foreigners and natives.

Hayti, therefore, and her independence show bright gleams as well as dark shades, and it will be for the honest and impartial judgment of mankind to decide, whether a nation, which has demonstrated that under fair circumstances she would amply and in all respects acquit herself, does not justify the best hopes as to the future. For it is not to be supposed, that either civil wars or military revolutions can become the permanent order of things.

Contact by means of general commerce with foreign nations has already done much for Hayti; and with this fact before us, hope must become yet much brighter, as peace shall consolidate all interests, and commerce extend itself, which must ultimately be the case.

The evident order of God, with regard to the human family is, that no nation should live apart, or simply to itself. Whether, therefore, any nation has a right to be permanently exclusive, in the sense in which this was once essential to the independence of Hayti, is perhaps questionable. Certainly such a principle in a righteous order of things amongst nations, is not to the interest of any country—all throughout the earth, within reasonable limits, would rather appear to be mutual.

The independence, therefore, advocated here, is in no sense isolated, but is perfectly compatible with the most distinct identity; the highest national independence being in perfect harmony with the most complete commercial dependence upon each other.

Perhaps we are safe in the statement, that no country, once sunk in a moral sense, ever yet recovered itself, of itself. Hence the nations of the past have simply disappeared; their ruin, beyond all doubt, having commenced in the corruption of the moral element, certainly not from any want of intellectual capacity or general intelligence.

The healing of the nations is truly a beautiful thought; but it nevertheless suggests the idea, that the whole of humanity is sick, and that the heart of the world is faint, while at the same time it reminds us that the healing element for the world is not in itself. It is not, therefore, in any special sense, derogatory to a nation that, morally, she cannot heal herself. There is not and never was a nation that has done this; nor is it to be supposed that Hayti will be an exception; in this she is in the same case with humanity at large. Her independence or dignity are not interfered with by the frailties that flesh is heir to; her guilt is in the "love of darkness rather than light."

That there is a healing power for the nations, all true Christians believe, and that the command to preach the Gospel to every creature, had essentially in view the healing of the nations cannot be doubted. Men cannot heal themselves, but heaven will, by their consent. The great business of Hayti, therefore, is, to accept the help of the universal Father. And as far as religious toleration is concerned, it must be admitted, that as a nation, she has rather encouraged than spurned religious truth.

Help abounds; the press, with all its moral corruption, pours nevertheless an unceasing flood of light upon the value and necessity of sound moral principle.

Science, also, well directed and developed, is a

revelation of God, and is not without a moral, elevating power.

Above all, religion, in its light, its life, and power, constitute the main-spring of human welfare. Nor is this a mere matter of national creed or pompous forms, which rather engender pride than humility; but that power of God, in and amongst men, which alone can give stability to that independence in which the Haytians so justly glory.

Nevertheless, there is a weak point in the governing genius of Hayti, and this unquestionably exists in her revolutionary tendencies. It is, however, a weakness which the bare exercise of common sense would cure. For where is the common sense of habitual reforms by the sword? The fact of want of national solidity takes its rise here. The entire life and energy of the nation are exhausted in revolutionary struggles, which are far worse than useless. Changes in men simply, without any in principle, except that a bad man has often been exchanged for one much worse, and this worse has gone on, until despair has almost quenched the nation's hope.

Still, from the preceding pages, it will be quite evident that a great amount of general intelligence is found amongst the Haytians, and that this has been the case from the beginning of the Republic down to the present time. Those, too, who have had anything to do with education in this Republic, are convinced of the entire capacity and aptitude of the Haytian youth of both sexes for every branch of literature.

A fit subject here offers for serious study. A grand question presents itself to our attention in the fact now before us, which is, that general knowledge is possessed, the pen is wielded, and the general principles of language are mastered, with much besides; yet all is paralyzed. Nor is it to be denied, that many other nations have been, and still are, in the same case. Where and what is the true solution of this great question, that nations possessing all needful intelligence, become mere wrecks?

This question, although great, and involving the best interests of mankind, is singularly simple. All is said, as to its solution, in the plain fact, that human beings cannot live together in peace without moral culture, and the universal admission is, that this, in a national sense, has been neglected in Hayti.

Here is the only hope of man; here, therefore, is the only hope of Hayti. We are then driven to the conclusion, whether we will or no, that mere intelligence, however developed, however cultivated, never did and never will suffice for the right and efficient government of human beings. And in this, perhaps, may be understood the saying of a celebrated infidel of the last century, that, "If there were no God, it would be necessary to make one!" Doubtless he meant for the right management of human affairs.

The nature and constitution of man evidently demands more than mere intelligence. Nor will or can our hope, in any moral sense, ever be realized by a mere national creed, however pure or good. A power must be brought to bear upon the conscience, which will mould and form it; an element must be brought into human hearts, which will create a love of good, and a horror of evil; truth must be loved, for it to have full power; a moral state of things to be brought about, solely by the knowledge of God and His eternal truth, together with His love and life within.

The great Missionary efforts of the age, therefore, by all and every means, constitute the great hope of Hayti. The age itself is in a sense missionary; hence the telegraph and steam are great auxiliaries to the amelioration of mankind.

But the great missionary work, as commenced by Christ, belongs to men who have given their lives in a religious sense for the salvation of their fellow-men, wherever they may be scattered over the face of the earth. That the Christian church has been charged by its great and glorious Head with the conversion and salvation of the world, is plainly expressed in the last command of the Redeemer, to "go into all the world, and preach the Gospel to every creature." That this church is guilty before God, is equally evident.

Christian faith and hope look for the day when the Christian foreign merchant will feel far more deeply than ever that his moral influence and bearing, in the community where his lot has fallen, are of incalculable importance both to the people themselves, and his own honest aims and hopes of wealth.

Christianity, thus publicly sanctioned and sustained by foreigners on foreign shores, both by merchants and ambassadors, would strike into silence many a taunt which is often thrown at the Minister of the Gospel—" Your own people are but rarely, if ever, with you in the public worship of God."

On the subject of appeals for help to the public generally, it will be seen by the preceding pages that the foreign merchants, as well as the representatives of foreign Governments in Hayti, have ever done generously; but the materials of the great temple of God among men consist rather in "living stones" than in gold and silver, notwithstanding the erection of edifices, and the support of schools, require the latter.

Differences of creed, doubtless, tell here; and these differences are numerous among foreigners in Hayti; but will men never feel that they are brethren? and that the worship of God by every creed is, "in spirit and in truth"? Will intelligent men never cease to be sectarian?

Such a Missionary power brought to bear upon the world would become a moral lever of irresistible power, which would ultimately lift up mankind from the dregs of vice. Such a power would, long ago, have told on Hayti; nor ought it to be forgotten that the foreign element throughout the world has often been a grand stumbling block and rock of offence. Men leaving their Christian homes, and finding themselves in a truly moral isolation, have yielded to the pressure of various customs, and in many cases have been driven on by the overwhelming torrent of evil, until they have been whirled off the stage of life without living out half their days.

If the moral element of God within us is needful for one part of the human race, it is needful for all; and if there be greater need in one class than in another of mankind, of the power and life of God within those who have the greatest amount of human wisdom are, unquestionably in such a matter, the most necessitous of all men, as will be seen in the simple fact, that true religion is not mere knowledge, but that great power within which is called the Love of God!

Hayti's hope, therefore, is in God. Let those who can point her to Him, do it by all and every means; nor let her forget that she, too, must save herself.

www.ingramcontent.com/pod-product-compliance
Lightning Source LLC
LaVergne TN
LVHW020938110826
845150LV00004B/896

9781425551933